STREETWISE®
SELLING
on eBAY®

How to Start, Manage, and Maximize
a Successful eBay® Business

SONIA WEISS

Adams Media
Avon, Massachusetts

Published by Adams Media, an F+W Publications Company
57 Littlefield Street
Avon, MA 02322
www.adamsmedia.com

ISBN: 1-59337-610-3

Library of Congress Cataloging-in-Publication Data
Weiss, Sonia.
Streetwise selling on eBay / Sonia Weiss.
p. cm.
Includes index.
ISBN 1-59337-610-3
1. eBay (Firm) 2. Internet auctions. I. Title.
HF5478.W45 2006
658.8'7--dc22
2006005211

This publication is designed to provide accurate and authoritative information with regard to the subject matter covered. It is sold with the understanding that the publisher is not engaged in rendering legal, accounting, or other professional advice. If legal advice or other expert assistance is required, the services of a competent professional person should be sought.
—From a *Declaration of Principles* jointly adopted by a Committee of the American Bar Association and a Committee of Publishers and Associations

Many of the designations used by manufacturers and sellers to distinguish their product are claimed as trademarks. Where those designations appear in this book and Adams Media was aware of a trademark claim, the designations have been printed with initial capital letters.

Screenshots by Larry Brody.

This book is available at quantity discounts for bulk purchases.
For information, please call 1-800-872-5627.

CONTENTS

Dedication

To my husband, for tolerating the clutter caused by writing and selling.

And to you, the reader. May your eBay career be auspicious, wonderful, and everything you ever dreamed of.

Acknowledgments

In my six-plus years as a member of the eBay community, it's been my pleasure and joy to get to know a number of the talented sellers at the site. Many of them graciously allowed me to use their experiences in various ways throughout this project, and it's an understatement to say the book you hold in your hands would not be the same without their contributions. Others assisted me more directly through their willingness to serve as a somewhat unofficial advisory panel or as technical editors.

There isn't enough space to thank them all individually here, nor do all of them wish to be publicly acknowledged. That said, particular thanks go to the following for their help: Joan Blake (catbooks1940s), Sylvia Petras (swedishdrama), Cathleen Lola (tialeyvintage) and Lesley Feeney (lesley_feeney).

To anyone I've omitted, please accept my apologies and know that not appearing on this list in no way diminishes your contributions; it just reflects my organizational shortcomings.

Special thanks also go to the amazing group of individuals who post regularly to eBay's Vintage Clothing and Accessories Board. The sea of knowledge among them is vast, and they freely offer it up. They've welcomed me and many others with open arms, and they truly personify the community values that are at the heart of eBay.

Shoshanna Grossman at Adams Media is as fine an acquisitions editor as an author could wish to work with; my thanks also to the other members of the Adams Media team who worked on this book, including development editor Larry Shea, book designer Sorae Lee, and cover designers Paul Beatrice, Matt LeBlanc, and Erick DaCosta. William Bond, my go-to guy, provided key research assistance on several of this book's more technical chapters. Thanks also go to Jacky Sach at Bookends LLC for this and every other project she's swung my way over the years.

Introduction

I met eBay for the first time in 1999 when researching and writing a book on collecting antiques. The site was still in its infancy, having started just four years earlier. It was known more as a venue for collectibles buyers and sellers, but almost every antiques dealer I spoke with mentioned it. Most weren't sure how online sales would work for the things they sold, since being able to judge condition close up and personal is so important to people who buy antiques. Still, they knew, or perhaps sensed, that somehow, someway, they would have to move some part of their business online sooner than later.

Based on their input, I knew I had to discuss online auctions—and specifically eBay—in my book, so I registered at the site and went shopping. Things were very different back then. One of the biggest differences was the lack of images—since the marketplace was so small, the competition was far less stiff than it is today. If you were lucky, you might see a picture or two of an item you were interested in. Many sellers relied solely on descriptions.

After an hour or so of browsing various categories, I found a listing for a nice piece of mid-twentieth-century pottery. What's more, the seller included a couple of pictures so I could see what the piece looked like. I registered, I bid, and then I waited. In my innocence, I thought I had won the bowl when my bid remained in first place as the auction wound down. Then I watched with horror when, in the last few minutes of the auction, the bid amount shot up far beyond my proxy amount. I didn't know enough about eBay to understand what had happened (a sniper—someone who bids on auctions at the last minute in an effort to win them at a good price—had outbid me), but I knew I wanted the bowl badly enough to pay a little more, so I frantically tried to up my proxy. Sadly, I was on a dial-up Internet connection, and my bid increase didn't register before the auction ended.

The bowl went to a buyer in Canada, and I was hooked on the eBay concept from that moment on. It was lots of fun to be able to browse what amounted to a gigantic online garage sale, but what really intrigued me was eBay's global reach.

Everything I had read and written about the emergence of a boundary-free economy now made sense, and it did so on a very personal level. Here, like never before, was the opportunity for anyone—small business, big business, and me, even—to establish a presence in this new economy on what was for all intents and purposes a level playing field. What this represented, especially for small business owners, was beyond exciting; it was revolutionary.

It didn't take me long to jump onto eBay as a seller, and I've done my fair share of that, particularly in the vintage clothing and accessories division. Among other things, I'm an avid collector of women's clothing from the late 1950s through the early 1970s and of purses from the Victorian era through the Roaring Twenties, and I've been at it long enough to be considered somewhat of an expert in both areas. But what I like better is using my twenty-plus years of experience as a small business owner to help others realize their dreams on eBay.

If I could point to one factor that hampers the progress and success of eBay sellers—beginners or the more experienced—more than anything else, it's their failure to treat their business like a business. Some of this might be because of what eBay started out as—a site for hobbyists to meet and greet and maybe sell a few things. Part of this might be because of where these sellers started out, as it can be difficult to make the paradigm shift from hobbyist to business owner, especially for anyone new to the world of small business and self-employment. Part of it might be because the concept of doing business online is still relatively new, and it sometimes doesn't seem like a "real" business either to those who do it or those who hear and read about it.

If you still don't think of selling on eBay as a real business, all you have to do is go through all the selling-related material eBay makes available at its site to see the emphasis on doing business, and doing business better. While the virtual garage-sale concept is still at the heart of eBay, the site has evolved far past this, and the best sellers have kept up with this evolution regardless of their level of involvement.

Simply put, I believe (and I'm far from alone on this) that selling on eBay is a business like any other, and the basics of how business is done are the same wherever you do it—on land or in cyberspace. Yet for some reason, a good number of people try to reinvent the wheel when it comes to selling online. When they realize that the basics of doing business are always fairly constant and perfectly applicable to selling on eBay, too, they can do great things with their businesses. This belief is what led to this book and, hopefully, what prompted you to pick it up.

In keeping with the overall philosophy of the Streetwise series to provide savvy reference books for business professionals who think big, *Streetwise® Selling on eBay* is geared toward individuals who are serious about doing business online and making a success of it. If you are more of a hobbyist, or you simply want to use the site occasionally to clear some clutter from your garage or basement, you'll find lots of good stuff here too, but most of the information in the pages ahead is geared to readers who want to make a go of it online.

Since its inception, eBay has spawned many new businesses, including many businesses that sell at the site and nowhere else. According to the results of an eBay survey from July 2005, more than 724,000 Americans are making eBay their primary or secondary source of income. And another 1.5 million people supplement their income by selling at the site. In the first six months of 2005, eBay members sold merchandise worth approximately $10.6 billion.

The numbers tell the story. No matter what your vision is, you can realize it on eBay. In the pages ahead, you'll learn a great deal about how to do it.

If you're a beginning seller or you're not that familiar with the site, I encourage you to start at the beginning and work your way through the book from there, as the sections and the chapters build on one another to a certain extent.

If you're already familiar with the site, you might be tempted to skip the chapters that provide a general overview of what the site is all about and how to use it. However, you'll find good information sprinkled throughout this book, and there might be something in those early chapters that you didn't know about or had simply forgotten.

I wish you good reading and, more important, good eBaying!

Getting Started
on eBay

Financial Freedom Through a Second Income

The reasons for selling on eBay are as varied as the millions of people who are registered at the site, but one of the most compelling for becoming an eBay seller is the desire to supplement existing income. This desire could be driven by a short-term need—say, to cover some unexpected medical bills or wanting to pay cash for the annual family vacation instead of running up charge cards.

For many people, however, the desire goes much deeper. Their short-term goal might be to generate more income in the short run, for whatever reason, but their long-term goal is to own and operate a successful eBay business and to turn their part-time, second-income business into the one they work at full time.

eBay offers the opportunity to satisfy whatever goals you have. You might start like the many new sellers who underscore eBay's early reputation as a virtual flea market and who hold what's very much like an online garage sale—periodically going through your home, gathering up everything you don't want or need, and auctioning it off. A fair number of sellers stay at this level, hopping onto the site from time to time to sell single items that they want to get rid of for various reasons.

Making a Living on eBay

According to eBay's estimates, in July 2005, some 724,000 of the site's 114 million active users earn a living as eBay sellers. Many of them are small business owners who also have brick-and-mortar stores, who maintain separate Web sites, and who only earn part of their income on eBay.

Other sellers establish an ongoing presence at some level and rely on eBay for a certain portion of their income. Typically, this means going beyond what they have on hand for inventory and obtaining items from other sources. Some of these sellers start small and stay small, preferring to build a business they can easily manage themselves, with maybe some involvement from family members or other help from time to time. Others jump right in with a full-blown business plan and a huge amount of inventory and establish a large presence right away.

The majority of eBay sellers end up somewhere in between, and find happiness doing what they want to do, when they want to do it. They might grow their businesses at times, or cut back at times. They might focus on just one category, or spread their offerings across many. They might sell items of their own that they've acquired for resale through various channels, or sell on consignment for others, or both. The unique nature of the eBay marketplace affords this flexibility, which is just one of many reasons why it works so well for so many people.

It is possible to build a million-dollar business on eBay; it's the model that's allowed more of these businesses to be built than at any other time in history. That said, small businesses can easily compete against big ones on eBay, thanks to the site's emphasis on offering a level playing field for all. As such, you can set your own sights and your goals at any level, and, if you do things right, find happiness and success selling on eBay.

The Numbers Tell the Story

For many small business owners, the sheer volume of business conducted on eBay is reason enough to join the party, as not doing so can quickly leave them in the dust. Numbers like these make a compelling argument for establishing an eBay business: 2,000 to 3,000 new users register at the site daily, on top of the 114 million current eBay users worldwide, of which 90 percent are buyers.

Establishing a New Business

Many eBay sellers choose the site to establish a new business, either as their solo concern or as an adjunct or offshoot of a going concern. And for good reason, as doing things "the eBay way" is one of the easiest ways to start a new business. Here's why:

1. The startup costs are incredibly low. Unlike spending thousands leasing and outfitting a brick-and-mortar store, hiring salespeople, and covering all the other costs that go into running a traditional retail store, it is possible to get a business up and running on eBay for as little as $100 or so, depending on

the resources you already have on hand and your inventory acquisition costs.

2. You don't have to spend time and money developing your own online commerce site and getting it up and running. When you sell on eBay, most of the work is done for you. Should you want to set up your own selling site—it can be a very good idea to do so, by the way, and you'll read more about why in the chapters ahead—one of eBay's newest service offerings will even help you do it.

3. It's a great place to test the water if you're new to online commerce. You can test drive your existing products and services to see how well they translate to online sales, and you can try out new offerings to see how they fit into your product mix.

4. You can see if you really like sales without making a huge investment in it as a career. Retail sales isn't for everyone, but if you've never done it before, you won't know if it's a good fit for you. eBay is just about the easiest, lowest-risk way to find out if retailing is something you like to do and like well enough to do for the duration. If you don't, you can say "Oops!" and leave without too much grief and aggravation. What's more, if you have inventory left when you say goodbye, you might be able to minimize your losses by hiring an eBay Trading Assistant to sell it for you.

Is eBay Overpopulated?

Do the hundreds of thousands of sellers already on eBay make the atmosphere so competitive that it's a barrier to entry? Clearly, you can find yourself going up against some stiff competition, certainly in eBay's most popular categories—consumer electronics, clothing and accessories, camera equipment, computer equipment, and the like. It's hard to find hot selling niches that aren't overrun with other sellers trying to do the same thing you are.

This doesn't mean there isn't room for you on eBay. As the number of sellers has gone up, so too has the number of buyers, and these numbers will keep going up in the years to come. There is truly no limit to the online empire that is eBay. For this reason alone, it's worth some time and effort to test things out and see if it's the right fit for you.

The competition is only a problem if you let it be. While it can be intimidating to read the success stories of multimillion-dollar sellers, it should also be encouraging, as their stories and experiences can be very similar to yours.

It's been said more than once that the best success stories on eBay are still to be written. Yours might be one of them. But it won't be if you're not a part of the show.

Is eBay Still Worth It?

If you've ever met a veteran eBay seller, maybe someone who sold during eBay's early days but has since left the site, you might hear a pretty bad rap on what eBay is like today. Back in the old days, they'll tell you, things were easier. Competition wasn't as stiff, prices realized were higher, buyers weren't as demanding, fees were lower, you didn't have to work as hard on your listings, you didn't have to have pictures, and so on and on.

You know what? They're right. Things were decidedly different in eBay's early days. It was easier to sell, and sellers could offer less and make more. But here's a simple truth: Everything changes over time. To think that eBay wouldn't follow suit is simply silly.

Most of the changes, to be honest, benefit sellers. Yes, they come with a price. It does cost more to sell on eBay now. There is more competition. ▶▶**You do have to put more time and effort into your listings if you want to realize the best possible prices for your merchandise.** But there isn't another place in this universe where business is done quite like eBay does it. Yahoo! Auctions, eBay's closest competition, has one-sixth the market that eBay captured during its first decade of operation. Other auction sites command an even smaller presence.

Reasons for Starting an eBay Business

This one factor mentioned above—eBay's overwhelming market presence—makes the price of doing business on eBay well worth the price of admission. The following sections describe some of the other advantages of selling on eBay that have made thousands of people realize what a great business opportunity it provides.

Expanding an Existing Business

Sellers flock to eBay to expand existing businesses. Again, it's one of the cheapest, lowest-risk approaches to growing an operation that retailers could possibly take. What's more, their expansion plans fit right into eBay's own. The company is always looking for ways to expand its existing business footprint. As it does, it increases the business opportunities for sellers at the same time.

According to eBay's own estimates, the company has penetrated less than 5 percent of its potential market. Increasing its market penetration through developing new markets and channels has been a significant focus of the company's business plan from the get-go, and it will continue to be so in the future.

Accessing a Global Market

Online commerce has revolutionized retail selling like nothing else. No longer are sellers confined by the brick and mortar of their retail stores. No longer are buyers in one part of the world relegated to merely dreaming about things they'd like to own. They can jump on eBay and buy them! Geographic limitations are few; for the most part, you can ship almost everywhere in the world. In other words, if you can get it there, and it's legal for you to sell it there, you can.

As of this writing, eBay links to auction sites in twenty-six countries. No other online commerce site comes anywhere close.

Networking with Others like You

It's been said time and time again that imitation is the sincerest form of flattery. On eBay, the flattery flows both ways, twenty-four hours a day, 365 days a year. Not only can buyers and sellers come to eBay and find people with similar interests, they can also learn from each other and become better buyers and sellers when they do.

eBay abounds with people who have established themselves as successful sellers. Due to the nature of online selling, the secrets to their success are much more easily mined than in the brick-and-mortar

Small Business and the Internet

Almost three-quarters of American adults have thought about starting their own businesses, and 75 percent said the Internet makes it easier to do so, according to a study released in April 2005.

The study, conducted by Yahoo!, Register.com, and Harris Interactive, also reported that 51 percent of the adults who characterized themselves as having entrepreneurial goals anticipated launching their business within the next five years. Of the individuals polled who have considered starting a business but haven't yet, 47 percent said they never thought they'd be too old to do so.

environment. On eBay, it's not only possible to determine what works and what doesn't work for other sellers and then to learn from their successes and failures, you can even get a sense for what it costs them to acquire their inventory and how much they clear when they sell it.

Calling Your Own Shots

Are you a night owl? eBay, like other e-commerce sites, never sleeps. It's open for business twenty-four hours a day, seven days a week, 365 days a year. If you're most productive during the late evening or the wee hours of the morning, you can work on your listings then. You can even take pictures if you have lights set up for it.

Do you want to be able to stay home with your kids? Build a business they could work at if they want to? Do you want to execute your own dreams instead of someone else's? eBay is where you can do all of this, and more.

Turning Passion into Profits

Many people work at jobs day in and day out that they're not thrilled about doing, but they put up with them and keep at them, often because the money makes it worth their while. Of all the advantages of starting an eBay business, one of the greatest is this: On eBay, it's possible to have both a job you like and a job you can make money at.

Looking at turning passion into profits from another perspective, it's also possible to build your business around the things that you're passionate about and to provide a valuable service to like-minded individuals who want and need products related to their passions, and who will be more than happy to buy them from you on eBay.

Finally, another approach to turning passion into profits is to support your favorite cause by donating part or all of the final sale prices of your items to charity. Participating in eBay Giving Works, the program eBay established to coordinate these efforts, allows you to list items to support worthy causes. Donate at least 90 percent of the item's final sale price to a certified nonprofit organization, and eBay will donate the insertion and final value fees on the item as well.

A Day in the Life of an eBay Seller

Since no two eBay sellers are exactly alike, there's really no such thing as a completely typical seller with a completely typical day. ▶▶**eBay sellers are as varied as the range of different marketplaces they trade in.** A lot of what takes place during normal business hours—and afterward—depends on what they're selling, how they run their business, and the systems, or lack thereof, that they have in place for things like inventory management, client contact, and so on.

That said, there are some common factors that characterize what it's like to be an eBay seller. Most sellers will tell you that the hours are long and that they typically work harder being self-employed than they did when working for someone else. That's standard for the game, regardless of the business you're in and where you do it. But they like what they're doing, their enjoyment level is far higher, and this, plus lots of other perks—such as flexibility, doing what you love, and more—makes it worthwhile.

Cathleen Lola, who has operated on eBay as Tialey Vintage since 2003, would agree with the above. She came from the retail world and was accustomed to long hours, but she wasn't used to having to do everything herself. That said, the freedom of being able to own and operate her own business and do it her way more than makes up for the amount of work her business requires. Asked if she'd ever consider going back to work for someone else, she smiled broadly and gave a one-word answer.

"Never!"

Here's what life as an eBay seller is like for her:

❝ On days I'm staying home, meaning that I'm not shopping for inventory, I start at around 6:30 A.M. I check the site for questions, make changes to auction durations if needed, reply to any e-mails, make coffee and breakfast, do the laundry, take a shower.

Between 8 and 10:30 A.M., I take or edit photos, whichever is needed. After this, I work on auction listings for another hour and a half or so. I generally get between five to eight done, depending on the items and how much research I have to do.

I break for lunch around 12 P.M., and do any household tidying that's needed while waiting for lunch to heat.

Afternoons are spent on general eBay business. I check e-mails again, get items ready for shipping, work on listings or photos, and maybe do item research. When things go right, I can take about 164 pictures of twenty items. I can write about six to eight listings a day. If I can recycle old listing copy, which I try to do as much as possible, I can write more.

My day ends at 5 P.M. with a post office run if I'm shipping internationally. Then I might hit the dry cleaners or the bank, if needed. This generally is the end of my day, but if there's nothing interesting on television during the evening, I might do some photo editing.

Thursdays are typically buying days for me. I start early—6 A.M. is fairly standard, but it depends on sale times or areas. I usually visit an average of six to eight (or more) estate sales or four to six thrifts on my regular weekly routine. I try to fit in more if I'm feeling lucky.

If the day's not going well and I finish my buying rounds early, I'll come home and write listings, research items, or take pictures. For inventory purposes, I also work up a list of everything I've bought, with what I paid and where purchased, before doing any other eBay business. It's too easy to let picky stuff like this go, and I don't like doing it, so I try to force myself to do it as soon as possible.

I really do try to stick to these hours, give or take a few minutes, but sometimes life does get in the way. On weekends, I usually have to force myself not to do anything eBay related, but if the week turned ugly, I will work on photos, shipping, research, and sometimes writing ads, but at a more relaxed pace.

Paperwork is the one thing I hate to do, which isn't good, and I tend to leave it to last because of this. I'm thinking of taking on an employee to help with the filing and paperwork, which you can see isn't really scheduled, and possibly even work toward delegating shipping to someone else. I do try to automate my systems as much as possible—I have a system for tracking the status on transactions, and for tracking income and expenses. But this is an area I can definitely improve on, and I'm determined to streamline my operations in the year to come.

My family supports my business, even when it overflows into their lives more than it should, and I'm thankful for that. There are times when I can see how easily things could get out of control, and I'm determined not to let them. Life's too short for that. **99**

▶▶ **TEST DRIVE**

Think about what you would do for a living if you could do anything you want and price was no object. Try to come up with more than one possibility, but if you only have one, that's fine, too. Is there a component of your dream job or jobs that you could do on eBay? For example, if you're a graphic designer, could you put your skills to use coming up with great auction templates for something you want to sell? Could you develop a niche market selling graphic arts supplies? Maybe offer your services through eBay's services division? Offer customized T-shirts or other items that display your designs? Or let's say you like to restore old MG automobiles. Could you sell MG parts? MG memorabilia? Service manuals? Make a list of the possibilities, and start thinking about how you might be able to turn your passions into profit on eBay.

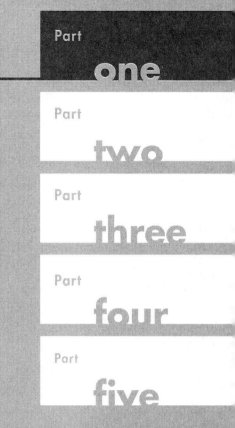

Part

one

Part

two

Part

three

Part

four

Part

five

Registering as a Member

The first step in becoming an eBay seller is registering at the site. There's no charge for registering as either a buyer or a seller, but you will need proof of your identity to register as a seller. This typically means providing a credit card and checking account information.

The Registration Process

All you have to do is go to eBay's home page at *www.ebay.com*. At the top of the page, right under the horizontal menu bar, you'll see a line that says "Hello! Sign in or register." Click on "Register." This will take you to a screen where you'll enter your personal information, including your full name, address, city, state, country, phone numbers, and e-mail address. For confirmation purposes, you'll be asked to enter your e-mail address twice; this is to make sure you've entered it correctly as eBay will use this address to confirm your registration. If there's an error, you won't be able to complete the registration process.

Below this information you'll see eBay's User Agreement and Privacy Policy. In order to complete your registration, you'll have to click on a box that confirms that you have read and agreed to this document.

Another Way to Prove You're You

If you don't have both a credit card and checking account, or for some reason you don't want to provide this information, ID Verify is another way to satisfy eBay's need for proof of identity.

ID Verify is run by Equifax, the same company that does credit checks. You submit your information, and Equifax runs it through its verification network. There's a fee of $5 for the service, which you'll only pay after your information passes muster. If for some reason you don't complete the verification process, you don't owe a thing.

ID Verify has other advantages for new eBayers, especially if you want to start selling right away. After you're verified, you can run Buy It Now auctions with fewer than ten feedbacks, and you can sell items in the Mature Audiences category. You can also place bids higher than $15,000.

After you've navigated through the personal information and indicated that you agree to abide by eBay's rules and regulations, you'll be directed to a screen where you'll choose your user ID and password. Simply follow the directions there.

Registering Multiple Accounts

There's no limit to the number of accounts—or identities—you can have on eBay. Many users have at least two, one for buying and the other for selling.

When you're first starting out, it's probably best to limit yourself to one or two active accounts at the most. You'll also be using them to build your reputation, give and get feedback, and gain the trust of other members. Having too many identities in use will slow down this process. Plus, keeping track of multiple identities can be confusing, especially in the beginning.

Once you're up and running, and if your plans include selling in more than one category, having multiple personalities can be a very good idea. Here are just a few ways they can come in handy:

1. Establishing a strong reputation in different categories: Let's say you start out by selling children's clothing. You're doing great, and then you happen to stumble across a huge lot of old fishing lures that screams "Buy me!" It's going to take you a while to sell all of them, and there's more where they came from, so you're thinking about making them a staple in your auction lineup. Fishing lures and children's clothing? Probably not the best combo, as they appeal to two very different audiences. Set up another ID for the lures.

2. Testing a new product or supplier: Maybe you're thinking about taking on a new product line, but you're not entirely sure it's for you. Selling items in the new line under an ID other than your main one will let you test-drive it without diluting your main identity. Doing so will also protect the feedback on your main ID, just in case your new venture doesn't go as well as you thought it would.

3. **Testing a new market niche, auction format, marketing idea, and so on:** In these situations, selling under another identity is a good idea for the same reasons as above. Again, why risk damaging the feedback on your main selling ID when you're in test-drive mode?

4. **Concealing your supply sources:** If you plan to acquire inventory on eBay for selling on the site, buying on one ID and selling on another can hide your tracks from your buyers. It can also make it more difficult, if not impossible, for your buyers and your competition to know what you spend on your inventory.

5. **Dumping inventory that doesn't sell:** We all make mistakes, but we don't necessarily want the entire world to know when we make them. If you're in an "oops" situation, you can cloak your misfortune by selling the merchandise that didn't do well under a secondary ID.

6. **Selling on consignment for others:** If you decide to do this, either on your own or as part of eBay's Trading Assistant program, establishing a separate ID for these sales can help you organize and manage them better.

You don't need a separate credit card for each ID you set up. Nor do you need a separate PayPal account for each one, as PayPal lets you accept payments for up to seven different e-mail addresses on a single account. But you will need a separate e-mail address for each. Most online services will let you set up multiple screen names and e-mail addresses under one account. If you have your own domain, you can set up all of your e-mail addresses under it.

If you think you're going to sell under multiple User IDs, you might want to reserve the names on eBay right away. Doing so will prevent others from taking names that you want to use. You can register IDs as buyer-only accounts at any time, and you can upgrade them to seller accounts at any time.

About Posting IDs

Many eBayers establish one or more User IDs for posting on eBay's discussion boards. This can be a good idea when posting or discussing delicate or controversial subjects, and it can protect you from people who single out sellers and interfere with their auctions, which, unfortunately, can and does happen.

If you're concerned about this happening to you, you can register a posting ID at any time. You can use it solely for posting and never buy or sell a thing with it, but you'll be limited to just ten posts a day on the discussion boards if you take this approach. If you want to participate more, you'll have to do some buying to push your feedback score to ten or above.

Choosing a User Name

Since people can't see or hear you in cyberspace—for the most part, anyway—they have to get to know you in other ways. For this reason, user or screen names—known as User IDs on eBay—are a big part of online identities.

There are differences of opinion over the elements of an effective user name, and what someone else likes might not be to your taste at all. That said, here are some generally accepted guidelines to go by:

1. **Keep it simple.** Long or complicated strings of letters and numbers are difficult for other users to remember.
2. **Make it distinctive.** This is for an obvious reason—you want your name to stand out. But don't go overboard. A name chosen for its shock value might offend some bidders and alienate others.
3. **If possible, have it reflect what you're selling.** Let's say you're selling custom children's clothing, pieces you design and sew yourself. A name like suescustomkids is cute, but it doesn't exactly tell potential buyers what you're selling. Try something like customkidclothes or customclothesforkids instead.
4. **Don't go crazy with original spellings.** Millions of User IDs have been registered before yours, which can make it difficult to come up with a name that's distinctive and original. This

means you might have to come up with a spelling variation to get a name that's even close to what you want. This can be okay—if you go back to the previous example, kustomklothesforkids can be kind of cute—but it can also make User IDs harder to read and remember.

5. **Keep it short.** eBay only gives you thirty-five characters for a User ID, so you couldn't go on forever even if you wanted to. It's a good idea to keep names fairly short regardless. Long, drawn-out names are difficult to read and to remember, and they can wreak havoc with screen displays. At the same time, don't make your name so short that it doesn't say anything about you or what you're selling.

6. **Stay away from ambiguous combinations.** Some things like the letter O and the number 0 in combination can be confusing. So do the lowercase letter L and the number 1. Yes, they look different here, but eBay displays all letters in User IDs in lower case, regardless of how you type them in.

7. **If you think you'll expand your offerings in the future, try to pick a name that's broad or generic enough to allow for that expansion.** Again, going back to the custom kid's clothing theme, if you're going to start by making baby clothes, you might think it a good idea to choose a name that reflects that. But if you plan to offer clothes for older children in the future, using the term "kids" instead of "babies" is probably a better bet.

8. **Keep punctuation to a minimum.** Because there are so many users at the site, it can be tough to come up with a name without punctuation. If you have to use it, hyphens and asterisks work the best, such as custom*kids*clothes or custom-kids-clothes. Underscores and periods—custom_kids_clothes or custom.kids.clothes—can be difficult to see, especially when User IDs are displayed as links.

9. **Incorporate your User ID into your branding if at all possible.** For more on the importance of branding, turn to Chapter 19.

10. **If you already have a business name, and you're establishing your eBay business as a part of your existing business, think about using all or part of your business name as your User ID.**

eBay also has some rules on the words and symbols that User IDs can and can't include. There aren't any surprises here—basically, you can't use profanity or in some other way violate eBay's guidelines. You can't use certain punctuation marks or open spaces, although hyphens or underscores are okay. You can't use an e-mail address or URL or include a third-party trademark or brand. As an example, if you're going to sell Converse shoes, you can't include Converse in your ID.

If you want to learn more about what you can and can't include in your User ID before you start the registration process, go to the Help area, then "New" to "eBay>Registration Process>Choosing a User ID." Otherwise, just jump in. If the name you want to use isn't in compliance, you'll find out right away, as you won't be allowed to register it.

Registering Your Password

You'll also have to register a password with your User ID. The standard cautions about computer passwords apply here:

➲ Don't go with the obvious; that is, anything that someone else might be able to figure out and use to hack into your account.

➲ Try to pick a password that has meaning to you, and only you.

➲ Whatever password you end up with, try not to forget it. However, if your password does slip your mind, you can retrieve it at the site.

You can have the same password regardless of how many User IDs you register. eBay will prompt you to enter it, along with your User ID, every time you access the site unless you tell the system to keep you signed in until you sign out.

For privacy and security purposes, you might want to change your password from time to time, but you don't have to.

Changing Your Identity

If for some reason you end up not liking the name you choose, or you feel you need a name that better reflects what you're selling, you can exchange your old User ID for a new one at any time. When you do, eBay suspends your old ID for thirty days. After that, it's up for grabs, which means you or anyone else can use it. For this reason, it's a good idea to think twice before changing your User ID. If for some reason you want to reclaim it, you might not be able to if someone else beats you to it.

Establishing an eBay E-mail Address

Each ID you establish on eBay has to have a separate e-mail address defined for it. If you receive e-mail through your Internet service provider, eBay won't require anything more than that address. If you use a free e-mail service such as Yahoo or Hotmail, you'll have to register a credit or debit card number and billing information along with the address. This is for identity verification. Free services don't require it, which is one of the reasons they're popular, but eBay wants to make darned sure that the name and address you provided when you registered are valid.

The credit/debit card information must match your eBay contact information. It's only used to verify this information; your card won't be charged.

Understanding eBay's User Agreement and Privacy Policy

This document stipulates how you can use the eBay site. It also details what eBay does and doesn't do.

If you're like most people, you'll skim through part of it, get bored, and accept its terms without reading it all the way through. And that's probably okay. But it's important to realize that this document is a binding contract. When you click "I Accept," you're agreeing to its terms. It's never a good idea to agree to something without knowing what you're locked into. For this reason, you'll want to read it in more detail at some point, and it's a good idea to read it sooner than later.

The User Agreement and Privacy Policy is too lengthy to detail here, but here's some information on parts of the document that, for various reasons, sometimes trip up new users:

Eligibility: eBay can only be used by individuals who can enter into legally binding contracts. For the most part, this means adults over age eighteen. If you're under eighteen, you can use eBay, but you have to do it while supervised by parents or guardians.

Account ownership: You, and only you, can own and operate your eBay account, which includes your User ID and feedback. This means you can't transfer or sell either entity to someone else. eBay also stipulates that if you're registering as a business, you must have the authority to enter into the agreement as your business's representative.

Using other people's information: To facilitate transactions, eBay gives users limited access to other users' contact and shipping information. You can only use this information for eBay-related communications and for services offered through eBay. You can't take it and put it into another database for your own use elsewhere unless you get permission from the other users.

Dispute resolution: Agreeing to the User Agreement stipulates that you'll hold eBay harmless from "claims, demands and damages (actual and consequential) of every kind and nature, known and unknown, suspected and unsuspected, disclosed and undisclosed, arising out of or in any way connected with such disputes."

Your obligations as a seller and/or buyer: Simply put, you're obligated to complete your transactions, regardless of which side of the table you sit at, unless there's a good reason why you can't. For sellers, good reasons include such things as breaking the item when you pack it or having something else happen that renders the item unsellable. They don't include things like offering products that aren't really available, seller's remorse, or simply deciding you don't want to sell because you didn't get enough money.

Fraud: If you engage in fraudulent activity, such as not following through on auctions, shill bidding, selling fake merchandise and the like, or you're suspected of doing so, eBay can suspend or terminate your account.

Selling infringing items: eBay has a program called Verified Rights Owner, or VeRO, which protects copyright, trademark, and other rights of various parties. If you sell items that infringe on these rights, such as "designer-inspired" or fake handbags, VeRO program participants can ask eBay to yank your listings. Other eBay users can also report your auctions, with the same results if the things you're selling aren't the real deal.

Price manipulation and auction interference: You can't inflate auction prices or otherwise interfere with auctions by bidding up your or anyone else's items, entering and then retracting bids, or enlisting others to do the same.

You can see a copy of the complete agreement at *http://pages.ebay .com/help/community/png-user.html.*

Make It Easy—Print it Out

You can print out eBay's user agreement, and it's not a bad idea to do it so you can read it offline at your leisure. It's a little dry and full of legalese, but it also contains good information about your rights and responsibilities as an eBay member and about eBay's rights and responsibilities as well. If—well, more likely, *when*—you encounter problems on eBay (you'd definitely be the exception to the rule if you never run afoul of eBay's rules and policies), chances are pretty good that whoever handles the problem on eBay's end will refer at least once to this document or direct you to it for further review.

Setting Up Online Payment Accounts

As a seller, you'll want to offer as many payment options as possible. Doing so makes it easy for buyers to do business with you. As a buyer, it's also a good idea to have a few options, which includes being able to make payments online.

Of the eBay sellers who offer online payment (not all do), the majority use PayPal.

eBay owns PayPal. As such, it's fully integrated into the site. You'll see it everywhere—in auction listings (when sellers offer it), on your My eBay page, you name it.

You can go directly to PayPal's site at *www.paypal.com* or simply access it from any eBay area that provides a link to it. When you get there, you'll be asked to register a user name and password, just like you did at eBay. Have your checking account and credit card numbers handy, too. PayPal will want to know how you're going to pay for the items you win or buy. Until you start selling and you deposit some funds into your PayPal account, the money for your purchases will come out of your bank account or, if sellers accept it, off your credit card.

PayPal offers three different types of accounts with different bundles of services. If you're new to eBay, a personal account, which is the lowest and most basic level, might be all you'll need. You can send and receive payments, but you can't accept debit or credit cards. There are no fees for personal accounts.

When you start selling, you'll want to upgrade to a premier or business account. You'll find more information on these in Chapter 14.

All about the "Me" Page

The "About Me" page—often just referred to as the "Me" page—is where you can tell other eBayers who you are. You can also use the page to promote your business.

As a buyer, having a "Me" page is a nice touch, but it isn't critical. It's more important for sellers.

Some sellers wait a while before putting their "Me" pages together, but it's really something you'll want to do as soon as possible, even if it's just a

Why Not Me?

Every so often I come across a really fantastic seller who doesn't have an "About Me" page. I always feel kind of cheated when this happens. For me, and for countless other eBayers, part of the fun in trading on eBay is meeting interesting people you wouldn't otherwise come across, and the "About Me" page is prime territory for learning more about them.

When I come upon these sellers, I also wonder why they're not willing to be more forthcoming about who they are and what their business is all about. The way they present their auctions, as well as their feedback scores and comments, can give you some of this information, but you can only glean so much. Just a few lines about how the seller got started in the business, why they sell what they sell, and maybe a short explanation of their business philosophy can make newbies feel more comfortable when buying. If there are problems with feedback scores and/or comments, the "Me" page is also a good place to explain what's going on.

In an ultracompetitive business arena like eBay, I don't think you can afford to cast doubt in your customers' minds by not telling them a little about yourself. You might feel awkward writing about yourself—if so, get someone else to do it for you—or you might think you should wait until you have something more to say about yourself. On the contrary, getting your "Me" page up early is really one of the best things you can do to get off on the right foot right away.

bare-bones version. Having one up and running at the beginning of your trading career will tell everyone you're serious about doing business on eBay and that you buy into the site's basic philosophies. You can always expand on it later.

Building Your "Me" Page

Putting together a basic "Me" page is fairly simple. All you have to do is go to the Community tab at the top of any page. Scroll down to "More Community Programs," and then down to "Create an About Me Page." Follow the directions from there. You'll be able to choose from several basic layout options, which you can personalize with eBay's HTML tags or your own.

"About Me" pages are great advertising tools for sellers, and the fact that they're free makes them an incredible value. What's more, you can do just about anything you want to with your page. You can tell people a little bit about how you started your eBay business and where you want to go with it. You can talk about your business philosophies, what you like to collect, your hobbies—you name it. But remember, this is a promotional tool. While it's a nice touch to tell people a little bit about yourself, don't bury or neglect important information about your business.

You can even include a link to your own Web store or Web site on your "Me" page. But you can't directly offer any non-eBay merchandise on your "Me" page, such as telling buyers you have more of the same items for sale privately. eBay frowns heavily on off-site trading.

Things you'll want to stay away from on your "Me" page include the following:

- **Fancy graphics:** They take too long to load, and they're distracting. Also nix excessive animations and screen effects like slow dissolves, wipes, and so on. They're distracting, and they can do weird things to computer operating systems.
- **Music:** You never know where your customers might be when they decide to take a look at your "Me" page. If they're at work, they won't want a blast of unexpected music to herald the fact that they're doing something other than their jobs.
- **Too much information:** Remember the KISS acronym: keep it short and sweet. Two to three paragraphs is usually just about right.

One thing to consider including on your "About Me" page are your terms and conditions of service, or TOS. TOS tell bidders what they can expect when they buy from you. They also include information on payment forms, shipping, feedback, return policies, how and when you communicate with buyers—basically anything having to do with how you would like transactions to take place.

You'll include a short form of these—the basics that buyers need to know—in your auction listings. Many sellers expand on them a little (or a lot) on their "About Me" pages. You'll find more information on writing your TOS in Chapter 11.

"Me" Page No-No's

There are some restrictions for what you can include on your "Me" page. The following things are not allowed on your "Me" page:

⟳ Links to merchandise or information not available or not permitted on eBay

⟳ Links to other online trading sites

⟳ Links to sites offering the same merchandise at the same or lower price

⟳ Links to commercial Web sites that compile listings from other sellers

A Typical "About Me" Page

The following text is an example of what can be included on a simple yet effective "About Me" page. It's straightforward and to the point; the copy tells buyers what the seller specializes in and gives them a taste of the seller's personality and style.

Welcome to the SWEDISHDRAMA Zone . . .

We like all kinds of things, but especially beautiful linens, vintage clothing, retro kitchen items, and pretty much anything that's got great design or is too much fun to pass up.

Architecture and Design Books are a Favorite!

We both belong to the genus *packratus maximus*, but eBay gives us the perfect opportunity to find and collect great, groovy, weird and funky stuff and pass it on to you . . .
We hope you enjoy the great mid-century modern, funky stuff, treasures of the past, and just plain cool junque that you'll find here at Swedishdrama. We love having it, we love passing it on to a good home—we hope it's yours!

Protecting Your Online Identity

Online communities like eBay have many things in common with the brick-and-mortar retail world. Unfortunately, some of these things are as unsavory in cyberspace as they are on land. Identity theft can and does happen online. So does stalking.

Most of what you do online is visible to others. When you post to a discussion board, it's not just the participants on that board who read what you write. Your comments can be quoted in other forums, cut and pasted into other discussion boards, and even made accessible to search engines. Always be smart about what you do online.

It's always a good idea to err on the side of caution when communicating online. Be careful about what you say and do. Don't include too much personal information on your "About Me" page. And never give out personal information, including your name and address, to anyone you're not involved in a transaction with.

▶▶ Test Drive

You can access eBay as a guest and do almost anything a registered user can at the site. If you haven't already done so, go to eBay now and start looking around. Pull up some auctions—any auctions—and analyze them along these lines:

1. User name: Easy to remember? Does it match what the seller is offering? If not, does it work anyway?

2. Auction title/gallery photo: There's a reason you chose the particular auctions you looked at. Was it the title? The gallery picture? Both? Would you be as likely to pull up the listing if it didn't have a gallery picture? What was it about the title that grabbed you?

3. Auction appearance and language: Are things easy to read? Confusing? Is the description well written? If not, how would you improve on it? Do the pictures show you enough about the product?

Finding Your Way Around

eBay is a fantastic and fascinating marketplace, and it's also an amazingly complex one. For this reason, it's often not all that easy to navigate, especially when you start poking around beyond the site's topmost layers. Finding certain content areas, such as the links for reporting questionable auctions or contacting eBay directly, can seem like deep space exploration.

To use the site to its fullest potential, you have to get to know it, and the best way to do this is to dig into it. This might seem simplistic, maybe even kind of silly, but seasoned sellers will tell you that they spent a great deal of time getting to know the site before they listed their first items. Following their example will cut down on the amount of time you feel dazed and confused, keep you from asking too many embarrassing newbie questions on the discussion boards, and give you a leg up as a seller that much faster.

There's a link to eBay's site map at the top of every page. Click on it, and you'll see how the site is laid out. eBay recently reorganized its site map into five main subject areas: Buy, Sell, My eBay, Community, and Help. Whether the reorganization makes things easier to find can be debated, as it's still nearly impossible to locate certain information, but the current layout is simpler and easier to read.

---

eBay A to Z

If you need to find something on eBay but you're not exactly sure what you're looking for, try this tip suggested by an eBay PowerSeller: Start with the A-Z Index in the Help section on eBay's site map. Seeing the help topics in alphabetical order can make it easier to find what you're after.

Still, seeing everything in one place like this can be overwhelming, and, to be honest, it's probably more than you ever want or need to know about eBay. In the future, maybe out of curiosity, you might want to visit more of it. For now, here's a short list of the areas you should explore sooner than later:

⊃ **Common Keyword Searches and Common Keywords:** If you want to see actual search terms or test the effectiveness of various keywords, this is ground zero for that information. If you're still researching what you're going to sell, these areas might also give you some ideas.

⊃ **Categories:** This is a top-level index of every eBay category, with subcategories organized behind each link.

⊃ **News:** Links to announcements, the eBay newsletter, and other community-wide information can be found here.

⊃ **Help:** You'll find links to areas that answer some of the most frequently asked questions here.

▲ Going to a help page (like the typical one shown here) is often the easiest way to answer any questions you have about eBay or any other online auction site.

Learning How to Use eBay Search Effectively

Mastering the ins and outs of eBay's search system can help you find deals, both for yourself and for resale. It can also be a great way to comparison-shop prices and research possible selling categories.

You'll find more in-depth information on configuring searches for research purposes in Chapter 4. For now, let's just take a look at how to make searches yield the information you really want to see.

Turning General into Specific

New eBayers often just enter in the first search word or two that pops into their heads. This is okay, but doing so typically doesn't get the best results, especially if the words you choose don't really describe what you're after. As an example, let's say you're looking for an old purse. The search terms "old" and "purse" are going to return thousands of listings, as they're fairly broad and vague. However, you won't see every old purse that's on eBay if you just use these terms for your search. Lots of sellers call them something else—bags and handbags are two other common terms—and they might not include the word "purse" in their listings. As such, you won't see these items unless you refine your search.

Here's how to make this search better:

1. **More specific words:** What kind of purse are you looking for? Add these terms to your search. "Beaded purse" will return more targeted listings. So will "deco purse," "Victorian purse," "flapper bag," "Lucite handbag," and so on.
2. **Different words:** "Old" and "purse" might not be the best search terms. Try different combinations—"old handbag," "old bag," "vintage purse," "vintage handbag," and so on. Keep the number of words short—two or three at most—if you want to see lots of listings and a good variety of them.
3. **Date matches:** Let's say you want to see old purses from the 1920s. Enter "old purse 192*." The asterisk is a wild card, and this search will return all listings from this decade. It also works if you're not sure about the spelling on an item, or you think sellers might misspell it. As an example, let's say you're searching for

Barbra Streisand memorabilia. Many people think she spells her name the conventional way—Barbara—and that's how they list their items. Type in Barb*, and you'll get auctions containing any word beginning with these four letters.

4. **Color match:** This one's pretty easy. Just type in the color along with your primary search term. The same thing goes for style searches. If you want a fringed purse, type that in.

5. **Brand match:** Let's say you want a Whiting & Davis purse. Type that in. If you want one from a specific era, say the 1930s, enter "Whiting & Davis purse 193*."

6. **Quote it:** Putting your search terms in quotes, such as "Whiting & Davis purse" will limit the search to the exact phrase inside the quotes.

7. **Search titles and descriptions:** eBay's basic search only looks at titles. But you can ask the search engine to look at descriptions too. You'll get lots more results if you do. This search only works for active listings.

8. **Singles and plurals:** Search "bag." Then search "bags." You'll get results both ways.

Using words like "or," "the," and "and" can mess up searches unless you're searching for items that contain them, as the example above did, because eBay's search engine searches for them as it does with any other words. If you're not, leave them out. Punctuation is another search scrambler. Only use it if it's part of the item you're looking for.

Other search approaches to know about include these:

⮕ **Separating words with commas instead of spaces:** This method tells eBay's search engine to look for items related to the word on both sides of the comma. It's a good one to know about if what you're searching for does include punctuation, or, again, if you're unsure of the spelling on an item.

⮕ **Parentheses:** These searches will return results based on both versions of the word in parentheses. It's good for combining key words with single and plural variations, such as vintage (bag, bags).

➲ **Minus sign and parentheses combination:** This approach will tell the search engine to find the words before the parentheses, but it will exclude any words inside them. As an example, say you're searching for a St. John jacket. Configuring your search like this, "St. John –(Bay)" will cut down on the number of listings you get for J. C. Penney apparel.

If all else fails, or you're not looking for anything specific, just browse through the category listing pages. You never know what you might find.

▲ Advanced search pages, like this one, allow you to refine your searches to find items within very specific parameters.

Pre-Set Searches

eBay has a number of preconfigured searches. You can tell the search engine to return results based on item location, type of listing, and so on. For eBay sellers, "Search Completed Auctions" is one of the best preconfigured searches to know about, as it lets you see how well items

Welcome to Your New Job

When I started my first business in 1986, I also bought my first PC. Back then, personal computers were far from being the ubiquitous business tools they are now. I had experience with dedicated word processors, but this machine scared me—and so it sat in its boxes for two weeks. When I finally dug it out and set it up, I realized I didn't know what to do next. I was also afraid I would do something wrong and break it.

My father's company manufactured computers (yes, that's where I bought mine). When I told him I wasn't using it, he told me to quit being silly. There wasn't much I could do that would break it, he said. "Just turn it off if you think you've done something wrong." Then he told me to locate my user's manual (computers came with them back then) and get serious about learning the machine. "Do it this weekend," he said. "Think of it as part of your orientation for your new job. Now that you're self-employed, there's no one else to show you the ropes but you."

If you're pretty savvy about using Web sites, spending hours poking around eBay might seem like the last thing you need to do. But it's really one of the first, especially if you're serious about building your business. You're starting a new job, and you're playing every role, including that of the person who's responsible for showing you around.

Learning the site is a big part of your orientation, and there's no one to show you around other than you. So, take the time and orient yourself. Yes, you might feel silly, but you don't have to tell anybody about it. You'll be glad you did this. Honest.

the same or similar to yours sold, and for how much. But it only lets you see about two weeks' worth of completed listings. Due to the volume of transactions at the site, eBay only stores that much data.

This is okay if you're looking for in-season items or if you want to sell items that are always in demand. If you're not, then it could be a problem, especially if you're doing your research during the off-season. If so, you'll have to rely on other sources of information to tell you what you need to know about your items, or you'll have to wait until your items come back into season. This might not seem as far-fetched as you may think. Some very successful eBay sellers waited as much as a year to launch their businesses, or to offer new products, after they made the decision to do so. They spent a lot of that time researching categories and products.

Searching eBay Stores

eBay's basic search doesn't display offerings from eBay Stores. If you want to look for items in them—which you should, as it can give you a more complete picture of what the competition looks like in your category—you can do a separate search to grab these listings. eBay has recently redesigned its search engines to make this kind of search very easy, and you can do it a couple of different ways. You can go to eBay's home page and click on Buy, which will take you to the front page for this area. Enter your search terms, then choose how you want to search—by category, title and description, or in eBay Stores.

You can also simply click on the link prompting you to look at the offerings in eBay stores that appears at the bottom of search results pages. You'll also see a link to items available from sellers in other countries down there. This can also be an interesting source of information—remember, you're dealing with a global marketplace.

Saving Searches

If you're going to check the competition in certain areas on a regular basis, save your search as a favorite search. Doing so will let you launch the search any time you want to directly from your My eBay page without having to reconfigure it each time. You can even configure the search to notify you when new items become available.

Understanding Selling Categories

There are tens of thousands of selling categories on eBay, and new categories are added when necessary. They're arranged in a fairly linear style. As an example, if you want to buy a pair of boots, you'll find your best selection in the logical category—clothing and accessories. Let's say you're looking for English riding boots. They might be listed in clothing and accessories, but if you're looking for the real deal, not fashion boots that look like riding boots, "equestrian equipment and apparel" in the

Sports category will be the better place to search. Maybe you're passionate about old fishing lures. You might find them in the fishing equipment category. But they could also be listed as collectibles.

Gaining a basic understanding of how product categories are broken down will help you know which ones will work best for you when you're ready to sell. And knowing which categories to list in can make a big difference in your sales. While many eBay buyers use keywords to configure their searches, many others love to browse categories just to see what they might come across. You'll want to be sure they find your listings when they're browsing.

▲ Understanding the categories available at online auction site will help you both in researching the market for your goods, and in placing your items in a place where possible buyers can easily find them.

Exploring Half.com and eBay Motors

These are eBay's two big specialty selling areas. Half.com is for books, DVDs, and other media. eBay Motors is, well, what it says it is. Cars, motorcycles, campers, things with motors. You'll also find accessories and parts here.

The rules for selling in each area are a bit different than for the rest of eBay. For Half.com, you have to register a separate seller account even if you're already an eBay seller. This is for eBay's accounting purposes, as they bill Half.com transactions separately from eBay sales. However, you can use the same User ID and password, and your feedback from both sites will go to the same name.

At this time, only U.S. residents can sell on Half.com. But you can live anywhere and buy.

eBay has developed an excellent online tutorial about selling on eBay Motors. If you're thinking about selling in this area, you'll want to go through it in detail. As a seller in this category, you'll have to deal with things that other sellers don't, such as warranties, financing, shipping, vehicle inspection, title transfer, and so on. The tutorial is the best place to learn how.

Delving into Discussion Boards

eBay is more than buying and selling. It's truly an online community in every sense of the word, and the company devotes a fair amount of resources and room on the site to promoting community spirit. If there's any question about eBay's position on this, the company's following statement of community values should make things very clear:

> We believe people are basically good.
>
> We believe everyone has something to contribute.
>
> We believe that an honest, open environment can bring out the best in people.
>
> We recognize and respect everyone as a unique individual.
>
> We encourage you to treat others the way you want to be treated.

Participating in eBay's discussion boards will help you realize how much of a community really does exist around eBay. Working in cyberspace can be lonely. Discussion boards put community at your fingertips.

If you're a complete newbie and you literally don't know where to start, there's a board that can help you. Want to know more about the category you want to sell in? Chances are there's a board for this, too.

eBay's community discussion boards are divided into three broad categories:

➔ **Community help boards** that provide assistance on subjects ranging from writing good auction descriptions to trouble-shooting problems with buyers.

➔ **Category-specific boards,** which can be great resources for asking questions about the items you're selling and getting answers from others in the same category.

➔ **General discussion boards** are the lighter side of eBay. Check these out if you're interested in meeting fellow eBayers and carrying on general conversations.

Not all eBayers get involved in discussion boards, but a good number do. If you're going to follow suit, do it judiciously. It can be far too easy to spend more time on the boards than you should, especially when you're connecting with a group of people with interests similar to yours.

▸▸**Remember that the more time you spend on the boards, the less time you'll have to devote to your business.** Try to set a reasonable limit on your participation—maybe half an hour a day—and stick to it.

The general tenor of the boards ranges from polite and supportive to boisterous and cutthroat, and it can vary quite a bit by board. Some boards will feel open and welcoming, while others will seem like they're run by a small group of individuals who have been there for a while, know each other well, and speak the same language. Oftentimes, these boards can be intimidating for new users, as they seem less than welcoming. They might very well be, but you can always lurk and just watch the discussions. You don't have to join in. If you do, you might want to use a posting ID—discussed in Chapter 2—to protect your identity until you feel more comfortable.

Another word of caution about discussion boards: Never forget that they're open forums, and that anything you say on them can be seen by the public. It's a very good idea not to divulge too much about yourself, your loved ones, where you live, what your daily schedule is, and so on. Also be careful what you say about others. You can delete posts once they're made, but you'll never know how many people saw what you wrote before your words disappear.

Finally, never post in anger, and always take a moment to reflect on what you've written if there's a chance that your words will offend. Undoing the damage done by a seemingly innocent comment gone wrong can take a long time, and the board that was once so welcoming and friendly might no longer be.

Trolls and Train Wrecks

Spend enough time on the boards, and you'll encounter an unsavory aspect of the Internet world called a troll. These are people who lurk in discussion boards and chat rooms, looking for a chance to start an argument. If they hit on a particularly hot button, boardies—other board participants—will pile on. Discussions can escalate until they get out of control and turn into train wrecks. Some people survive these. Others don't. Getting "pink slapped"—receiving a cautionary e-mail from one of eBay's board monitors about what you can and can't do on the boards—is the typical outcome of a train wreck. Participants can also be forced to go on a brief vacation, during which time they can buy and sell on eBay but can't participate on the boards.

The Internet, because it's so anonymous, is prime hunting ground for trolls. If and when you encounter one, your best bet is to ignore it. This won't make it go away—it can always lurk without anyone knowing about it—but trolls are less likely to cause problems if you don't feed them.

Meeting eBay Members via Groups and Chat Rooms

Groups and Chat Rooms are other eBay community-building areas. Groups are what the name suggests—special gatherings of eBayers with the same interests and passions. Interest areas can range far beyond what eBay has defined for discussion boards. Anyone can start a group, and most groups are open to anyone who's interested. You can also be invited to join a group.

Chat Rooms are live chat areas. There are general chat rooms and category-specific rooms. They're very much like Discussion Boards, only in real time.

Even if you don't think these areas are for you, it's not a bad idea to drop by and see what they're all about. You might come across good information that you won't see anywhere else, and they'll definitely tell you what's on the minds of other eBayers.

How eBay Keeps You Informed

eBay likes to have an informed community, and it disseminates information in a variety of ways. It's up to you how much or little of it you want to read; eBay makes this information freely available and very accessible.

Areas you'll want to keep an eye on include the following:

➔ **Announcements:** This is fairly fluffy stuff for the most part, but every so often eBay will let a little bomb drop in this area. If there are fee increases in the works, you'll often find information about them here. Also here are announcements on things like site enhancements, category realignments, technical issues, and so on.

➔ **Community and Workshop Calendars:** This is where eBay lists events, workshops, and other things of interest to the eBay community.

⤳ **The Chatter:** This is eBay's monthly newsletter. It's definitely a promotional tool, but the articles can be interesting and informative.

The granddaddy of them all for eBay information is eBay Live! This annual event gathers eBay members, employees, and vendors for three days of seminars, presentations, workshops, product demonstrations, and networking geared to sellers at all levels of experience. You have to pay to go, but the price is extremely affordable, and past attendees will tell you that what you get is more than worth the money.

eBay Live! 2005 celebrated the company's tenth anniversary and was held in San Jose, California, eBay's home city. Las Vegas is the site for eBay Live! 2006.

 ▶▶ **Test Drive**

Pick an item you want to research on eBay, and try a variety of different approaches. At a minimum, do the following searches:

⤳ Active listings
⤳ Completed listings
⤳ Broad category search
⤳ Specific category search
⤳ Stores search

Compare the results, and note the differences in what turns up.

Buy Before You Sell

You can start off immediately as a seller on eBay—many people do—but you might find it rough going. Since you're new to the marketplace, people don't know who you are. You could have great merchandise and fantastic auction listings, and buyers might still pass you over because you're missing something: feedback.

Obviously, every eBay seller has to start somewhere. Buyers realize this, which means they'll give sellers with low feedback numbers a chance as long as they like what they see—the feedback that has been received is positive, listings are well presented, and they're interested in what the sellers have to offer.

But why do things the hard way? You'll get to where you want to go much faster if you get a leg up on feedback by doing some buying first.

Putting yourself in the buyer's shoes is also one of the best ways to get a feel for how eBay works and for how you want to do things when you start selling. Also, building your feedback score past ten allows you full privileges at the site. You can post Buy It Now auctions, you can sell items in the Mature Audiences category, and you can participate in the Community Forums to your heart's delight.

Learning from Others

eBay offers more opportunities than any other forum in history to see what others are doing and learn from them. Why not use this to your advantage? If possible, buy from sellers in the category or categories you want to sell in. Watch and learn how they run their businesses. If you like what you see, take away their best stuff for yourself—don't make an identical copy of it, of course, but just let it shape your efforts. If you don't like what you see or how you're treated, make notes so you can avoid doing the same things to your customers.

Since your primary goal is building your feedback, what you buy doesn't matter all that much. Many new sellers buy some of the things they need to set up shop, like shipping supplies, display pieces, photography backdrops and lights, and so on. Others buy some of the inventory they'll use when they start selling. Have some fun with this if you want, and buy some things that you either need or just want to own. But be a little picky about who you buy from. Make your first transactions as positive and fruitful as possible by buying from reputable sellers who follow through on their transactions and post appropriate feedback. Be sure to check their terms of service to see if they mention how they handle feedback. Many sellers wait until buyers post it first. Knowing this will keep you from waiting weeks for feedback that's not going to get posted unless you go first.

And, check their feedback, both what they've received and what they've left for others. Some sellers aren't well versed in the fine art of leaving feedback, and what they leave might not be as helpful as what you'd get from those who are. Others simply don't leave it. Checking what they've left for others will tell you if they do.

Finding the Feedback

The easiest way to check any eBayer's feedback is to click on the number following his or her User ID. This will take you to the individual's Member Profile, which displays the member's feedback score, percentage of positive feedback, length of membership, and so on. Click on the tab marked "Left for Others," and you can see what the member has to say about his or her trading partners as well.

Researching Products and Prices

Buying before you start selling is an excellent way to research products that you're thinking about selling. You can also use this pre-selling buying time to research the categories you plan to sell in.

As is discussed in more detail in Chapter 3, this research will have its best payoffs if you configure your search to return items that are as closely matched as possible to what you're going to sell. As an example, let's say you're thinking about selling a specific type of shower head. It's a high-end piece, very attractive and very distinctive. As such, you're not going to learn much about the demand for it by comparing it to shower heads that are inferior, of a different style, or that don't sell for as much. Given this, you'll want to search on the make, the model, and the model number, if there is one. You'll also want to see if there are other brands competing for the same customers. Configuring your search based on specific features might not be the most targeted search you can do, but it should return listings for products that are at least somewhat similar to yours.

▶▶**As for prices, there are two ways to research them on eBay: through current auctions and completed listings.** Current auctions will give you the most up-to-the-minute read on market conditions. Completed auctions will let you compare current market performance to sales over a two-week period.

One of eBay's neater features is the ability to sort listings by price. You can look at items based on highest prices first, or start at the bottom and work your way up. This can tell you two things: where to start your items, and what they might sell for. It can also help you determine starting prices, Buy It Now prices, and reserve amounts.

Getting to Know Auction Formats

eBay has a number of different auction formats. Of them, the following are those you're most likely to use, both as a buyer and a seller. Trying them out as a buyer is the best way to get a feel for how they work:

> **Auction:** This is the classic eBay auction format. No frills, no fuss, just an offering of an item that will go to the highest bidder.

> **Reserve price auction:** As the name suggests, these auctions allow sellers to set a reserve, or minimum, price. If bidding doesn't match this amount, no sale takes place. Reserve price auctions don't reveal the reserve amount, but sellers can choose to do so in their listing copy. This might seem like it goes against the nature of these auctions, but it really doesn't. If you know the reserve, you at least know if it's worth your while to bid.

> **Buy It Now:** Buy It Now, or BIN, gives bidders the option to buy items immediately at a set price instead of waiting for the auction to end.

Best offer: This is a fairly new auction format. It lets bidders make—you guessed it—their best offer. Sellers can take the offer or not. It's only available if sellers choose this format for their listings.

Private listing: These auctions cloak bidder identities from other prospective bidders. Sellers typically use them for items that might be somewhat sensitive in nature, such as lingerie or other more adult-oriented merchandise. Private listing auctions are the same as others in all other ways.

Fixed-price auctions: This format simply offers items at a set price. If you want it, you pay the price. No bidding, no haggling involved. Store listings are always fixed-price auctions.

You might also come across Multiple Item or Dutch auctions. This is a fairly confusing auction format that's something of a holdover from eBay's early days. These auctions offer multiple items in one listing. You decide how much you want to pay per item, and how many items you want to buy. At auction close, you get your items at the lowest bid price.

As an example, let's say you found an auction for a certain type of notebook that you like to use. The seller is offering ten of them at a beginning bid of $1 each. You decide you'd like five, and you're willing to pay $1.75 for each, so you enter the bid amount and the quantity you want. Now, let's say there's another bidder, and she wants eight notebooks. However, her bid amount is only $1.50 each. At the end of the auction, her bid is the lowest, so you both win your items at $1.50. However, since winning bids are selected in the order of bid price per item, and your bid price was higher, you'll be able to buy all five notebooks at the $1.50 price. Bidder B can have the rest at the same price. She can also choose not to complete the purchase as the remaining quantity doesn't match the number she wanted to buy.

Confused? So are most bidders, which is why you don't see too many of these auctions. If you think they might make sense for what you plan to sell, test-drive them as a buyer first.

You'll find more information on auction formats from the seller's point of view and suggestions for choosing the right format for what you want to sell in Chapter 10.

Selling for Charity

If you want to sell items for charity on eBay, you can do so on in any auction format. Simply go to the Sell Your Item form. When you get to the Pictures and Details section, click the "Add" link in the area titled "Donate percentage of sale." For more information on charity auctions, click the Community tab at the top of any page, and then go to More Community Programs.

Bidding Versus Buy It Now

In general, eBay auctions fall into two basic categories: bidding and Buy It Now.

Some buyers love the thrill of competing against others for items. For them, there's nothing like eBay's traditional auction format, which lets them ride the emotional roller coaster while winning (or losing).

Buy It Now auctions give buyers the option of bidding on items and seeing what happens or buying items right away at a set price. This format is great for people who don't want to wait. They might get a better deal if they go through the auction process, but they're willing to pay more for the convenience of not doing so.

The Bidding Process

If you haven't bid on auction items before, parts of the process might seem a little confusing. Going through the steps of an imaginary auction can help eliminate some of that.

Here's the scenario: You want to buy a headset for your cell phone. It's a snazzy wireless one, and you've found the exact one you want on eBay. Actually, you've found several. One is listed as a standard auction, one is a Buy It Now auction, and one is listed in a Multiple Item auction. Let's go through the process for each auction.

The Tale of the Snipe

Sniping, which refers to the practice of knocking out high bidders by entering bids at the last possible moment, may seem extremely sneaky and maybe a little smarmy, especially if you're on the losing end of one. However, it's a bidding approach that can deliver fantastic deals, and it's not a bad idea to learn how to do it for this reason. Since sniping pits high-speed connection against high-speed connection in the last moments of the auction, the person (or service) with the fastest connection usually wins. As such, final bid amounts on these auctions tend to be lower as bidders with slower connections can't get in fast enough to drive up the price.

Snipes can fail if other bidders have placed decent proxy amounts. Given this, it's a good idea to place a proxy bid for the full amount you're willing to pay on any item you really want to win. Doing so is the best protection against snipers. Even still, it won't guarantee a win.

Some bidders love the excitement generated by last-minute bidding and enter snipe bids manually. It's fairly easy to do as long as you have a good high-speed connection. Simply go to the auction you want to bid on. Open three screens (a shortcut for opening each screen on many computers is by hitting Ctrl+N on your keyboard). You'll use one screen to check the status of the auction; the other two are for placing your bids. Refresh the first screen and time how long it takes for the new screen to appear. This is the amount of time you'll have to place your bid. Enter the amount you want to bid using the second screen. As a backup, in case a sniper outbids you, you can enter a higher bid amount in the third screen. If you're not willing to go over the amount in the second screen, simply close the third one. Keep refreshing the first screen—this will show you the time left on the auction and the current bid amount. When the auction reaches its final seconds, hit "Send" on the second screen. If you're outbid by another sniper and there's still time to bid, you can switch to the third screen (if you've left it up) and hit "Send" again.

Others hire sniping services to do their bidding for them. If you'd rather go this route, you'll find a couple in Appendix Three.

Here's what happens in a standard auction:

1. You place your bid. It will be for at least the opening bid price. You can also elect to enter the highest amount you're willing to pay for the item. (If you did your research, you'll know what similar pieces are going for, and you'll know the price range.) This proxy bid format lets you enter the total amount you'll pay when you place your first bid. The system will bid on your behalf until you've been outbid. You don't have to manually enter each incremental bid.

2. The auction runs for a couple of days. You're still the high bidder.

3. The final day of the auction arrives. With about two hours to go, you receive an outbid notification via e-mail. You decide to bid against the highest bidder, so you enter another bid amount that's just slightly above his. You get a message back telling you you're still outbid. This means the highest bidder's proxy amount is higher than your latest bid. At this point, if you want to stay in the running, you can raise your proxy bid to the next highest increment. This might be higher than the other bidder's amount. Or you can enter a figure higher than this. Again, the system will automatically bid on your behalf.

4. The auction winds down to the last couple of minutes. You're in the lead, but wait a minute. A new bidder has chimed in, and you've been outbid. You bid again, and you're once again the high bidder.

5. You sniped the other bidder by squeaking your bid in during the last few seconds of the auction. You win the headset.

Here's what happens in a Buy It Now Auction:

1. First, you decide whether you want to buy the item or bid on it. If the former, simply click on the Buy It Now button and you're done. If you want to bid, enter in a starting bid amount. This will eliminate the Buy It Now option.

2. Bidding commences as before. You either win the item or you don't, based on who might be bidding against you.

And, finally, here's what happens in the Multiple Item (also called Dutch Auction) format:

1. You decide you want to buy two headsets. The seller is offering five headsets at a minimum bid of $79 each. You enter a bid of $80 for two. This auction format, by the way, doesn't allow proxy bidding. If you decide you want to improve your chances of winning by increasing your bid, you have to do it manually.

2. Buyer B enters a bid of $85 for two.

3. Buyer C enters a bid of $82 for three.

4. At this point, Buyer B is in first position and Buyer C is in second position, as they both bid more than you did and bids are ranked in order of bid price per item. They'll both get the number of headsets they want, too. You, unfortunately, won't get a thing unless you raise your bid amount above $85.

5. You decide the headsets are worth all that, so you increase your bid to $90 for two. This puts you in first position for two headsets at $82 each, which is now the lowest successful bid. Buyer B will also get his two headsets for $82 each. Buyer C will only get one at $82.

6. Bidder D decides to join the action and also places a bid for two headsets at $90. Your bid takes precedence as it was there first.

7. The auction ends. You get your two headsets at $82 each. Bidder D gets his two, also for $82 each. Buyer B has the option to buy the remaining headset at the same price.

Completing the Sale

You always want to complete your transactions as quickly as possible—it's just simple courtesy and doing business right—but it's especially important when you're new. As a newbie, you want to establish a reputation for being someone others want to work with, and what you do after the sale is over is a big part of this.

First, read the seller's terms of service if you haven't already done so. They should specify what the seller does after auctions are over—how you'll be contacted, when she expects payment, preferred payment methods, and so on. Knowing what's there will keep you from panicking if you don't hear from the seller minutes after the auction ends. Most sellers send out invoices right away, but not all do. It might also keep you from asking newbie questions like "When will you ship?" and "Will you take a check?" Sellers get questions like these all the time, and, frankly, they get a little tired of them, especially when the information is in their TOS for everyone to see. So stay on their good side and check things out before you start firing off e-mails.

▶▶If you have questions that you can't answer on your own, then an e-mail is definitely in order. Be courteous, be brief, and give the seller a chance to answer. A good seller will answer in a reasonable amount of time—say a day or so at the most—or send an automated response telling you when your e-mail will be answered.

If it's been more than a couple of days since the auction ended and you still haven't heard from the seller, sending another e-mail is appropriate. Again, keep things courteous. Simply state that you'd like to complete the transaction as quickly as possible. One e-mail is enough; sending more might make you feel better, but it won't have any effect on the seller.

If it's been a week since the auction ended and the seller still hasn't contacted you, it's time to see if there's something wrong. Here's how to do it:

- 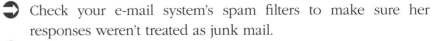 Check your e-mail system's spam filters to make sure her responses weren't treated as junk mail.
- Make sure your own contact information is correct. If it isn't, correct it right away, and ask the seller to resend the information.
- 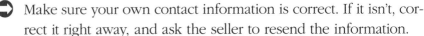 Request the seller's contact information and call her.

If your attempts to contact the seller are unsuccessful, you might have a nonperforming seller on your hands. If it's been ten days since the auction ended, you can and should alert eBay to the problem. Remember, both you and the seller have entered into a contract, and you're both expected to perform. eBay doesn't treat these situations lightly, but they can't do anything if you don't tell them about it.

Sellers who fail to honor their side of the agreement and who don't have a good reason for doing so can lose their trading privileges and possibly even be reported to law-enforcement officials.

What are acceptable reasons for not honoring a sale? There aren't many in eBay's book. In fact, there are just a couple—if the item is no longer available for sale, or if something happened to the item that significantly altered its condition from when it was listed. Neither is an excuse for a seller to ignore you, however, and good ones won't.

Paying for Your Purchases

Ideally, you're going to make sure that you can meet the sellers' terms of service before you place your bids. This will ensure that you can pay them on their terms. As discussed in Chapter 2, you'll want to have your PayPal account set up, as most sellers accept it, but be prepared for those who don't.

While many buyers avoid sellers who don't offer electronic payment, it's easy to overlook this when you're first starting out. Also, you might find items that you really want to buy from sellers who don't offer this service.

Sending a check extends the amount of time you'll have to wait to get your items. Sending money orders does the same thing, and having to go buy them is inconvenient. Remember this when you start selling. It should be all the convincing you need regarding the value of electronic payment systems and your motivation for offering this option to your customers.

Giving and Getting Feedback

Feedback is a very big deal on eBay, and for a very good reason. It's what measures your success, both as a seller and a buyer.

eBay's feedback system was launched in February 1996, not even six months after the site itself came into being. Here's how eBay founder Pierre Omidyar expressed the importance of having a forum for rating buyers and sellers:

❝ I launched eBay's AuctionWeb on Labor Day, 1995. Since then, the site has become more popular than I ever expected, and I began to realize that this was indeed a grand experiment in Internet commerce. By creating an open market that encourages honest dealings, I hope to make it easier to conduct business with strangers over the Net.

Most people are honest. And they mean well. Some people go out of their way to make things right. I've heard great stories about the honesty of people here. But some people are dishonest. Or deceptive. This is true here, in the newsgroups, in the classifieds, and right next door. It's a fact of life. But here, those people can't hide. We'll drive them away. Protect others from them. This grand hope depends on your active participation. Become a registered user. Use our feedback forum. Give praise where it is due; make complaints where appropriate. For the past six months, I've been developing this system single-handedly, in my spare time. Along the way, I've dealt with complaints among participants. But those complaints have amounted to only a handful. We've had close to 10,000 auctions since opening. And only a few dozen complaints.

Now, we have an open forum. Use it. Make your complaints in the open. Better yet, give your praise in the open. Let everyone know what a joy it was to deal with someone. Above all, conduct yourself in a professional manner. Deal with others the way you would have them deal with you. Remember that you are usually dealing with individuals, just like yourself. Subject to making mistakes. Well-meaning, but wrong on occasion. That's just human. We can live with that. We can deal with that. We can still make deals with that. Thanks for participating. Good luck, and good business! ❞

From the beginning, feedback has been optional and voluntary. It's not considered part of the transaction, as it comes after money and goods are exchanged. You don't have to give it, and others don't have to leave it for you.

Most sellers wait until buyers post feedback before doing it themselves. They'll say they do so because it's the best way to know if buyers received their merchandise and if they're happy with it. There's some truth to this, but here's the real reason why they go second: doing so puts them in the power seat. If a buyer registers a neutral or a negative, they can neutral or neg right back. If they go first and leave glowing feedback for a buyer only to have the buyer respond with anything less than, there's not much recourse beyond responding to the buyer's feedback. This is something most sellers would rather not do as it can make matters look worse.

That said, almost every seller you'll deal with will wait for you to go first, and you should for that reason alone. But don't use the feedback system to express your unhappiness with what you've bought, if indeed you are dissatisfied with it. Try to work it out with the seller privately and directly first. If you reach a positive conclusion, it merits a positive for the seller regardless of what happened. If you didn't, then you're justified in leaving the appropriate feedback. Or, if you choose, you might leave no feedback at all. Remember, it is voluntary. **▶▶Sometimes it's better to say nothing at all if it's simply a transaction gone bad.**

Some eBay members never leave feedback. This undermines eBay's basic principles and, if enough people were to follow suit, it would erode marketplace confidence over time. So leave feedback. Don't get into the "Well, they didn't, so why bother" frame of mind. Base your actions on how you want to business, not on the poor business decisions of others.

Building Your Reputation

Everything you do on eBay—your transactions, your participation on discussion boards, what have you—will take you either one step closer or one step farther away from being a trusted, reputable member of the eBay community. If you approach your dealings with this basic philosophy, you'll do fine in the long run.

That said, there will be times when you'll have to make some choices. A disgruntled buyer might leave you neutral or negative feedback no matter how hard you try to please him. Someone might misconstrue a comment you made in a chat or on a discussion board and decide to teach you a lesson by interfering with your auctions.

Taking the high road, no matter what, is always the honorable choice, and it's the one that will serve you in good stead over the long run. It's also the option that will garner the most support, both from other members of the eBay community and from eBay itself.

▶▶ Test Drive

Start building your reputation by bidding on some auctions if you haven't already done so. Pick at least one in each format. Research the sellers before you bid. Look at their feedback, both what they've received and what they've given. Make the best choices you can.

If you find some sellers you really like, add them to your favorite sellers list so you can keep an eye on what they're doing. Learning from other sellers is one of the best ways to become a good seller in your own right, and it's how many other eBay sellers before you have become the successes they are today.

" Feedback is a very big deal on eBay,

and for very good reason. It's what measures your

success, both as a seller and a buyer. **"**

2

Setting Up Your eBay Business

Selling What You Know

Many successful eBay sellers began by simply selling things they knew intimately—oftentimes, their own belongings or those of their family members. All they did was go around their homes, gather up things they no longer needed or wanted, and offer them for sale.

While it's not the most glamorous approach, and it's probably not one that will get you to PowerSeller status (unless you have some great stuff around your house and lots of it), it accomplishes a number of goals:

- It clears some clutter.
- It finds new homes for unwanted items (and keeps them out of landfills, also a good thing). Chances are you'll get more money for your castoffs than you would at a garage sale.
- It helps you learn what selling on eBay is all about.

Selling what you know can mean selling items in a category that you know well. It could be related to your profession or your passion. The items you sell might not be things you bought for yourself, your family, or your household, but instead items you acquired specifically for resale.

For example, let's say you've collected vintage rhinestone jewelry for some time. You now know what's desirable and collectible, and you know values, so you know how much is too much when you're buying. You're not interested in selling your collection—maybe just a few pieces to make way for new acquisitions—so you decide to look for vintage jewelry to sell.

Get to Know Your Category

Knowing your category intimately, and especially the particular segment or segments in which you plan to sell, is essential for success. This doesn't mean you have to stick to things you already know, but if you're going to branch out into a new area, research it thoroughly and carefully. You can do a lot of this online, but don't limit yourself to just online resources. Other resources can include pricing guides, auction catalogues, style and mark guides, historical references, collectors' guides, museum displays and exhibitions, collectors' and special interest groups, fashion and special-interest magazines, and so on.

Intimate knowledge of your market will tell you what's trendy and what's not. Pairing your knowledge with category searches on eBay will help you determine the relative health and dynamics of the market segments you want to sell in. As an example, some arts-and-crafts categories look like they're flooded with items at first glance. But if they're commodity items, meaning there's a steady demand for them, and the flood isn't indicative of a short-lived trend, then there might be plenty of room for you there.

If product offerings are slim in the category you're thinking about, you'll need to do some more exploring. Slim pickings could be a good thing if you've truly discovered an untapped market. It could be a bad thing if there's little or no demand for what you want to sell.

Selling What You Love

Selling what you love is similar to selling what you know, and it too is a great way of turning something you're passionate about into a business. Working with things you have a special connection with can bring a certain spark to your selling approach that sets you apart from other sellers in the same category. What's more, your passion can fuel your efforts and keep you going when things are a little slow or down.

However, there can be a downside to this approach. You have to be willing to part with the things you love. Stories abound about sellers who are fantastic at finding great merchandise to sell, but they like it so much themselves that they have a hard time putting it up for auction.

Things You Make Yourself

Selling what you love might mean selling your own creations. This can be a fantastic approach, especially if your items are unique and exclusive or if you can put a unique spin on something trendy, as buyers who want them will have to come to you to get them.

If you're going to offer handmade items for sale, keep these points in mind:

1. Make sure your offerings don't infringe on anyone else's copyright. If you have any concerns, you'll find some additional information on this subject in Chapter 11.

2. Be sure there's a steady source of supply for your raw materials. If you can, arrange for two good sources so you have a backup in case you need it.

3. Gauge the costs of the raw materials. If there isn't enough profit in the final object to make it worth your while, then you might want to find something else to sell.

4. Be sure you can turn out enough of what you're making to satisfy demand. There's nothing worse than an item taking off and not being able to keep up with orders because each item takes so much time to make.

5. Try to gauge the "trendiness" factor (or more technically, the product life cycle) as much as possible. This can be difficult, as the very nature of trends means they come and go quickly. If you're near the peak or on the downside of a product's life cycle, you might be okay if you can use the raw materials to make other things, or if you can sell them to other eBayers. What you don't want is to be stuck with a bunch of stuff that no one wants.

6. Consider other similar or related items you could sell if your creations are OOAK—one of a kind—and you can't offer very many of them at any one time. As an example, let's say you knit gorgeous sweaters from wool that you spin and dye from sheep that you shear yourself. You can only make maybe a dozen sweaters a year, but you have a nice little herd of sheep and they're producing lots of wool, more than you can use. Selling the excess wool will not only bring in more revenue, it will help maintain your visibility in a related category when you don't have sweaters to sell.

The Perils of Passion

A former eBay seller once asked me to help liquidate her inventory. She had been a PowerSeller, primarily selling small antiques and collectibles, before starting a new, non-eBay related business. When the new business took off, she no longer had time for eBay and stopped selling. The problem was, she never stopped buying.

By the time she called me, her house was so full of stuff that it was literally impossible to access parts of it. It took me several days to weed through the piles, and I never did get through everything. There was easily $20,000, maybe $30,000 worth of inventory in her home, much of it items that would easily sell on eBay and for good money.

We went through what I had sorted and discussed some options. She seemed serious about clearing the clutter at first, but the more we talked, the more I realized she really wasn't. She was in love with her stuff, and it was going to take an act of God to get her to part with it. In the end, she sold very little of it.

Being passionate about the items you sell is a good thing. It will carry you through what can be very long hours working your business, and it can make things like dealing with snarly customers more bearable. But somewhere along the line, you'll have to separate your emotions from your items. If you don't, you'll end up with a house full of inventory and nothing to show for it.

Determining What's Hot and What's Not

If you're going to ride trend waves, you'll have to get good at figuring out what they are. Even better is figuring out what they're going to be. This can be difficult to impossible, but success in this area can also be very lucrative. Getting in on the front end of a trend is definitely preferable to jumping in when it's starting to peak or when it's dying down. If at all possible, you never want to invest in merchandise that you can't move because the demand for it has passed.

The following resources might point you in the right direction for determining what could spur the next great trend.

➲ **Foreign fashion magazines:** It can take awhile for trends that launch in other parts of the world to catch on in the United States.

➲ **Movies:** There are one or two movies every year that seem to drive trends.

➲ **Teenagers:** There's incredible buying power in this age group, and these buyers definitely drive trends.

➲ **Celebrities:** All it takes is one glitterati to show up at an opening or a concert sporting a new accessory or clothing style for it to take off.

➲ **Specialty business publications:** In particular, you might check out those that cover such industries as furniture, health and beauty aids, jewelry design and display, and so on.

Selling in trend-driven market segments definitely has its pluses and minuses. Competition in the sector can send prices into a nosedive, which can impact margins that are already achingly slim. But remember, you have a gigantic global market at your fingertips. Items that might be past their selling prime where you are could do well halfway around the world, where the trend might not have caught on yet.

eBay's Biggest Merchandise Categories

Trends are definitely behind some, if not all, of eBay's top-ranked selling categories. Today, eBay has ten merchandise categories that each generate $1 billion or more in annual auction sales. The biggest is eBay Motors, with $7.5 billion including sales of vehicles, car parts, and accessories. Other top-grossing categories are consumer electronics ($2.6 billion); computers ($2.4 billion); books, movies, and music ($2 billion); clothing and accessories ($1.8 billion); sports ($1.8 billion); collectibles ($1.5 billion); home and garden ($1.3 billion); toys ($1.5 billion); and jewelry and gemstones ($1.3 billion).

Mining Market Niches

Mining a market niche means going beyond the obvious in a particular market sector. As an example of this approach, let's go back to our vintage jewelry example.

Jewelry might be your main focus, but if you concentrate solely on jewelry you might miss out on some great ways to increase your revenues and meet the needs of those in this sector at the same time. Here are some other things that you could consider selling in this category:

- Loose rhinestones for repairing pieces
- Findings, also for repairing pieces
- Jewelry adhesive, also for repairing pieces
- Jewelry cleaning cloths
- Liquid jewelry cleaner
- Loupes (magnifying lenses) for inspecting pieces
- Books on buying and collecting vintage jewelry
- Jewelry storage and/or display cases
- Silk, velvet, or silver keeper bags for storing pieces

Branching Out into Niche Categories

You can take the niche concept a step further and decide to branch out into subsets of the same category. Doing so can keep you active and visible in your category, let you focus on a hot area, and leave the others behind until they rebound.

Going back to our vintage jewelry concept, let's say our seller has primarily specialized in rhinestone jewelry dating to the 1950s and earlier. Recent fashions based on vintage designs have driven a huge demand for certain items from this period, most notably brooches. But the fad has died down, and only pieces with high collectible appeal are bringing much money.

She decides to start researching a couple of subcategories. She has always liked clean-lined, mid-century jewelry, so she starts there. While there's always a dedicated market for these pieces, and pieces by certain designers have always been collectible, they haven't been what you'd call hot. She checks current and completed auctions and notes a steady demand and good prices. She also does some research on other sites that specialize in items from this era, and checks out a couple of books from the library. All of this convinces her that this could be a viable market niche to mine.

Knowing What You Can and Can't Sell on eBay

You can sell a nearly endless variety of things on eBay. But there's also a fairly lengthy list of things you can't sell. At a minimum, violating the rules in this area will get your listings canceled. At a maximum, your account will be suspended and you won't be able to sell at all.

▶▶**Prohibited items run the gamut from alcoholic beverages to satellite television signal descramblers.** For a complete rundown on what you can and can't sell, go to eBay's Help Section and look for the heading "Help>Selling>Listing Your Item>Is My Item Allowed?" If you can't find information pertaining to what you want to sell here, get in touch with eBay directly, either by e-mailing or calling. If for any reason you can't sell the items you want to sell, it's better to find out about it before you invest any time or money.

Finding Inventory

As previously mentioned, many new eBay sellers start by offering individual items that they already own. Or they seek out individual items to sell outside of the home. This can be a fun way to explore what it's like to sell on eBay. It can also be a good, fairly low-risk way of trying out various eBay categories and testing the waters for the same or similar items you might want to sell in volume at some point.

If you're going to go the individual item route, you're probably going to have to spend a fair amount of time acquiring your inventory, and you'll probably have to find items in a variety of places and ways. This too can be fun, especially if you enjoy the thrill of the hunt. However, it can also burn you out fairly quickly.

The following are just some of the places to search for things to sell if you take this approach:

- Your house, room by room.
- The homes of your parents, relatives, and friends. They might not want you riffling through their drawers, but then again, they might not mind.
- Trash cans and Dumpsters. If you take this approach, be sure to protect your eyes and extremities. You never know what you'll come across. Don't limit yourself to residential trash, either. Retailers don't dump as much merchandise out as they once did, for a variety of reasons, but some still do.
- Garage sales, estate sales, rummage sales, and so on. Yes, they might be flooded with other eBay sellers also looking for merchandise. This doesn't mean there aren't things for you to buy.
- Thrift stores.
- Clearance racks and bins at department stores and other retailers. If you're going to do this, look for season-end items that you can buy for pennies on the dollar and store until next year.

Whether these approaches will work for you or not is hard to say. Some sellers are exceptionally good "pickers"—people who glean things from various sources, and they seem to come up with a limitless amount of inventory. Others don't have as good an eye, at least when they're first starting out. And, there are simply more people taking this approach than there used to be.

Other potential inventory sources include the following:

- Manufacturers' overstock
- Going-out-of-business sales
- Government surplus sales

Some sellers place ads in their local papers that say they'll buy estates, collections, old clothing, and so on. Another approach to try is to contact consignment stores and see if they're open to consigning some of their merchandise to you for sale. Many store owners would like to sell some of their merchandise on eBay but lack the time and the skills to do it, and they might be willing to strike a deal with you.

About Wholesaler Lists

You'll find a lot of wholesaler lists available on eBay. Are they worth anything? As a rule, no. If you can get your hands on one and compare the prices to items already being sold on eBay, you'll likely find that the prices wholesalers charge for their merchandise are higher. It's virtually impossible to buy from these sources and sell for a profit. If you want to buy from wholesalers, search the Internet for them instead. Don't pay good money for something that won't benefit your business.

Stocking Versus Drop Shipping

Drop shippers—businesses that stock merchandise and sell it to you, but ship it directly to your customers—might seem like a dream come true, but they may not be. Oftentimes their prices on merchandise don't compare favorably with wholesalers, which means there's little room for you to make any profit when you use them. Their inventory sources might not be as steady as you'd like. This is something you don't want to worry about when you have a bunch of sales that you need to fulfill.

Shipping problems are another concern. Since you're not doing it yourself, you have to trust that the drop shipper you're working with will and can fulfill your orders as they come in.

If you're thinking about going this route, know that there are honest, reputable companies that do drop shipping. They can be difficult to find, however. When you do find them, ask for references and ask to see actual samples of the merchandise. Make sure you're getting what you bargained for.

Drop shipping can work well if you're selling large, bulky items that would cost you a lot to warehouse. Again, however, be sure you're working with trusted sources. If you have to, go visit them.

▶▶ Test Drive

Pick five items from around your house, and research two things: whether they'd be worth selling on eBay, and whether you can legally sell them. Try to select items from different categories—as an example, here's what I came up with during a quick look around my office: a Palm Tungsten T3, slightly used; a pair of pants from Banana Republic's spring 2004 line that fit once and probably never will again; a custom-beaded dog collar; a Red Willow Band CD; and Microsoft's Streets & Trips 2004.

Setting Goals and Objectives

// **I**f you don't know where you're going, you'll probably end up somewhere else." You've probably heard this saying time and time again, and there's a good reason why. It's true.

Lots of people have tried to do business without a clear sense of direction. Some are successful in spite of themselves, but many others fail. Oftentimes they don't even know why they failed, which illustrates the reason they did: They didn't know where they were going because they didn't have a plan.

Setting goals and objectives is the first step in developing a business plan, and a business plan is one of the best protections against failure you could ask for. If you're serious about being more than just a hobbyist on eBay—you want to build a new business or expand an existing one—you'll want one of these.

The Difference Between Goals and Objectives

Many people use these terms interchangeably, and they are parts of the same thing, but there are differences between the two, as the following chart illustrates:

Goals	Objectives
Broad	Narrow
General	Precise
Abstract	Concrete
Immeasurable	Measurable

As an example, stating that you want to have a successful eBay business is a goal. All the elements of a goal are here: it's broad, general, abstract, and immeasurable. It's a broad and general statement of what you hope to accomplish, but it doesn't say anything about how you're going to get there.

Turning Goals into Objectives

Goals can be fairly easy to come up with because they're so broad and abstract. You almost can't go wrong with them. Objectives are more difficult because they pin things down, but this is also why it's so important to develop them, and it's why they're such a valuable part of a business plan.

Let's say your goal is to become an eBay PowerSeller. This goal is a little more specific than just saying you want to have a successful eBay business, but not much. It still doesn't say how you're going to do it.

Using the PowerSeller goal as an example, here are some possible objectives:

1. Becoming the number one destination for whatever it is you plan to sell.
2. Reaching a certain amount in sales the first year.
3. Reaching and maintaining a gross profit margin of a certain percentage for the first year of operations.
4. Growing the business by 25 percent per year for the first five years.

Each of these objectives narrows the goal, defines it, and makes it measurable. They state what you're going to sell, how much you want to sell, what your profit margins will be, and how much you plan to grow the business.

The best time to start writing your plan is before you start selling, but don't feel like you've missed the boat if you've already started and your plan isn't in place. You can still do one. What's more, you should still do one, and the sooner the better.

Turning Glimmers into Reality

Every business, no matter how large or small, starts as a glimmer of an idea in someone's head. Even if you're still in the glimmer stage, writing a business plan is the best way to turn your thoughts into reality. Seeing things in print—or on a computer screen—makes them more tangible, and more real. Plus, if you write things down, you won't have to worry about remembering all of your great ideas.

The Elements of a Business Plan

Business plans can be as simple or complex as you want to make them. A classic business plan includes these elements:

- **Executive summary:** This is your business plan in a nutshell; a quick read on everything there is to know about where you are, where you want to go, and how you're going to get there.
- **Company overview:** What your company is all about. How long it's been in business, what its goals are.
- **Description of products and/or services:** What your company makes or sells.
- **Industry and marketplace analysis:** Your competition, both in your industry in general and in your specific selling arena.
- **Marketing strategy:** How you're going to get the word out on what you do, and how you plan to compete against others in the marketplace.
- **Operations overview:** How your company runs, and who runs it.
- **Development overview:** If you're going to develop new products, how you're going to do it.
- **Management overview:** Who's running the shop.
- **Financials:** What you're making, what you're spending, and some projections for what the future holds in both categories.

You don't have to go into great detail, but using these bullets to organize your information will help you write your plan.

A Sample Business Plan

As mentioned, business plans can be as simple or as complex as you want to make them. The following sample business plan is an example of a fairly simple one. It was written for a fictitious eBay seller with the User ID barkandmew who plans to market natural pet treats and other products for dogs and cats.

Barkandmew's plan is based on the suggestions in this chapter, but it was modified to meet her particular needs. It's looser than a formal

Making Your Plans

eBay is a selling venue unlike any other. But this factor doesn't make the basics of operating a business on it that much different from anywhere else. You need to approach your eBay business just like you would any other. This means spending some time building a business plan, ideally before you start selling.

Here's what one long-time eBay PowerSeller has to say about the importance of a business plan:

"Doing a business plan can make a big difference in your success, and can help you become successful faster, as you'll have a better idea of where you want to go and how you'll get there. It can also keep you from making costly mistakes that can hamper your progress and your success.

"If you've never written a business plan before, the task can seem daunting. But you can't let your fears derail your efforts and keep you from doing one. They're just too important. They can be complex and they can take a long time to write. But yours doesn't have to be. Mine wasn't. What's more, it probably shouldn't be, especially if you're just starting out. At this stage, it's always best to keep things as simple as possible. If necessary, you can make your plan more complex later on. You also want to keep your plan flexible and allow yourself plenty of room to make changes to it as you go. One great way to do this: put it in a loose-leaf binder so you can put things in and take things out when necessary.

"Think of your business plan as a road map. It'll have twists and turns along the way, there might even be times when roads will be closed and you'll have to take detours. But it will still help you get to your destination. What's even better, it can also show you how you got there."

business plan would be, as it illustrates a working plan that's done more for the individual's needs, not for fundraising. Finally, this plan includes a branding plan, which you'll read more about in Chapter 19.

1. Executive Summary

Barkandmew is an online purveyor of natural, wholesome dog and cat treats. It's an expansion of an existing small pet bakery business that has offered a select product line based on natural and organic ingredients. It is owned and operated by one individual—me—and funded by me, too, although I might have to look for outside funding so I can expand my product line, which I plan to do in the months ahead.

2. Company Overview

I have always loved animals, and I've always loved to bake for them. Over the past five years, I've developed a number of pet treats based on natural and organic ingredients that not only taste good but are good for dogs and cats. I've made these products for friends and family and started to get requests from others who wanted to buy them, so I started selling them direct at places like craft shows, neighborhood fairs, farmers' markets, and in a couple of local pet stores. This has been a nice source of additional income for me, although it also takes a lot of time to prepare and bake the treats.

My business philosophy has always been to do what you love and to do it well. I love animals, and I love baking for them, and this love results in an excellent product that pets and their humans love. My business has grown, but it's reached a point where I have to establish an actual selling presence to grow it more. Plus, I'm getting tired of the shows and markets. A traditional retail shop doesn't make sense, especially in the small town I live in, and I don't have the money to open one anyway, so I've chosen to start selling on eBay.

3. Description of Products and/or Services

Barkandmew produces and markets natural foods for pets. At this time, the majority of the company's products are made by me. Over time, I plan to add other natural pet foods from other suppliers. Eventually I'd like to launch an eBay store with an expanded product line from other manufacturers, and I'd like to establish a separate e-commerce site as more of a natural pet-foods portal that other boutique pet-food manufacturers could join in on.

4. Industry and Marketplace Analysis

The pet industry is big and getting bigger—estimated at $31 billion annually. It kept growing through the 2001–2003 recession, which shows that people are willing to spend money on their pets even when that money is tight. Industry analysis also shows that much of their expenditures are now going to buy natural pet food and treats, especially over the past several years. Sales in the natural food and supplements category are increasing by double digits each year as people are becoming more aware of what goes into mass-market pet food.

Because natural pet foods and treats contain higher-quality ingredients, they are more expensive than mass-market products. For this reason, it's important to educate consumers on the reasons why natural pet food is such a better choice. Some sort of educational approach will be an important aspect of my online sales.

5. Marketing Strategy

My target market/customers are pet owners who love shopping for their best friends and buying them special treats. I plan to brand myself as the leading seller of natural pet treats on eBay in the following ways:

- ➲ Develop a distinctive look and feel for my listings, my "About Me" Page, and my store.
- ➲ Have a logo professionally designed and use it to brand all pages.
- ➲ Develop a separate page with information on why natural treats are a good choice when I open my eBay store.
- ➲ Participate on animal-related discussion boards (eBay has a good one), with my main emphasis on food-related questions.
- ➲ Have business cards made up with my logo and URL information.
- ➲ Make up little doggie treat bags. Attach business card to them.
- ➲ Include business card and pamphlet on natural dog food in all auction wins.

6. Operations Overview

I am currently the only employee of barkandmew, but that could change. Based on demand, I might have to hire additional baking help, or packaging help. I also plan to use a bookkeeper and outside accounting firm to do my annual books.

At present time, I mix up and bake everything at home, and I do all the packing and shipping there myself. As mentioned, as the business grows, I might have to find a larger kitchen with better equipment—my oven can't handle more than two cookie sheets at a time—or hire someone else to bake for me.

7. Development Overview

At present time, I plan to stay with my current product line, which includes twelve different baked goods for cats and dogs. I will continue to develop new recipes as warranted, and will add other natural food products from other manufacturers when I open my eBay Store.

8. Management Overview

I am barkandmew, and barkandmew is me. My boyfriend helps me mix up some of my treat dough and is my chief pack-and-ship guy.

My two pets, Lucky and Doodles, are by my side all the time and are an essential component in my product development process.

9. Financials

After expenses, I netted about $5,000 from my pet treat business last year. This was an increase of $450 over the previous year's earnings.

I expect to triple my revenues by selling on eBay, which should deliver more profits, too. However, my expenses will also go up, as I'll have to buy more raw ingredients. Also, I might have to hire some help.

Determining a Budget

"Budget" is one of those words that often makes people cringe. They don't like doing them, and they find it hard to adhere to them. But a budget is another essential element in moving from eBay hobbyist to eBay seller. Simply put, you have to know how much you need to operate your business, and you need to know how much you can spend on things like inventory acquisition, packaging materials, auction management programs, and the like.

There are two aspects to budgeting. The first is determining what your start-up costs are going to be. The second is figuring out what your ongoing expenses are going to be.

Here are some of the factors to consider for both:

Overhead: How much it costs you to run your place of business

Inventory: Buying it and shipping it

Supplies: Things like paper, pens, tape, packing materials, and so on

Equipment: Computer, camera, scanner, postage scale—basically everything you need to operate your business

Marketing and promoting: What you pay for getting your name out, including Web site development and maintenance

Fees: eBay, PayPal, and any other ongoing fee-related expenses

Education: What you need for learning how to run your business, including classes, books, and magazines

When you're just getting going, you'll probably have to guess at some of this until you have a few months' worth of expenses as a basis. ▶▶**Save your receipts, and start entering them into an accounting program so you can pull this information when it's compiled.**

There are other budget categories, but this will get you started. For a more complete list, go to *www.irs.gov* and print out a Schedule C and the instructions that accompany this form. It's the one you'll file to report your self-employment income and expenses, and it includes a list of expense categories as well as an explanation of what goes where. If you get into the habit of thinking about and organizing your expenses based on this list, it can make tax season much easier to get through.

> ### Paying Yourself
>
> Your business budget should include a salary for yourself. That said, this particular line item is somewhat wishful thinking for most start-ups. You might not be able to take much out for yourself during your first year. You might not be able to take out anything at all. But paying yourself should be part of the program. If you can't, you might like what you're doing, even love it, but it will be a labor of love. It won't put food on your table or a roof over your head.

Funding Your Business

Cash on hand is the typical funding source for many new business owners, and it will probably be yours, too. If your personal funds are a bit slim, you might have to look beyond your bank balances at other assets you might be able to liquidate or use as collateral for a loan.

If you plan to use your business plan to raise money, such as applying for a bank loan or a small business loan, you'll want to develop a full-blown plan with as much detail and information as possible. Potential investors will want to see exactly how you plan to make money. They'll also want to see financial projections based on solid data.

Potential investors might include friends and/or family members. For the best results, approach them as you would banks or other lending institutions. Present your business plan, and describe what you want to do. Instead of just telling them you need money to fund your business, present it as an opportunity for them to make an investment in a new business venture that's part of a business model that has rewritten the face of doing business.

Shoring Up Your Resources

As you build your business plan, you're probably going to see something happen pretty quickly. There will be all these jobs for all these different people, but there's only you in the room. You'll need suppliers, workers, packers, shippers, writers, photographers . . . the list goes on.

For the most part, all these people will be you, at least in the beginning. But it doesn't have to be. Before your first day of operations, figure out who you'll need on your team. This can include any or all of the following:

- The UPS delivery person
- Your mail carrier
- The people at your local business services store
- Your banker
- Your spouse and kids
- Your Wednesday morning yoga class
- Your hairstylist
- Your babysitter
- Your dog groomer
- The reference librarian at the library
- The kid down the block who's a whiz at working with computers

The people on your list may or may not be directly involved in your business, but they're all part of your life. Sometimes you'll need to remind yourself that you're not completely alone in this venture. Just reviewing the list might be all the reminder you need. If not, get out of the house and go see someone who's on your list, or choose someone on it, pick up the phone, and connect with someone for a few minutes. You don't even have to talk about business if you don't want to.

Going It Alone Versus Hiring Help

Many successful eBay sellers start out as solo acts, and a good number of them stay that way. There are lots of advantages to doing everything yourself—one of the largest being that you only have to worry about yourself. Plus, you're a known entity. You know your strengths and weaknesses—if you don't, you'll learn them fast when you're your own boss—and you can work with them or around them, as necessary.

You also don't have to do any of these things:

➲ Pay employment taxes for anyone but yourself.
➲ Carry workers' compensation insurance. (The requirements for this vary by state—in most states you can have up to three employees before you have to have it.)
➲ Increase your business liability insurance coverage.
➲ Hire and train anyone. Doing both well takes time and resources that might already be in short supply.

If you're not an experienced manager or you simply don't like managing others, and you want to keep your business small, operating alone might be ideal for you. However, if you plan on growing your business, you should plan on hiring help at some point. The good thing is, you don't necessarily have to have employees. Depending on the kind of assistance you need, you could also consider hiring temporary help.

▶▶**Don't bring anyone else on board to help you until you really need it.** Really needing it means you are so busy that your business is either suffering now because you can't handle everything yourself, or it's going to start suffering very soon.

Answering the following questions will help you determine if you've reached that point:

1. I process orders promptly and according to my TOS.
Yes   Most of the time   Sometimes   No

2. I answer all ASQ (ask seller a question) inquiries within a half day of receiving them.
Yes   Most of the time   Sometimes   No

3. I have enough time to source inventory on a regular basis.
Yes   Most of the time   Sometimes   No

4. I have enough time to sort, inventory, and store my merchandise.
Yes   Most of the time   Sometimes   No

5. I have enough time to pay my bills and do other office work.

Yes   Most of the time   Sometimes   No

6. I'm comfortable with the number of hours I work each week.

Yes   Most of the time   Sometimes   No

7. I have enough time to do things for myself and my family.

Yes   Most of the time   Sometimes   No

8. I get enough sleep.

Yes   Most of the time   Sometimes   No

9. I don't feel like I'm tied to my computer.

Yes   Most of the time   Sometimes   No

10. I like what I'm doing.

Yes   Most of the time   Sometimes   No

Scoring: Give yourself 3 points for every yes, 2 points for every most of the time, 1 point for every sometimes, and 0 points for every no.

Scoring key:

27–30: Your life is under control. You manage your time well.

22–26: Things are pretty good now, but there might be trouble ahead. Go back through the quiz and note any areas of concern. See what you can do now to address them.

17–21: You manage things pretty well for the most part, but there are times when certain aspects of your business feel like they're not going as well as they should. You might need a helping hand from time to time or assistance in smoothing out some areas of your operation.

15–20: Things are verging on being out of control. You're not getting things done in a timely manner, and your family life might be suffering. You need to take a close look at your business systems and possibly make some significant adjustments in areas that need it.

10–15: You definitely need some help, but maybe just temporarily or seasonally.

5–9: You need to hand off some of your responsibilities to someone who can assist you regularly on at least a part-time basis.

0–4: Yikes! Your life is out of control. If you really scored this low, do yourself and everyone else in your life a favor and stop selling until you get things straightened out.

If you're going to hire help, determine in advance the areas where having someone assist you will benefit you the most. It might make sense to hand off your bookkeeping to a professional every week. Maybe you just need a neighborhood kid to help you pack and ship.

Finding Good Help

Chances are pretty good that if you just put the word out that you're looking for help with your eBay business, at least a couple of people will pop up, tell you they've always wanted to sell on eBay, and would love to work with you because they find the whole eBay thing so, well, fascinating.

Would they turn into good hires? Maybe, maybe not. Being interested in eBay doesn't mean they'll like the business once they see what it entails. Then again, it might. Enthusiasm plays a big role in how people approach a new job. If they're excited about the prospects of learning about something as intriguing as eBay, their enthusiasm might make them great to have around and committed to you and the work you need done. The question, however, is not whether they like or dislike eBay or want to learn more about it. The real question is if they have the skills and qualities you're seeking.

▶▶**Remember that your eBay business is a business like any other, and it shouldn't be run much differently than any other.** Before you even think about hiring someone, write a job description that clearly defines your expectations and defines the job's duties and responsibilities. The more time you spend thinking about the best person for the job, the better your chances of finding that person.

Developing a Fall-Back Plan

There are always going to be ups and downs in your business—it's simply part of what being in business is all about. Sometimes things just happen, and sometimes you do something to cause them to happen—like making a bad buying decision that leaves you with hundreds of widgets you can't sell.

It can be difficult to plan for things you can't predict, but you can put some fail-safes in place to protect you and help you weather the vagaries of doing business. Here are a few suggestions to get you thinking:

1. Find a good computer tech or consultant before you need one. Computers always fail at the worst possible time. Don't ignore warning signs that your system is having problems or think they'll just go away. They usually don't.

2. If you're selling a commodity item, and you've established yourself as a player in this category, look for alternative supply sources. If your usual supplier has a problem fulfilling your order, you'll have someone else to place orders with.

3. Cash flow can be maddeningly irregular when you're running a small business, especially if you're used to drawing a regular paycheck. Arrange for a line of credit through your bank or get a credit card with a high limit to help you through the lean times.

4. Find a mentor or someone like a mentor whom you can talk to when it feels like nothing is going right and you're ready to throw in the towel. Your friends and family will get tired of hearing about eBay long before you get tired of talking about it. Having someone you can go to who's a little removed from your usual circle can keep everyone's sanity levels nearer to where they should be. It can also prevent the eye rolls and the groans you hear from your friends when you launch into the latest problem you've encountered with your goofy buyers.

▶▶ Test Drive

The field test for this chapter should be crystal clear to you by now. If you haven't already done so, start writing your business plan! Start with a simple statement that sets out your primary goal. Then break it down into objectives.

If you don't know where to start, there are some good online resources and some good books. You'll find suggestions in Appendixes Two and Three.

Internet Access

You can't trade on eBay without Internet access. If you don't have an Internet connection in your home, and your budget doesn't permit getting one right away, you have at least two options: using a friend's or one in a public place. However, going this route really isn't a good idea. Not only are you at the mercy of others when it comes to gaining access to these systems, but you'll also find that many public facilities have various methods of discouraging people from using their computers in this manner, typically by limiting the amount of time users can spend on them.

Having Internet access in your home is the best approach, and really the only recommended one.

Dial-Up Service

If you're on a tight budget, you can opt for a dial-up connection, which connects to the Internet via a modem and telephone lines. It's cheap and widely available—if you have phone service and a modem, which is standard issue in today's computers, you're good to go. And, it might be the only option available if you live in an area where high-speed services aren't yet available.

Dial-up service used to be achingly slow, but technologies have been developed to make it significantly faster than in the past. Look for companies that offer optimized or high-speed dial-up, which can deliver connection speeds faster than traditional dial-up.

The Need for Speed

Internet users are demons for speed, and for good reason—faster connections do a far better job than slow dial-up connections of handling today's content-rich Web files. There's no denying that fast service is great, but don't let the lack of it hold you back if it's not available where you are. Many good sellers have done just fine with old-fashioned dial-up connections. Such connections are certainly slower than newer technologies, and therefore they're a bit cumbersome and frustrating at times, but they do work.

High-Speed Access

If you're in or near a major metropolitan area, chances are you can choose from more than one high-speed service provider and more than one high-speed technology. In many cases, it comes through the same cable that delivers your television signal and telephone service. It's more expensive than dial-up, but often not by all that much, as providers typically offer special promotional packages to new subscribers. Also, competition tends to keep prices reasonable. Regardless of the cost, most high-speed users will tell you that not having to deal with the frustrations that come with dial-up service makes it well worth the money.

Digital subscriber line (DSL) service might be another option. This technology delivers high-speed access over telephone lines. Unlike dial-up, you can be online and talk on the phone at the same time. However, the technology's drawbacks—it works best if you're near the provider's central office, and it receives data faster than it sends it—often puts it in second place to cable service.

If you have a choice, investigate high-speed cable first, then DSL, then dial-up if necessary.

Hardware Needs

Launching an eBay business can be an equipment-intensive venture. Apart from inventory acquisition, this category might be your highest expenditure area.

To avoid having to repeat the same advice for each category, here's a caveat: Buy the best equipment you can afford, but not necessarily the newest and/or most expensive. There's nothing wrong with last year's digital camera or a used scanner as long as the technology isn't obsolete, the equipment is in good working order, and the item has the features you need.

Computer

Having a computer goes hand in hand with Internet access. Again, you might be able to get away with using someone else's machine when you're just getting started. But, like Internet access, it's much better to have your own.

If you already own a computer, chances are it will meet your needs just fine, even if it's a little old. As your business grows, you might decide to upgrade to a faster system, or maybe exchange an older monitor for one with a large flat screen to make things easier on your eyes. Or you might decide to add a laptop or notebook computer to your setup so you can work on your auctions wherever you are.

You have two basic configuration choices in this category: desktop or laptop. Here are the chief advantages and disadvantages for each:

Desktop	
Advantages	**Disadvantages**
Cheaper.	Takes up more space.
Component based—if something fails, you're not dead in the water.	Not portable.

Laptop	
Advantages	**Disadvantages**
Portable—set up a wireless network, and you can work almost anywhere you'd like.	More expensive.
	If something breaks, the entire machine might have to go in for repair.
	Fragile—needs a solid protective case when transported.

Features to Look for on a Laptop

There are good laptops and then there are, well, better laptops. If you're going to buy one, look for features that separate "better" from "good." These features include the ability to pop out the hard drive, optical drive, and batteries for easy swapping. Should any of them fail, it's easy to find another one (on eBay, perhaps?) and just snap it in place. Built-in wireless (Wi-Fi) is another good feature, and you'll find it standard on most newer laptop machines.

Your other choice is the platform you want to use: PC or Macintosh. Again, there are pros and cons for each, with strong arguments on both sides by people who swear by their respective systems. Doing a side-by-side comparison really isn't fair to either system, but here are some things to consider that might help you decide between the two:

1. Many people simply find Macs easier to use, thanks to their sleek design and the synergy between the machines and their operating systems. The technology is developed by Apple, which results in as close to a perfect fit between machine and operating system as you're going to find in computerland.
2. Macs typically come loaded with more software than PCs do. As such, they're usually easier to set up and run.
3. Many users find the user interface on the Mac easier to use and less obtrusive than Windows. PCs have come a long way since the days when users had to enter lines of code to boot up their systems, but the Windows interface still isn't renowned for being user-friendly.
4. In general, Macs are more expensive than PCs. However, if you're buying a PC designed for business use, or you're buying an ultra-portable laptop, you might find less difference in price. In general, the prices for PC and Mac laptops can be competitive, and they can be extremely competitive when it comes to the smallest, thinnest, and lightest PC laptops.
5. The open architecture of PCs can make them easier to expand when it comes to things like adding memory or drive space.

6. If the machine develops mechanical problems or software incompatibilities, it can be easier to find a PC technician than a Mac technician. This is where Apple's proprietary systems work against it to a certain extent. Just about every town, no matter how small, has at least one guy who builds and fixes PCs. If you don't live near a Mac dealer, you might have to send in your machine to get it fixed.

7. Most experts agree that Macs are more stable than PCs when it comes to things like hardware failures and system crashes, again thanks to the synergy between hardware and operating system.

8. Ninety percent of the world's personal computers are Windows-based, which is one reason why they're such a popular target for hackers. Since Macs have such a small market share, and they're not Windows-based, they aren't as prone to viruses and other problems encountered online.

9. PCs have traditionally been considered more of a business machine than Macs. Many leading business software programs were and are developed first for the PC, then the Mac. Because of this, some of it doesn't run or look the same on Macs.

10. Some special-purpose and/or industry-specific software—notably eBay's Turbo Lister—only comes in PC format. However, there are special software programs called PC emulators—Virtual PC is a well-known one—that allow Windows applications to run on Macs.

11. The higher price of Macs puts them out of reach for many buyers, and cost can make it difficult to upgrade. Prices on PCs—in particular, full-size desktop setups—are at historic lows, which make them almost disposable if they crash or need upgrading.

How much of a system do you need? Again, if you already have a computer and it's fairly new—let's say you bought it in the last three years or so—you probably have all the computing power and speed you need.

If you're buying a new computer, here's a basic configuration that will do everything you need and more. If your current system falls far short of these specifications, you might want to consider buying a new one:

- ➲ **Pentium 4, Celeron D or AMD Athlon 64 processor (for PCs); PowerPC G5 (for Macs):** These are the standard processors on new computers as of this writing. If you're buying a laptop, look for machines with mobile versions of these processors. They use less power and generate less heat than the others. If you plan to keep your machine plugged in and you're working in a well-ventilated area, a nonportable processor will work fine.

- ➲ **256 to 512MB of RAM:** You can get by on 128MB, but just barely. In the broad scheme of things, additional memory doesn't cost that much, it's easy to install yourself, and it will let you run multiple programs without crashing.

- ➲ **60 to 80GB hard drive:** Windows-based software hogs memory. So do picture, multimedia, and music files. The more hard drive space you have, the better your system will perform. However, you can definitely get away with a smaller hard drive, say 20 to 40GB, if you add an external hard drive or two to your configuration for storing nonessential files—anything other than the machine's operating system and software programs.

- ➲ **CD-RW drive:** You'll want this for storing data and picture files.

- ➲ **A good display screen:** This is one thing that's worth spending some money on. Running a successful eBay business usually means spending a good deal of time with your eyes glued to a computer screen, especially in the beginning. Larger displays are simply easier on the eyes. Many new desktop systems come standard with flat screens, which beat old-fashioned curved monitors hands down. If you're buying a laptop, and it's going to be your only machine, buy one with the biggest screen you can afford, even if the machine itself is heavier and bulkier than you'd like. Your eyes will thank you.

If you decide to buy a laptop, you'll also need to make some choices regarding size and weight. These days, laptops range from machines designed to replace full-sized desktop PCs to small, lightweight ultra-portables that make computing on the road a breeze. The smaller and more portable they are, the more expensive they tend to be.

If you're going to use it primarily at home, or if it's going to be your only computer, a bigger, heavier desktop replacement model will probably be a better bet than a smaller, lighter one, and it will be easier on your wallet, too.

Printer

You'll need a printer for printing out auction pages, invoices, labels, and many other things. For the cost-conscious, an inexpensive black-and-white inkjet printer will fit the bill. Color is a nice touch when printing invoices or checking out auction formats, but it's really not necessary. Read user reviews and comparison-shop to find a model that doesn't go through ink cartridges like mad. These machines can be notorious ink hogs, and you could find yourself spending all the money you thought you saved when you have to buy ink cartridges every couple of weeks or so.

Laser printers, which deliver sharper, clearer images than inkjets, used to be prohibitively expensive, but they've become much more affordable in recent years. It's now possible to buy a very decent small-office laser for less than $500, and if you shop around you can probably find one for anywhere from $100 to $200 less than that. Another plus for laser printers is that their ink cartridges last longer. However, the cartridges are more expensive, too.

If you're going to print postage at home, a thermal label printer is a great tool to have. It prints shipping and postage information directly onto crack-and-peel labels that you simply attach to packages. This eliminates having to tape over paper labels to protect them during shipping and can be a real time and expense saver. Plus, they give packages a neater, more professional look.

Scanner

This is an optional piece of equipment for many sellers; however, if you're going to convert photo prints into digital files or if you plan to sell flat items like old postcards, trading cards, or antique photographs, you'll want one as you can image the items directly on the scanner and skip taking pictures of them altogether. Some sellers even use them for taking close-ups of fabric, jewelry, and what not.

Scanners vary in regard to resolution and sharpness, with 300 × 300 dots per inch (dpi) being fairly standard. If you're going to buy one, get one with a legal-size scan area. You might not think you'll need it, but when you do (and you will) you'll be glad you have it.

You can find good scanners for less than $200, and sometimes even half this.

All in One or Separate?

Buying an all-in-one machine—one that scans, faxes, copies, and prints—might seem like a good idea. You're getting one piece of equipment that can do four things, and they can cost a lot less than individual single-function machines. While it's true that they can save you some money—space, too—there's one big drawback with these machines. If one function dies, you lose the others while the machine is being fixed. If you decide to go this route, think about having backup machines on hand—say, a cheap black-and-white inkjet printer or an inexpensive scanner—so you're not without the features you need the most.

USB/Firewire Hub

Newer computers come with USB and/or Firewire sockets, which allow you to easily switch out various devices such as cameras, scanners, and printers. However, many of them only have one or two of these sockets, meaning you have to switch things around if you have more of these devices than this. A simple remedy is a USB or Firewire hub. You hook it up to the appropriate socket, and then plug all of your devices into it.

These hubs are relatively inexpensive and worth the price for the convenience they add to daily operations. However, if you're on a tight budget, this is one purchase you can definitely skip.

Camera

Again, you're faced with two platform choices here: film or digital. Digital is far and away the more common among eBay sellers for a variety of reasons, and it really is the only way to go. Film cameras are not a viable long-term choice for anyone serious about establishing a solid eBay business. The costs associated with buying and processing film and then converting images to digital format are prohibitive. Also, using film simply requires more messing-around time than digital photography. ▶▶**With digital photography, you don't have to wait until you finish a roll of film to build your auctions and get them listed.** Instead of spinning through rolls of film and paying for prints that you can't or won't use, you can delete any images that you don't want, anytime you want.

Even if you're on a shoestring budget, a digital camera is one piece of equipment you'll want to have before you start selling. Fortunately, there are tons of cameras to choose from in all price ranges, all of them with bells and whistles that you may or may not need. Again, you don't have to buy the best, nor do you have to spend a lot of money. Older cameras will work just fine as long as they have the features you need.

Here's what to look for in a digital camera:

1. **At least 2 megapixels:** Pictures taken with a digital camera are made up of pixels, which are small, encoded bits of information that are arranged by digital software to make up images. As pixels go up, image quality gets better, and cameras get more expensive. For online work, it's not necessary to buy a camera with honking high pixels. Anything at 2 and above will work just fine. These days, 3 megapixels is considered the entry-level configuration for new digital cameras. This is enough for making good eight-by-ten prints and more than enough for your eBay pictures.

2. **Macro feature:** This is essential, as it lets you shoot detail close-up and in focus. Cameras vary widely on this feature; if possible, find one that will focus at about two inches. How close you want to get is up to you, but you'll probably find that you'll use this feature more than any other, so it's not a bad idea to put it at the top of your list when shopping for a digital camera.

3. **Autofocus and auto exposure:** Like 35mm cameras, most digital cameras come loaded with features that make using

them a breeze. These are two that just about every camera today has.

4. Digital and optical zoom: Both features let you focus in closer on far-away objects. It's not super important for online work, but it's a nice feature to have for general use. Of the two, optical zoom is the feature to pay more attention to as it actually magnifies images, which yields better results. Digital zoom relies on software, not optics, to enlarge images. The results can be close to optical, but they're typically not quite as sharp.

5. A variety of automatic settings: These settings let you dial up preconfigured settings to better capture specific types of images, such as portraits, landscapes, sunsets, party scenes, sporting events, and so on. Again, they're good to have for general shooting; you'll find them less useful for eBay work, but they can come in handy there, too.

6. White balance: This is a more advanced feature, but it's one you'll want to have as it lets you adjust the camera's settings for difference sources of light. Digital cameras typically adjust for white balance automatically, and this works pretty well for most things. However, if there's a big difference in color between what you see and what's captured on your images, you'll want to manually adjust the white balance to match the light you're shooting with—daylight, fluorescent, tungsten, and so on.

7. Exposure compensation: This feature lets you control the exposure on your shots, which is a very big deal when shooting certain objects. Unless you're manually adjusting exposure settings when you shoot, your camera's built-in light meter picks a happy medium between the various tones in an image. If what you're shooting has large dark areas, the camera will overcompensate for the darkness, pick a slow shutter speed and a wide lens aperture, and let in too much light. Or the exact reverse can happen. The result is overexposed or underexposed images, unless you can adjust the exposure setting to compensate.

8. **Image size and quality settings:** All but the cheapest digital cameras will let you adjust for both. Image size is the actual physical dimensions of the image as measured in pixels. You'll see at least three settings on most cameras; the bigger the megapixel count, the more settings you'll see. All you need for online work is the lowest setting—640 × 480. Image quality determines the amount of memory images use when you save them to disk or memory card. The lowest, or basic setting, delivers the most compression and is fine for online work.

Understanding Image Size

The science behind image size can be confusing, and it's not necessarily something you need to understand in great detail. Just know that for online work, shooting at the lowest image size—640 × 480—is ideal. This results in images that are easy to see and easy to load. Some sellers prefer to shoot at the next highest size—1024 × 768—as the image resolution is a bit better. However, this also results in larger picture files, which take up more memory on memory cards and can be a problem unless you plan to make them more manageable during the editing process.

Lights and Other Photography Equipment

Things like tripods, accessory lights, and backdrops aren't necessities, but they can make your images better and your life easier. For more detail on these items, turn to Chapter 13.

Software Needs

If you already have a computer, you probably already own most of the software you'll need. Here's what you should have on hand for basic day-to-day operations:

➲ **Some type of word processing program for writing auction copy:** You can write copy directly into your auction listings, but if there's a glitch, you run the risk of losing your copy. Writing

Zapped!

Years ago, I was living in the country and working on a magazine project when a summer lightning storm struck. It came up so quickly that I hardly had the chance to get my pets indoors and shut all the windows before it hit. Just as I was getting ready to power down my computer system and unplug it, I heard a huge crack of thunder. The storm was right on top of us, and it knocked out the power before the computer was off.

After the storm passed, I went outside and found that the tree in front of my house had been struck by lightning—the bolt had nearly cleaved the tree in two, and it was still smoking. Something told me my computer might not have made it through the storm, and I was right. It would power up, but the lightning's current had corrupted the hard drive. Everything I had been working on was lost.

I'm not sure that a surge protector would have protected my equipment from a direct hit, but it might have helped. From that day forward, I've used surge protectors—not just power strips, but heavy-duty protectors designed to handle a fair amount of energy—on all of my sensitive equipment, and I encourage you to do the same. Yes, insurance might cover your equipment loss, but once data is gone, it's often gone forever.

your descriptions in Word or another program and cutting and pasting them into your listings is a safer bet. Also, you'll have record of what you've written in case you want to reuse your descriptions.

➲ **Accounting software:** Turn to Chapter 9 for more information on these programs.

➲ **Scanner software:** If you're buying a scanner, it should come bundled with the software you'll need to run it or have the Web site information for downloading what you need. You'll need a few basic pieces of software—the driver, which tells your computer how to communicate with the scanner, a scanning utility, and image-editing software, which can range from okay to excellent. Some scanners will come with OCR software, which stands for optical character recognition. This lets you scan in words from a document and convert them in to editable text. It's a nice feature but not necessary for online selling.

⊃ **Photo imaging software:** Digital cameras typically come bundled with some sort of image editing programs. If yours didn't, you'll want to get some. For more information on this, turn to Chapter 13.

⊃ **Basic auction management software:** eBay has several systems. Many sellers start with these and stay with them as they suit their needs. For more information on them, turn to Chapter 11.

⊃ **A virus detector/spyware program:** Some systems come bundled with these programs. If yours didn't, buy one, either directly online or at a local store. And use it regularly. Don't risk data loss and an interruption in your business by letting a corrupted file or a virus crash your system.

As your business grows, you'll probably find you'll need to invest in some specialized software to help you do things like manage your auctions better, keep in closer contact with your customers, analyze your selling patterns and performance, and so on. Turn to Appendix Three for a list of programs that can automate many facets of selling on eBay and make your life easier.

Space Needs

Many successful businesses—online and off—have been started on little more than a folding table in a bedroom or dining room. If you're in a similar situation, don't let the lack of space hold you back. You can even work out of a clothes closet if you set things up right and you're serious about making your business a success.

That said, you'll feel more like you're really running a business (and drive yourself and the rest of your family members less crazy) if you can set aside an area where you can work at your business without worrying about having to pack things up at night. Even a corner of your living room can work as long as it's devoted to your eBay business and nothing else.

Photography Space

Many eBay sellers will tell you that they either have space set aside solely for taking pictures, or that they wish they did. If you can devote space to this function, it's highly advisable to do so.

Try to pick a spot with good natural light or enough space to set up light stands or clamp lights. For the best results, walls should be neutral in color. If you can, invest in some backdrops. For more information on both, turn to Chapter 13.

Inventory Space

If you're keeping your inventory at home, it's important to keep it well organized and safe from the elements. There are a variety of ways to do this, depending on what you're selling. Here are some options:

- **Storage containers:** Clear ones are great, as you can see what's in them.
- **Open racks:** Buy metal ones, not plastic. They'll hold up longer.
- **Moveable closets:** These offer more protection from the elements than open racks do. Again, buy the best ones you can afford.
- **Clothing racks:** If you buy freestanding racks, spend the money and get sturdy metal ones. Plastic racks don't hold up to anything but occasional use.

Office Equipment and Supplies

You'll need the basic equipment and supplies that any business needs, plus a few things that are specific to an eBay business. The following list will get you started:

- **File cabinet:** Necessary for storing business records that are in use.
- **Banker's boxes:** A good way to store business records that you no longer use but need to keep.
- **Desk and chair:** No need to get fancy here unless you want to. Buy whatever works for you, if you have to buy it, and whatever fits

in your budget. This is an area in which you might really be able to cut some costs by buying used at garage sales. Another place to look is the scratch-and-dent area in office supply stores.

➲ **Paper, pen, pencils, and other office supply basics.**

➲ **Postage scale:** Buy a scale that can weigh at least 35 pounds. Even if you won't be selling items that are this heavy, the construction on these scales makes them more accurate. Buy a digital one; a scale that can run on batteries or AC power is also nice.

➲ **Packing and shipping supplies:** Depending on what you're going to sell, you'll need things like boxes, bags, tape, and cushioning materials. You'll find a rundown on what you'll need, and sources for it, in Chapter 15.

Setting-Up-Shop Checklist

Here's a recap of the major items you'll need to set up shop as an eBay seller.

Mandatory:

➲ **Internet access:** Faster is better, but don't despair if you're limited to dial-up.

➲ **Computer:** The one you already have will probably be fine.

➲ **Printer:** Again, if you already have one, it will probably fit the bill. If you don't, consider spending the money on a laser printer—they're more expensive than ink-jet machines, but worth it. A label printer is another investment to think seriously about—when business takes off, having to cut and tape labels to bags and boxes will be one of the last things you'll want to spend precious time on.

➲ **Surge protector:** You spent good money on your equipment. Don't let a power surge or electrical storm wipe it out.

➲ **Camera:** If you're on a tight budget and already own a film camera, try it for a while. But know that you'll need to go digital as soon as you can.

Optional:

➲ **Lights, tripod, and other assorted photography equipment:** However, the sooner you invest in these, the better your pictures will be.

➲ **Scanner:** Only necessary if you're using a film camera and you'll be scanning your images in, or if you're selling paper items, ephemera, coins or other flat objects.

➲ **USB hub:** If you're going to be plugging in a lot of accessories, buy a USB hub so you don't have to keep switching out plugs.

▶▶ **Test Drive**

Using the list above, go through your house and see what you already have on hand that you can use to set up your business. If you need to buy equipment, start comparison-shopping now. There are a number of magazines and Web sites that review and rate electronics. Spend some time comparing products and features. Don't just walk into an office supply store and buy the first products you see.

If you're using equipment you already own for business, be sure you can prove what you paid for it, as you might be able to deduct these expenses on your tax return after you form your company. For more information, consult with a tax professional.

Naming Your Business

Naming your business is one of the first steps in giving it a life of its own and making it real. It's also one of the first steps in establishing your business as an entity separate from yourself. There are legal and financial reasons for doing this, which is why it's something you'll want to do as soon as possible.

You don't name your business to impress your online customers—they might never know you as anything other than your User ID. You do it as part of setting up your business the right way in the brick-and-mortar world.

If you're setting up your business as a corporation, limited liability company (LLC), or limited partnership, you'll have to make sure that the name you choose for it is available and not currently in use by another company. You can find this out by doing a name and trademark search in your state. You'll also have to be sure to comply with your state's rules for naming your business.

Choosing a Name

There's no right or wrong name for a business, and no formula will help you determine the name that's right for yours. Still, there is some basic logic when it comes to naming businesses that can help you name yours.

Good business names should be the following:

- Distinctive
- Memorable
- Easy to pronounce and spell
- Distinguishable from the competition
- Suggestive of the products or services you offer

The name you choose for your business can be the same or different from your eBay User ID or your store name. But choosing a name that ties into your online activities will make it easier to promote them in the brick-and-mortar world and can make it easier to do business in general. You won't have to juggle names or try to remember which name to use in various situations.

Fictitious, Trade, or DBA Names

If you're a sole proprietor and you're going to do business under any name other than your own, you'll want to do two things: check with your county clerk's office to make sure no one else is already using the name you've chosen, and register it with the county so it remains yours and yours alone. Typically, all you'll have to do is go to the courthouse, fill out a short form, and pay a small fee.

Starting Off Right

Knowing what you need to do to establish your business correctly and doing everything in the proper order can seem daunting. If it does to you, see what new business assistance services are offered by your state or local government. Another good place for help is the Small Business Administration, which operates Small Business Development Centers (SBDCs) in many cities across the United States. Local chambers of commerce can also be helpful; it never hurts to see what's offered where you live.

Choosing Your Business Structure

Business legal structures range from very simple to very complex. There are advantages and disadvantages to each. Which form is the best for you? Much of this answer depends on what you're planning to do with your business and how large you want it to be. Some will be a better fit if you want to keep things small and personal. Others are a good choice if you plan to grow your small business into a large one.

In general, the structure you choose needs to do three things:

1. **Provide an appropriate level of legal protection.** This varies quite a bit depending on the specific legal structure.
2. **Provide the appropriate structural organization.** If you're hiring employees and setting up divisions from the get-go, a sole proprietorship might not be the right structure for you.
3. **Be flexible enough to allow for changes in the future.** As an example, it's fairly easy to morph a sole proprietorship into a

partnership or a limited liability company. It's much more difficult for a corporation to go the opposite way and adopt a less formal structure.

There are many different business forms on the books. Of them, the following are the most common:

- Sole proprietorship
- Partnership
- Corporation
- Limited liability company

Sole Proprietorship

As the name suggests, this form of business means you're the captain of your ship. You own your business, lock, stock, and barrel. It also means the following:

- Your income—what you earn selling on eBay—is yours.
- The expenses you incur while doing business are also your responsibility.
- Your profits—your income after deducting expenses—are yours.
- You have complete control of your business. If you die, the business also ceases to exist. Your estate gets to handle the business's assets and liabilities.

Sole proprietorships are the most common and simplest business form in the United States. They're easy to form, easy to dissolve, and almost unregulated. All you have to do to set one up is obtain whatever licenses are required where you live and register a trade name. You don't have to hold annual meetings, issue annual reports, or anything like that.

With a sole proprietorship, you don't file separate tax returns for your business, as the IRS doesn't recognize sole proprietorships as separate entities. You just report your extra earnings on a Schedule C as part of your regular tax return.

If you're married, and your spouse is a joint owner of your business, you can still run it as a sole proprietorship as long as you also file a joint tax return.

▶▶**The biggest drawback to a sole proprietorship is the fact that you're responsible for both the profits and the liabilities of your company.** This means all of your assets, both personal and professional, are at risk. Should things go poorly, your creditors could go after everything you own, not just your business.

Partnerships

Two or more people going into business together often form partnerships. There are two types:

General: With this form, each partner is an agent of the partnership and can make decisions for the partnership without approval from the other partners. In general partnerships, all partners bear equal responsibility for partnership debts.

Limited: This form of partnership allows partners who are not involved in day-to-day operations to limit their liability to the amount they invest. This structure is often used when there are outside investors who don't want to participate in daily operations.

At the heart of partnerships are partnership agreements that specify each partner's obligations and responsibilities and define the legal aspects of the partnership. These documents are essential and should always be executed, regardless of the relationship among the partners.

Corporations

Corporations are separate legal entities that can own property and incur debt and are the most structured of all business forms.

There are two types of corporations—C and subchapter S. Both are owned by shareholders whose liability is limited to their investment amounts. They differ according to how taxes are handled, not according to their structure.

The level of asset protection afforded by incorporation is a significant advantage to this business form. On the downside, corporations require more record-keeping. In addition, annual meetings must be held, and corporate and personal funds must be kept completely separate, even if you're the only shareholder.

Limited Liability Company (LLC)

Limited liability companies combine the characteristics of partnerships and corporations. Like corporations, LLCs protect their members regardless of their level of participation in the business. Creditors can only go after the LLC's assets to satisfy claims. However, LLCs can be taxed like partnerships instead of corporations.

Can You Work from Your Home?

It's your castle, and you can do whatever you want in it, right? Well, maybe not. Depending on where you live, you might not be able to run your eBay business from home.

The rules and regulations governing home businesses can vary quite a bit depending on where you live and the type of business you have. What's more, it's up to you to know what you can and can't do in this respect. You can always try pleading ignorance should your cottage industry be out of compliance and the local authorities find out about it, but chances are it won't get you very far. Business owners are expected to do all necessary due diligence before they open for business, not after.

Noncompliance Can Cost You

Violations for not complying with municipal zoning laws are typically considered civil or noncriminal violations. However, they can be costly. Fines for zoning violations are often levied on a per diem basis, so the longer you're in violation, the more it's going to cost you. If you did something like build a little shed for storing inventory in your backyard, or add on to your garage, and the structure is found to be nonconforming, you might have to make the necessary changes to bring it into compliance, or you might be required to tear it down.

Protection from the Unknown

Someone trips and falls on your property, or your dog bites the kid across the street. Fortunately, you have homeowner's insurance, and you're protected, right? Yes, but if you're working from your home, you have a whole new set of liability concerns, and there's a good chance that your existing insurance coverage won't be adequate should something go wrong.

As a business, you're liable for things like customers suing you if they feel that something they bought from you injured them or caused them pain and anguish. If a delivery person falls when bringing a business shipment to your door, your homeowner's insurance might not cover it because it's a business-related injury. If you sell items on consignment for others, you also have to make sure these items are protected from things like fires or floods.

Before the unforeseen happens, take out a small-business insurance policy. Many companies that issue home insurance policies issue these too, and they can often be added on to your existing policy. Policy costs will vary depending on the type of coverage you need and how much liability you're willing to shoulder on your own. If you're manufacturing products for sale, you might need product liability insurance, too.

Don't assume that you're protected because you're small and no one will want to go after you. All it takes is one disgruntled customer armed with a good attorney and a sympathetic judge or jury to wipe out a small business. It can and does happen on a regular basis. Don't let it happen to you.

Flying under the Radar

The businesses that cause the most problems, and are the ones most heavily regulated, are those that cause neighborhood disruptions. That said, eBay sellers are usually pretty benign. While there aren't any firm statistics to cite, it's safe to say that many of them fly under the regulatory radar.

If you're mostly working alone, there's no one coming to your house on a regular basis, and you don't have inventory stacked all over your yard, chances are you can make it under the radar, too. But this doesn't mean you should. It's better to live by the law, not against it.

If you have a steady stream of people coming in and out of your home, or you're displaying signs that say things like "I buy estates. Call me" in your yard or window, you can pretty much bet on one of your neighbors filing a complaint and your getting a visit from your local officials sooner than later if these activities aren't allowed where you live.

How do you find out what the laws are in your area? Contact the governmental body that's responsible for making zoning decisions in your municipality. Usually this will be a local planning and/or zoning department. Many municipalities include this information on their Web sites; you might want to check there first.

Depending on where you live, you might have to obtain one or more of the following:

➲ Zoning approval
➲ A business license
➲ A home occupation permit

You might also have to pay a head tax and taxes on business equipment. The zoning laws in your area also might restrict how many people you can employ and your hours of operation, among other things.

Business Licenses—Required or Not?

As noted above, you might be required to have a business license to comply with the regulations in your area. The requirements for business licenses vary significantly; your best bet is to contact your local authorities to see what's necessary in your area. If you don't know who to contact, do an Internet search on your city and state. Most governmental agencies make this information available online.

Establishing a Business Checking Account

Most banks won't let you deposit or cash checks made out to your business name in your personal account. Instead, they'll require you to open a business account. Even if your bank lets you run business checks through your personal account, it's a better idea to set up a business account anyway, and to do it before you start selling.

Comingling business funds with personal funds might not seem like that big a deal, especially if you're not doing much business, but it really is. Unless you keep exceptionally good records, untangling the history on what went in and out of a comingled account can be a nightmare when tax season rolls around. Keeping separate accounts is also an easier way to get an accurate read on how your business is doing. Also, it's another way to prove the legitimacy of your business to the IRS.

Establishing a Business Address

If you're going to work out of your home, it's a good idea to set up a separate address for your business correspondence. Doing so will make your business feel more like an established, legal entity, and it will give you greater control over who knows where you live. All correspondence with eBay buyers, including any payments you receive in the mail, should go to this address.

The easiest approach is to go to the post office and rent a post office box. Rates for these are reasonable, and the extra measure of protection they provide is well worth the money. If you'd rather have a street address than a post office box, you can also rent boxes at business services stores or centers.

Street Address Versus P.O. Box—Which One Is Right for You?

Post office boxes are usually cheaper than boxes at the UPS Store or similar business services shops. However, having a street address instead of a post office box for your business address is another way to make your business seem more established, especially when you're first starting out. Also, business services centers can accept packages on your behalf. Delivery services like FedEx and UPS will not deliver to post office boxes.

Lines of Credit

A line of credit can simply be a credit card you open in your business name or one you convert solely to business use. Banks will also issue lines of credit for businesses with a strong financial history and a decent bank balance. Having one can make it possible to buy larger quantities of inventory than what you might be able to afford with existing funds, or to buy higher-ticket items than you usually do, as well as cover other business expenses when they come up.

If you can, get a line of credit in your business name, not your own. It will help you establish your business as a separate entity, and it will give your company greater credibility when dealing with manufacturers, wholesalers, and other potential inventory sources.

Business Versus Hobby—What the IRS Says

It takes many small businesses at least a couple of years before their income outweighs their expenses. The IRS realizes this and cuts small business owners some slack, but only so much. If your business loses money year after year, meaning that your expenses consistently exceed your profits from sales, the IRS might decide that your business is really a hobby, and your losses will only be deductible to the extent that they can be offset by your income.

The IRS uses two tests to determine if you're running a business or a hobby. First, you have to be able to show that you made money in three out of five years. If your profits don't pass muster, the IRS can also use something called a factors and circumstances test to reach a determination. This test evaluates the following:

- Whether you carry on the activity in a businesslike manner
- Whether the time and effort you put into the activity indicate you intend to make it profitable
- Whether you depend on income from the activity for your livelihood
- Whether your losses are due to circumstances beyond your control (or are normal in the startup phase of your type of business)
- Whether you change your methods of operation in an attempt to improve profitability
- Whether you, or your advisors, have the knowledge needed to carry on the activity as a successful business

➲ Whether you were successful in making a profit in similar activities in the past

➲ Whether the activity makes a profit in some years, and how much profit it makes

➲ Whether you can expect to make a future profit from the appreciation of the assets used in the activity

Formalizing your business by adopting a different legal structure can also help convince the IRS that you're really a businessperson, not a hobbyist. However, it's not a guarantee.

▶▶ **Test Drive**

If you haven't already started setting up your business the right way, now's the time to do it. Start with these steps:

1. Call the secretary of state's office in your state, your county, and the city where you live, or visit their Web sites, and determine what you're required to have in terms of business licenses, use permits, and so on.

2. Start working on a good business name.

3. When you have your business name figured out, and if you're going to operate as a sole proprietor, check with your county recorder's office to see if you can register it as a DBA.

4. Open a business banking account.

5. Talk to your insurance company about additional liability insurance for your business.

6. Open a post office box in your business name.

Understanding Basic Accounting Practices

Accounting. It's a dull, dry subject, unless you're an accountant. But you have to at least know the basics to run your business successfully. At the heart of all accounting practices is this simple formula:

liabilities + equity = assets

Liabilities are what you owe. *Equity* is the investment you've made in the business, plus your business's current and accumulated profits and losses. Add the two together and you have *assets*. This is your business's net worth.

If you're just setting up your eBay business, knowing its net worth might seem irrelevant. But it really isn't. **▶▶Keeping track of the information necessary to determine net worth is the only way to really know if you're making money.** Your sales might look great, but if your operating expenses are out of line or you're paying too much for inventory, you could be headed for disaster. The only way you'll know is by tracking what goes in and comes out of your business. You'll find information on software programs that will keep you on top of your finances and generate this information later in this chapter.

Another aspect of basic accounting practices is the systems you can use to account for your transactions. There are two of these. Double-entry accounting requires two journal entries—a debit and a credit—for each transaction. It's the more complex of the two, but it is also more accurate. Single-entry accounting just records one side of each transaction. When you make a journal entry, you just record it as a debit or a credit.

If your accounting experience begins and ends with balancing your checkbook, and maybe doing your own income taxes, this might seem intimidating. However, most accounting software programs will take care of the details for you.

Cash Basis Versus Accrual Basis Accounting

These are the two standard models for business accounting. They're fairly similar—the biggest difference between the two is when transactions are credited or debited. Either one will give you a snapshot of your business's financial condition. However, neither will give you the complete picture.

Which approach is right for you? Part of the answer depends on your business structure. If you're a sole proprietor, limited liability company, or S corporation, you can use either one. With some exceptions, other types of corporations and partnerships that have at least one corporation (other than an S corporation) as a shareholder must use the accrual method.

The other part of the answer depends on what you want or need to know about your business's financial health. If you need to keep an eye on your cash reserves, the cash method is better as it will tell you what you have on hand on any given day. If you're concerned about your long-term profitability, the accrual method is the one to use.

Cash Basis Accounting

Cash basis accounting—also called modified cash basis—is the simpler of the two approaches. If you use this system, every time you receive payment for something—*not* when you sell it—or pay out an expense, you immediately record it in a ledger book or in your accounting software. The only exceptions are expenses for certain capital expenditures like office equipment, which are amortized or depreciated over time.

As an example, let's say you sold twenty widgets on October 15, but you didn't get paid for them until November 2. You would not record the sale on October 15, when you sold the widgets, but on November 2, when you actually received payment for them.

The drawback to cash basis accounting is that it's based on cash flow instead of operations. It doesn't reflect outstanding payments—money you're expecting to get. It only reflects money you've actually received.

That said, this approach can be a boon when it comes to tax planning as you can sometimes time when you get money in or when you pay out on expenses to shift these items from one year to another. As an example, if you're having a good year, accelerating your expenses can help offset your income and minimize your tax burden. Or it might be to your benefit to delay some payments owed to you to the next calendar year.

Accrual Basis

Accrual basis accounting is considered the more accurate approach and is more commonly used, especially by businesses that carry inventory. With accrual basis accounting, you record revenues—in this case, sales—when they're made, not when you actually receive or spend the cash for them.

Let's go back to the example of the twenty widgets. Again, you sold them on October 15, but didn't receive payment until November 2. Under the accrual method, you'd record the sale the day it took place, not when you received the money.

If you use the accrual method, you'll break down your accounting into the following categories:

- **Accounts receivable:** This is everything you're owed.
- **Accounts payable:** This is everything you owe.
- **Accrued expenses:** These are expenses that you've incurred but not yet paid for during a given accounting period.

Your Company's Health Report Card

The financial health of a business or company is reflected in its financial statement. These documents contain a balance sheet, income statement, a statement of cash flow, and, in many cases, notes to the financial statement. Just about every successful, established business compiles this information regularly so they know what their financial health is at any given time. Publicly held companies are required to do so as part of their accountability to their stockholders.

Again, if you're just starting out, this might seem like more than you want or need to do. However, if you plan to grow your business, it's a good idea to get off on the right foot by learning about the process now and doing it right from the start. Plus, if you ever plan to go after outside financing for your business, potential investors and/or lenders will ask for these documents.

Tracking Inventory

Keeping track of how much inventory you have and where it is—just purchased, on its way, or being auctioned—doesn't necessarily require fancy automated systems, but it does require having some sort of system in place and using it regularly.

If you're not acquiring substantial amounts of inventory, you probably can keep track of it in a ledger book, on index cards, or on a simple computer-based spreadsheet program. Of course, if you're using a drop shipper, you won't have to keep track of your own inventory, but you will need to make sure they're fulfilling your orders as you transmit them. Some auction management programs include inventory tracking. If you need help in this area, it's a feature to look for when shopping these programs.

Tracking Taxes

Unless you live in one of the handful of states that don't charge sales tax, you'll have to collect and remit sales tax on any transactions that take place in your state. Currently, the only states that don't charge sales tax are Alaska, Delaware, Montana, New Hampshire, and Oregon.

This sounds complex, but it really isn't that bad. Remember, you're only charging sales tax to people who live in the same state that you do. You'll include information about this in your terms of service and in your auctions. When these sales happen, you'll collect the appropriate tax, and you'll send it in on a regular basis.

Sales Tax Licenses

In order to collect taxes, you'll need to apply for a sales tax license. These also go by other names, including a sales tax certificate, resale license, sales tax ID number, reseller's permit, or seller's permit. Talk to your state's department of revenue for more information.

There are some benefits to having a sales tax license. If you're buying from wholesalers, it allows you to do so without paying them sales tax, as you're buying for resale and you're not the end user. Instead, your buyers are, and you're going to be the one who's collecting tax from them—that is, if they live in your state, and if your state is one that levies sales taxes. Buyers who live in states other than yours (if they live in states that collect sales taxes) are responsible for paying the taxes on goods and services they purchase on the Internet. These *use taxes* are imposed to insure that the states receive funds from all purchases, regardless of where they take place.

Use taxes might be something new to you, but they've actually been around for a long time in most states. You can expect to hear more about them, and see more states make serious efforts to track and collect them in the years ahead, especially as Internet-based commerce continues to grow.

Sales taxes are typically regulated by the department of revenue in each state. Fees for tax licenses vary from state to state, but they usually aren't very expensive. You'll be expected to file your tax returns and any monies owed on a timely basis. Be sure to do so. Even if you have no local sales to report, you might be assessed a fine for not filing a report that states so.

Tax Collection Alternatives

You can sell on eBay and not collect taxes. All you have to do is not sell to people who live in your state. Deducting the taxes from the proceeds on items sold to people in your state is another option. This approach will wipe out some of your profit on these items, but it might be easier, especially if you don't have many customers in your state.

What You Can and Can't Deduct

Another aspect of tracking taxes relates to your own. When you're self-employed, you're both employer and employee. This means that no one else pays your taxes but you, and you're solely responsible for both computing them and remitting them. What's more, you're supposed to do this on a quarterly basis. Uncle Sam is definitely a "pay as you go" enterprise. The only way you can know what you owe is by tracking your income and expenses, and knowing what you can and can't deduct to offset income.

One of the big benefits to having your own business and being self-employed is that there are lots of things you can deduct that other taxpayers can't—things like books and magazines, office supplies, training, even a percentage of your house payments and your utilities, if you're working from home. All of these are business deductions, and you can use them to minimize your tax burden every year.

The following are just some of the expenses that you can deduct against income:

- Cost of goods, or what you pay for your inventory
- Mileage
- Car expenses
- Office supplies
- Shipping and postage
- Office equipment, including computers, telephones, cameras, and printers
- A portion of your entertainment expenses
- Tax preparation fees
- Legal and other professional fees
- Advertising and marketing

But you can't claim any of these deductions if you don't keep good records.

Waiting until April 15 or Paying As You Go

Many small business owners, and especially those used to having their taxes taken out of their paychecks, find it hard to make the paradigm shift to paying quarterly estimated taxes. As a result, they end up owing penalties and interest on what they didn't pay throughout the year.

Being able to use your money however you wish and settling up with Uncle Sam during tax season might be your preferred approach, but from a money management perspective you're better off making estimated payments instead of waiting until the bitter end. Even if you can't afford to pay everything you owe every time, at least you've paid something. Waiting until you file your annual return to determine how much you owe might also leave you with a nasty surprise—a big tax bill that you can't cover.

The IRS: Bogeyman or Best Friend?

IRS. Just the mention of this government agency is enough to strike fear in one's heart. And some even claim that that fear is enough to kill. Or, perhaps better put, it used to be enough.

The IRS was pretty draconian a decade or so ago, and it seemed especially so when it came to small businesses. In one well-publicized instance, it was claimed that the IRS literally hounded one business owner to death. The details of the case went something like this.

The owner of a small business in Houston was being pursued by tax collectors for possible nonpayment of payroll taxes. The man was battling cancer and heart disease, but he was still working a few hours a week to support himself and his family.

The lawyer representing this individual contacted the IRS and asked that all communications be routed to him due to his client's fragile health. According to the lawyer, the revenue officer on the case continued to make collection efforts directly to the taxpayer, including typing up a summons ordering the man to appear before him for interrogation and personally serving this document on the man's son.

The harassment didn't stop, no matter what the lawyer tried. In October 1995, his client received a notice of intent to levy from the IRS. He delivered it to the attorney, and died of a heart attack two days later.

With publicity like this, the writing was on the wall for the IRS. It had to change its ways, and it did. It became a kinder, friendlier agency. Taxpayers were even encouraged to come in and ask tax-related questions without fear of prosecution. The IRS figured it was better to clear up problems than to let them continue, and they were right.

Today, IRS regulations are far more reasonable when it comes to small businesses and their owners. Deducting things like home office expenses no longer sends up the big red audit flag, as long as the deductions are reasonable. Reasonable, however, is a key word. Go too far beyond reasonable, and you can bet on getting a letter from the kinder, gentler IRS sooner or later.

Accounting Software Versus Ledgers

For keeping track of daily income and expenses, you might find it easiest to just write things down in a simple ledger. For keeping your books and generating profit and loss reports, buy a good business accounting program and learn how to use it. Keeping track of this information manually is simply too time consuming. Many small business owners like Quick Books or Peachtree, but there are other programs to choose from.

Filing and Storing Your Business Records

To stay on the IRS's good side, you have to keep your business records for a certain number of years after you file your taxes. If there's any possibility that you might get audited, you pretty much have to keep them forever.

To keep from having to do a mad scramble should you have to gather these materials, keep them in one place. Banker's boxes, labeled by year, are ideal for this. Each box should contain the following:

⮑ That year's tax return
⮑ All bank statements for the year
⮑ All bills and receipts for the year
⮑ A printout of the year's ledger from your accounting software
⮑ Anything else that could support what you claimed for income and expenses for the year

Don't rely solely on your computer to store your financial information—if it crashes, the information might be gone forever. Print out at least one copy of your tax return (if you prepare it yourself) and your ledger for the year and put them in the box. Back up the same information to a CD-ROM, and put it in a safe place where you know you won't forget about it. Don't store it in the same box with all your tax records.

▶▶ Test Drive

Take a little time to think about which type of accounting—cash basis or accrual—will best match your company, and start setting up the necessary systems, including your accounting software, for the approach you choose.

3

Becoming a Successful eBay Seller

Researching Market Values

Now's the time to get serious about determining the values of the items you're going to sell. Doing this will tell you where to set your starting price, whether you should use optional listing features, set a reserve, and so on.

If you're dealing with commodity goods—things that are widely available—finding this information shouldn't be too much of a problem. If you're selling unique items, say antique silver or one-of-a-kind necklaces, it might be tougher going.

The easiest and best place to do your research is eBay itself. This is where you're going to find the most up-to-date and relevant information. Compare current and completed auctions of items that are the same as or similar to what you plan to sell. If you've spent enough time on the site, you should have been able to gather enough info, but remember, you only get about two weeks of closed auctions here. For some items, that's enough. For others, it isn't.

If you need to do additional research, here are a few other approaches:

➲ **Go through auction catalogs and price guides.** These can help establish values for things other than commodities—collectibles, vintage items, antiques, and so on. However, remember that auction prices, catalog prices, and prices realized on eBay can be very different. Use information from these sources to guide you, but don't rely on them alone.

➲ **Search other auction and/or selling sites.** Again, this information might be best simply for guiding pricing decisions. Keep in mind that the market conditions on other sites are often very different than what you'll find on eBay.

➲ **Subscribe to a pricing service.** Options to consider here include PriceMiner, which gathers historical price data for same or similar items from eBay and other sites. Pricing assistance is also a feature of Andale's auction management offerings.

Setting Starting Prices

In most cases, the starting price on any item should be the lowest amount you're willing to sell it for. The exception to this is reserve price auctions. With these, you can set your starting price low to generate interest. The reserve price is your protection, as the item won't sell unless the final bid amount is equal to or greater than the reserve.

There's definitely a fine art to setting starting prices, but there's no magic formula. Some sellers like to start low to generate more interest and to keep their listing fees reasonable. This can work well if you're selling high-demand items, as the demand for them keeps selling prices fairly consistent. If you're not in these categories, you risk selling your merchandise below its value if you take this approach. You might even end up getting less than what you paid for the item.

If after doing your research, you've come up with what seems to be a reasonable price range for the items you're selling, it's probably best to go with your findings if you can. Price your merchandise substantially higher, and bidders will look for cheaper items. Price it substantially lower, and you run the risk of undercutting and devaluing the market.

Most sellers will tell you that the best approach is the one discussed here— ▶▶**do your research, determine a reasonable starting price range, and set your beginning bid at the lowest price within this range that you're comfortable with.** Ideally, this amount will cover all your costs and allow you to make a little profit should the item sell for opening bid.

Understanding Listing Fees

eBay charges listing or insertion fees for every item that's listed on the site. For the most part, these fees are nonrefundable. If your items don't sell, you'll still be billed for them. However, if you relist the item, and it sells the second time, you'll get a refund for the insertion fee on the relist.

Remember, listing fees are what you pay for the privilege of using the site. They're different from final value fees, which are assessed and charged at the completion of each sale. You only pay final value fees if your items sell. These are the only fees that are refunded to you if buyers don't perform.

> ### Follow the Rules
>
> eBay only refunds insertion fees if you follow their rules for relisting items. This includes using the official "Relist Your Item" link, either in the original auction or on the Unsold Items area of your My eBay page. If you cut and paste the content from the original listing into a new one, the system won't pick up on the items being relisted, and you'll lose the credit. Items have to be relisted within ninety days of the last auction closing, and you only get the credit if the item sells the second time around. If you have to relist again, you won't get a credit. Relists also have to be in the same format as the originals; that is, you can't make a reserve item into a non-reserve or make the starting bid on the relist higher than the original one.

How eBay Computes Listing Fees

Listing fees are based on the starting bid for each item. They begin at 25 cents for a minimum bid of one penny and go up to $4.80 for items starting at $500 or more. For a complete rundown on what these fees are, go to "Help>Selling>Listing Your Item>Fees." The basic listing fees are the same regardless of what kind of auction you're running. For Multiple Item or Dutch auction listings, the fee is computed per item, not per auction. As an example, if you decide you want to offer ten items in a Dutch auction, you'll pay the appropriate listing fee times ten.

You can upgrade your listings in a number of ways, and there's more information on upgrades to consider later in this section. Listing upgrades results in higher insertion fees, but depending on what you're selling, the additional costs might be worth it.

Picture Services

eBay allows you to post one item picture and the item preview picture at no cost. After that, unless you make other arrangements, you have to pay eBay for additional photos. These fees range from 15 cents for each additional photo after the first one to $1.50 for eBay's Picture Pack, which includes such features as supersizing images, picture show (for viewing all item pictures) at the top of each listing page, and inserting up to twelve pictures.

Many beginning sellers use eBay's photo services. Doing so gives them one less thing to think about as they're learning the ropes. If you decide to follow suit, you'll want to investigate other options sooner than later as the charges for eBay's service can add up in a hurry. More information on photo hosts and services can be found in Chapter 13.

Listing Upgrades

eBay also offers a number of options for enhancing listings and drawing more attention to them. These range from Listing Designer—eBay's template package—at 10 cents per listing to Home Page Featured, which gives one of your listings a shot at rotating into a special display area on eBay's home page for $39.95.

Most of eBay's listing upgrades are great revenue sources for the company but are of lesser value to sellers. That said, the following are worth considering, again depending on what you're selling:

➲ **Subtitle:** This feature lets you add a second line under the item title. It's a great way to provide more information to potential buyers or highlight specific features of an item. Plus, listings with subtitles tend to stand out more in search results. Subtitle text doesn't show up on title searches, but it does show up on title and description searches. Cost: 50 cents.

➲ **Border:** Puts a border around a listing. Cost: $3.

➲ **Highlight:** Sets up the listing with a colored background. Cost: $5.

➲ **Bold:** This one puts titles in boldface type. Cost: $1.

➲ **Ten-day duration:** Lets you run auctions for 10 days. Cost: 40 cents.

➲ **Gallery:** Adds a thumbnail photo to listings in search results. Cost: 35 cents.

➲ **Gift services:** This feature adds a gift package icon to indicate that the seller offers gift wrapping/packaging services. If you offer these services, this is one to consider for the holiday season. Cost: 25 cents.

➲ **Featured Listing:** If you have something really special to sell, this enhancement will put it at the top of the search results in the category you list it in. Cost: $19.95.

Again, for a complete rundown on all listing enhancements and fees, go to "Help>Selling>Listing Your Item>Fees."

One upgrade that just about everyone agrees on is Gallery, which adds an image next to the title of the item. It gives potential buyers a preview of items as they browse search results, which is something most buyers really, really like. So don't consider this a listing enhancement unless you're selling commodity items that buyers are going to select more by price than by appearance. Consider it a listing necessity, and budget accordingly.

Choosing Auction Formats

As discussed in Chapter 4, the classic single-item auction format is by far the most prevalent and popular on eBay, and it works well for the majority of the items offered at the site. Other formats are available. With the exception of Multiple Item auctions, the other formats basically boil down to listing upgrades, as they're not much different from the classic format. They just add options. Fees for each option are added onto the basic listing fees.

Multiple Item Auctions

Unless you have a bunch of items that are exactly the same—and they have to be *exactly the same* to qualify for this auction format—this is one that you probably won't use much, if at all. If you do, you set them up just like you would any other auction.

What many sellers do when they have multiple items is to list them as a multiple-item fixed price auction. You simply enter the amount of items you have to sell and set a fixed price for each. Instead of bidding, buyers determine how many they want at the stated price and click on Buy It Now to purchase them.

Reserve Auctions

As previously discussed, reserve auctions are used to protect investments by ensuring items sell for a specific amount. If the bids don't meet the reserve, the seller isn't obligated to sell to the highest bidder.

To Reserve or Not?

I recently decided to sell off a number of first-edition children's books I had accumulated over the years. After researching one title—Roald Dahl's *Charlie and the Chocolate Factory*—I found that books similar to mine in condition had sold for as much as $500, so I listed mine with a low starting price—$9.99—and a fairly hefty reserve. After the first day, not only were there no bids, no one was even watching my auction, so I decided to take my chances and I dropped the reserve. Bingo! The first bids rolled in about two hours later, and the book sold at a nice price. It wasn't as high as the reserve I had set, but it was enough to make me happy.

Reserves are kind of a "Damned if you do, damned if you don't" proposition. Launching auctions at low prices is a time-tested approach to generating more interest and more bids, but combining that lower price with a reserve can wipe out the benefits of starting low. Listing things at the absolute minimum price you're willing to take might narrow the interest in your items, but you save a little on listing fees.

Go on boards frequented by buyers, and you'll see comments like "I hit the back button the second I see a reserve." This doesn't mean you shouldn't use them, but it does tell you that you'll turn off certain bidders if you do.

The best advice on reserves is to use them judiciously. Don't make the mistake that some newbie sellers do and put a reserve on everything. This just increases your costs and brands you a newcomer. eBay itself discourages reserve auctions by noting that items sold in this format typically sell for less than those without it.

Reserve fees begin at $1 for items up to $49.99 and increase to $2 for items between $50 and $199.99. After this, the reserve fee is 1 percent of the reserve price, up to $100.

Buy It Now

Buy It Now auctions, or BINs, allow buyers to end auctions early by buying items at a specific price. The fees for these auctions range from 5 cents for opening bids up to $9.99; 10 cents for opening bids from $10 to $24.99; 20 cents for bids from $25 to $49.99: and 25 cents for $50 or more.

BINs can be a great idea during the holiday season, especially as the holidays grow closer. They're also good for snagging impulse buyers and others who don't want to participate in auctions for various reasons.

They're also not a bad idea to put on high-demand items that buyers are clamoring for. Buyers don't have to wait until the auction ends to get their wins, and you know right away what items sold for.

How to set a BIN? Most sellers pick a price that reflects where they think the bidding would (or should) end up if the auction ran to its end. This is where doing your research on market values really pays off.

BIN auctions also have a Best Offer option that tells buyers you're willing to entertain offers on the items—in other words, they can name their price. When they do, you have forty-eight hours to decide whether to accept it. If you take the offer, the auction ends immediately.

You can add the Best Offer option to BIN listings by going to the Pictures & Details page in the Sell Your Item form. Go to the Pricing and Duration section and check the Best Offer box there.

Fixed Price Auctions

Fixed price auctions are basically the same as BINs. However, this format doesn't offer potential buyers the opportunity to bid on your items instead of buying them outright. They have to accept the fixed price.

▲ As seen in this sample page for setting up an auction, you will have to consider a number of options when putting even a single item up for sale.

Auction Durations

eBay auctions can run anywhere from one to ten days. ▶▶**Seven-day auctions are far and away the most popular and the most common.** Ten-day auctions, which are also fairly common, afford the opportunity of catching buyers over two weekends. You pay an additional premium for these auctions—40 cents—which is minimal in anyone's book, but the additional fees can add up over time and eat into your profit margins. The remaining auction durations—five-day, three-day, and one-day—cost the same as seven-day auctions do.

Choosing auction durations of shorter than seven days cuts down on the number of people who might see your items. What's more, these auctions cost you more when you factor how much you pay for them on a daily basis. As an example, let's say you're going to list a decorative mirror. You're setting the start price at $19.99, you're including a gallery image, and you're running a subtitle. Your listing costs will be $1.45. Divide that by seven (to find the cost to run your listing for seven days), and you find that the cost is slightly over 21 cents a day. Divide it by five, and you're at 29 cents. By three: 48 cents. And remember, as the number of days for the auction goes down, so does the number of people who might potentially see the item.

So, if you're going to pay the same regardless of auction length, does it ever make sense to run auctions less than seven days? It all depends on what you're selling and the audience you want to reach. Other factors, such as the time of year, can also factor in.

Here are some approaches to consider for determining how long to run your auctions:

⮕ For items where time is no object, seven-day listings work just fine. This choice will improve the chances of your items being seen by as many potential bidders as possible and will save you money should you have to relist. It costs more to relist a three-day auction twice than it does to run the item for a week to begin with.

⮕ Consider ten-day auctions for luxury items, unique items, and high-ticket merchandise that you want to expose to as many potential bidders as possible.

⊃ On items with more sensitive timelines, such as special-event tickets, choosing a shorter auction duration might be necessary to ensure that buyers receive their wins in time.

⊃ Consider three- and five-day auctions during the holiday season. Last-minute shoppers will thank you.

⊃ Use one-day auctions for special situations, such as fulfilling a request for a specific buyer.

Don't be afraid to experiment with auction durations. It's better to test-drive a few approaches and see what works best for you than to go with commonly accepted practices that might not match your buyers' needs.

Being Smart about Listing Fees

Something as simple as starting an auction for a penny less can save you a significant amount of money. As an example, you'll save 25 cents if you start an item at $9.99 instead of $10. You'll save 60 cents if you start an item at $24.99 instead of $25. Slapping BINs on auctions can add up, too. For items on which you want to realize a certain price, consider using the Fixed Price format instead of adding a BIN. Doing so can save you 5 cents per listing.

▶▶ Test Drive

There are two test drives for this chapter. If you're not yet selling on eBay, do an item search and analyze how various sellers set things like starting prices, auction formats, and auction durations. See which ones make the most sense to you, and which ones you like the most from the buyer's perspective. Use the results of your analysis for your own auctions.

If you're already selling, it's easy to fall into a rut and use the same approach on everything you sell. Consider testing the effectiveness of your approach by running two auctions simultaneously with different formats or durations. As an example, if you don't use BINs all that often, list one item with a BIN, the other without. For the best comparison, choose the same or very similar items if possible.

Copyright and Trademark

All eBay sellers are responsible for ensuring the legality of their auctions. This not only means making sure you're offering items that are legal to sell, it also means ensuring that the images and the copy included in your listings don't infringe on anyone's copyright or trademark.

Copyright and trademark law is complex, and there's no need to go into either area in any great detail here. It is, however, important to know the basics, which pretty much boil down to this: If the words and images you use are of your own creation and not taken from another source in any way, shape, or form, you're in the clear. If you borrow copy and/or images from other sources, including other sellers, you're asking for trouble unless you know for sure that the material you're using is in the public domain; that is, no other entity holds the rights to it. You can even run into trouble if your words and/or images are original but close to another's content and/or style.

Sellers often alert other sellers to infringements when they come across them. Injured sellers sometimes take it easy on newbies by contacting them via e-mail first and asking them to cease and desist. Others simply report listing violations directly to eBay without prior warning. eBay does not take these infractions lightly, and violations can lead to suspension of the seller's account.

Participants in eBay's Verified Rights Owner (VeRO) program will also report listings that violate their rights. Such listings can include unlawful use of copyrighted images, selling fake merchandise, inappropriate trademark use, and so on. Again, these are things eBay does not take lightly, and there's very little investigating done, if any, before auctions are pulled. If this should happen to you and you feel it was done in error, you can appeal it to eBay. If you can prove that you're in the right, eBay can and does reinstate auctions. If there's a question of whom to side with, however, be assured that VeRO participants trump others. It's therefore in your best interest to create listings that won't get you into trouble.

"Oops" Is Not a Defense

I was selling for a nonprofit organization a couple of years ago that had received a donation of a large assortment of Beanie Babies. The big Beanie Baby craze had ended, but certain Beanies were still in good demand. After doing a little research, it looked like about half of the Beanies we had were worth auctioning, so I started building auctions for them.

Back in the day, the mad frenzy over some of the more collectible Beanies had led to counterfeiting, but I was pretty sure the ones I had were the real deal. Or, perhaps better put, I had no reason to think they weren't. None of them were all that collectible, which in itself was enough to support their being real (or so I thought). However, since I hadn't bought them myself and I didn't know exactly where they came from, I couldn't be 100 percent sure, so I included wording to this effect in my auction listings.

Every one of them was pulled. The e-mails I received notifying me of eBay's actions simply stated that I couldn't sell counterfeit merchandise.

I thought the wording in the auctions made it pretty clear that the items were authentic, at least as far as I could tell, so I responded to one of the e-mails and asked what I had done wrong. What I had written about not being entirely sure of the Beanies' authenticity is what shut me down. As the follow-up e-mail put it, "Sellers may not disclaim knowledge of, or responsibility for, the authenticity or legality of the items offered in their listings. Sellers should take steps to ensure that their items are authentic before listing them on eBay. If a seller cannot verify the authenticity of an item, the seller is not permitted to list it."

That was a big oops, but on eBay oops is not a defense. Sellers are expected to do whatever's necessary to ensure that their auctions are in compliance with the site's rules and regulations. It was my responsibility to verify the authenticity of the items. If I had any doubt at all, I shouldn't have listed them. Or I should have authenticated them before I did. Lesson learned.

You'll come across auctions that are clearly in violation. Sellers will write things like "I can't guarantee the authenticity of this item, and have set the opening bid to reflect this," or "It looks like a Louis Vuitton Speedy, but I don't know for sure." Or they'll put question marks in their auction titles. Neither approach is acceptable.

eBay doesn't patrol listings looking for ones that break the rules, but other users do, and many of them report violations. While you're not expected to know every eBay rule and regulation, asking questions before you list anything you have doubts about is a far better approach than risking your reputation and your trading privileges.

Here's how to do it:

- ⮩ Make sure that everything you sell is authentic. If there's the slightest doubt, either get the item authenticated or don't list it.
- ⮩ Write your own listing copy. It's more than okay to look at other auctions to see how other sellers do it. However, when it comes to your own listings, make sure you put things in your own words.
- ⮩ Take your own pictures. Unless you've received permission from the photographer or the person who owns the rights to the images, all pictures in your auctions should be ones that you took yourself or had someone else do for you under your direction.
- ⮩ Use trademarks and brand names appropriately. As an example, if you're selling a pair of Keds, it's fine to say so. If you're selling a shirt that maybe looks like one you saw in a Bebe store a year ago, you can't include the brand name in your title to draw more potential bidders to the listing. Yes, you'll see lots of other sellers who do this, but that doesn't give you permission to follow suit. eBay does allow item comparisons in descriptions, but to only one other similar product.

More information about copyright can be found on eBay at "Help>Rules and Policies>Rules about Intellectual Property."

What Is Acceptable Use?

Acceptable or fair use is a sticky area of intellectual property law that you won't see discussed much on eBay. This is primarily because a fair number of sellers violate its precepts when they use artwork and other images that they themselves have not created to promote their businesses and/or listings.

Even if an image or a description doesn't carry a copyright symbol, it's still someone else's property unless you can prove otherwise. As such, "borrowing" it in any way for your own use is against the law.

Here's what the U.S. Copyright Office has to say about fair use:

66**Section 107 contains a list** of the various purposes for which the reproduction of a particular work may be considered 'fair,' such as criticism, comment, news reporting, teaching, scholarship, and research. Section 107 also sets out four factors to be considered in determining whether or not a particular use is fair:

1. the purpose and character of the use, including whether such use is of commercial nature or is for nonprofit educational purposes;
2. the nature of the copyrighted work;
3. amount and substantiality of the portion used in relation to the copyrighted work as a whole; and
4. the effect of the use upon the potential market for or value of the copyrighted work

The distinction between 'fair use' and infringement may be unclear and not easily defined. There is no specific number of words, lines, or notes that may safely be taken without permission. Acknowledging the source of the copyrighted material does not substitute for obtaining permission.

The 1961 Report of the Register of Copyrights on the General Revision of the U.S. Copyright Law cites examples of activities that courts have regarded as fair use: 'quotation of excerpts in a review or criticism for purposes of illustration or comment; quotation of short passages in a scholarly or technical work, for illustration or clarification of the author's observations; use in a parody of some of the content of the work parodied; summary of an address or article, with brief quotations, in a news report; reproduction by a library of a portion of a work to replace part of a damaged copy; reproduction by a teacher or student of a small part of a work to illustrate a lesson; reproduction of a work in legislative or judicial proceedings or reports; incidental and fortuitous reproduction, in a newsreel or broadcast, of a work located in the scene of an event being reported.'

> Copyright protects the particular way an author has expressed himself; it does not extend to any ideas, systems, or factual information conveyed in the work. **99**

In a nutshell, using someone else's words or images always runs the risk of stirring up trouble. If you want to completely avoid potential hassles, stick to your own work. Create your own logo, or base it on an image that's in the public domain. Take your own pictures unless you have written permission to use copyrighted images. Be careful about including quotes or excerpts from other sources in your listing copy. If you do, it's typically best to keep it brief—a sentence or two is good—and be sure to say where the quote came from. Or you can paraphrase the quote; for example, try saying something like "*PC Magazine* gave this computer five stars in its *Fall Buyer's Guide*" instead of directly quoting the review.

Timing Is Everything

You can launch eBay auctions at any time, day or night, on any day of the week, and during any season of the year. The best or optimal timing is a favorite topic of discussion among eBay sellers, and has been since the site opened. However, there's no clear consensus, and, to be honest, no single best time.

When eBay was substantially smaller, the timing of auction endings was much more of a consideration than it is now. Back then, sellers were encouraged to pattern their listing times after what was known about bidders' online habits—that is, when they were most likely to be shopping and bidding. Sunday evenings were determined to be prime time for both activities, and sellers timed their auctions to end then.

As mentioned, there really is no one "best" time to start and end auctions these days. It might be the middle of the night where you are, but they might be shopping with glee in Australia. Choosing listing durations and auction timing has more to do with knowing your audience. Knowing what works for others like you and patterning your scheduling after theirs works too. The bottom line is that you have complete control over when you want to end your auctions. Here are some approaches to consider:

➲ Pick a time and make it yours. As you establish yourself and your business, your listing patterns will become a part of how you do business.

➲ List something every day so you have auctions ending every day. Many sellers like to take this approach. Not only does it keep them online and visible at all times, it eases the burden of having tons of auctions ending on the same day.

➲ Stagger your hours. Doing so can catch bidders around the clock. Once again, remember the global aspect. If you want to sell internationally—and you should, as international buyers can be some of your best customers—when items end doesn't matter as much.

➲ Check the competition. If you're listing a specialty item, let's say a unique antique or collectible, it might not be to your advantage to be competing against other similar items. Then again, it might be just the thing to attract more attention to your items.

➲ Try a variety of different times and see which ones work best for you.

Many long-time eBay sellers recommend choosing times that work for you and that fit into your schedule. Bids often come in during the last minutes, as do questions, so being available to answer them as auctions wind down makes a lot of sense.

Ending the "End It on Sunday" Myth

Lots of people will tell you that ending auctions on Sunday evenings works the best. This might have been true in eBay's early days, but it isn't any longer. There's really no "best" day to begin or end auctions. What's more, people who still hold to the "end it on Sunday" tradition continue to flood the market with their listings on that day. Why try to compete during a time period that's overcrowded to begin with?

Nonetheless, Sundays are still the most popular item-ending days. Monday is the second most popular. Friday is the least popular day, followed closely by Saturday and Wednesday. Tuesdays and Thursdays are somewhat in the neutral zone. Keep in mind, however, that these rankings are more reflective of sellers' preferences than buyers' habits or desires.

Another big myth is to avoid listing or ending auctions during holiday weekends. This is another misconception that doesn't pan out at all. If you're willing to ship to international buyers, and you state this in your auctions, people around the world will be able to see your listings. When things are closed in the United States, many other parts of the world are definitely open for business. Plus, running auctions when others don't increases the chances of buyers finding your items.

It is a good idea to avoid launching auctions when eBay is running a listing promotion. Every so often, the eBay powers that be decide to pump up their revenues by giving sellers a break on fees. They'll announce a free listing day, a discount on listing fees, or discounts on various listing enhancements.

Listing promotions might seem like a great deal, but they really aren't, especially when it comes to free listing days and listing fee discounts. That's because sellers hot on saving a few bucks typically flood the marketplace with a lot of, to put it bluntly, junk. If you're selling in categories that are already saturated, the additional listings will only make market conditions worse.

Using Optional Listing Features

You've already seen the rundown on these in Chapter 10. How should you choose to use them, and when are they a good idea?

▶▶**Remember that every listing feature you add can potentially increase or decrease your profits.** Choose and use these judiciously, and do what you can to squeeze every last drop of value out of them. As an example, if you're going to do a featured listing on an item, parlay the increased exposure you'll get by running other auctions at the same time, having your store well-stocked, or both.

Using eBay's Seller Tools

Most sellers use eBay's "Sell Your Item" form when they're first starting out. This is a very simple form that takes you through all the steps of building an eBay auction. You can find it by clicking on the Sell button at the top of every eBay page.

Using the basic "Sell Your Item" form will teach you the nuts and bolts of how to build your auctions. It's not a bad approach to doing this, especially when you're new to selling. However, there are faster and more efficient approaches, and as your business grows you'll definitely want to automate and streamline the process as much as possible. You can do so in one of two ways: by using eBay's Seller Tools or subscribing to similar services from third-party vendors. You'll find information on other products to consider in Appendix Three.

eBay's seller tools range from fairly bare-bones offerings to more sophisticated programs that manage virtually every step of the selling process. They include the following:

- ⮕ **TurboLister:** This free program is designed for medium to high-volume sellers. You download it to your computer and use it to build listings offline. When you're ready to launch them, you can upload them all at once if you want. You can use TurboLister alone or with one of eBay's sales management tools.

- ⮕ **Selling Manager:** This is an online sales management tool for medium to large sellers that facilitates sales management and tracking. Features include sale status, e-mail and feedback templates, bulk relist and feedback, and printing labels directly from sales invoices. The cost is $4.99 a month.

- ⮕ **Selling Manager Pro:** Designed for high-volume sellers, the pro version offers all of Selling Manager's features as well as inventory management, listing statistics, automatic feedback and post-sale emails, monthly sales reports, and a free listing designer. The cost is $15.99 a month.

- ⮕ **Blackthorne Basic:** This newer all-in-one application offers bulk listing, sales status tracking, and customized templates for all customer correspondence, including payment and shipping notifications and sales invoices. Easy-to-use HTML listing templates make building auctions a breeze. The cost is $9.99 a month.

- ⮕ **Blackthorne Pro:** Another newer offering, Blackthorne Pro replaces eBay's Seller Assistant Pro (SAP). Designed for high-volume sellers, it offers the same features as Blackthorne Basic plus inventory management capabilities, multi-user settings, auction time scheduling, and a free listing designer. The cost is $24.99 a month.

Which one might be right for you? With the exception of TurboLister, which is a free program, all these programs offer free thirty-day trials, so you don't have anything to lose by trying any of them. ▶▶**Consider what your most important needs are and how much you're willing to pay for them, then match the service to your needs, your budget, and the size of your business.**

Establishing Terms and Conditions of Service

eBay's auction template includes several fields where sellers can detail the kinds of payments they'll accept, their shipping policies, returns policies, and so on. This is called terms and conditions of service, or TOS. Including your TOS in your auction listings tells potential buyers what they can expect from you and what you expect from them.

Basic terms and conditions of service is something that eBay expects all sellers to include in their auction listings, which is why areas for entering this information are part of eBay's auction template. Many sellers include additional TOS information in the body of their auction listings and on their "About Me" pages. You can, too, but you don't have to. What's more, it can be a good idea not to. Some sellers, and especially new ones, get a little heavy handed with their TOS. Or they think they have to spell out every little transactional detail. Not only is this not necessary, it can be a real turnoff to buyers. Yes, it's important to give buyers the information they need to complete the transaction and to let them know how you handle things. Making them wade through paragraph upon paragraph of details to find this information and/or beating them over the head with it isn't necessary. What's more, it's somewhat abusive.

The following TOS, taken from an actual auction listing (worse yet, from the top of the listing; it appeared before the item description and pictures), is a good example of this approach. It's nowhere near the worst you'll see, however. Some of the details have been changed for privacy.

Payment
*All payment is due within 7 DAYS of auction close.
*I PREFER PAYPAL!
*Money orders accepted on amounts OVER $20.00 ONLY. My bank is out of town and it's too much hassle to drive that far for such small amounts.
*NO PERSONAL CHECKS! THIS VIOLATES MY TERMS AND CONDITIONS AND CAN NEGATE THE SALE. SEND THEM AND I'LL RETURN THEM. IT'S AS SIMPLE AS THAT.

~~~~~~

Shipping
*I ship on Mondays and Fridays most weeks.
*I only ship USPS Priority Mail. Don't ask for other service, you won't get it.
*I will combine shipping at $2.50 per additional item on clothing items that end within a 7-day period only. Items MUST be paid for together to receive the discount.
*Shipping costs include handling and delivery confirmation.

****

Feedback
*I LEAVE FEEDBACK AFTER I'VE RECEIVED YOURS. This way I know you're happy with everything.
*If you are not happy about something, contact me BEFORE leaving feedback. I will work with you to resolve any problems, but if you just leave negative feedback without contacting me, I will return it.

Returns accepted only if I've very inaccurately described an item, in which case you may send the item back for a refund minus the cost of shipping. (The amount you pay for shipping is used to get your item to you). If you chose not to read my terms or the information in the auction then no refund!!

*EBAYERS WITH LESS THAN 10 FEEDBACK, NEW OR NOT, MUST EMAIL ME FOR PERMISSION TO BID. THIS MEANS EMAIL ME BEFORE YOU START BIDDING. I'M FED UP WITH NON-PAYING BIDDERS WASTING MY TIME AND MONEY. IF YOU CHOOSE NOT TO DO THIS, YOUR BID(S) WILL BE CANCELLED.**

Would you want to buy from this seller? Not only is she alienating bidders, newbies or not, by yelling at them IN ALL CAPS, her terms don't exactly position her as a friendly, accommodating seller, especially when it's the first thing you see when you scroll down to the item description. Not taking personal checks is okay, but telling people you don't want them because your bank is too far away might make them wonder if life in general is a little too much of a hassle. It's also okay to tell potential bidders that USPS Priority is your only shipping method. It's not necessary to tell them what you'll do if they ask for something else.

TOS should be kept short and sweet, friendly and informative, and should include the following:

- ⮫ Payment terms.
- ⮫ Shipping information, such as when you ship, how you ship, and if you combine shipping for multiple wins.
- ⮫ Your return policy, if you have one. (You'll find more information on this in Chapter 26.)

As mentioned, there's space for most of this information in eBay's basic auction template. You're prompted to enter it in the areas that describe your shipping, payment details, and return policy and payment methods accepted.

If you want to go beyond the basics, include the additional information on your "About Me" page or in your end-of-auction e-mail. If you do decide to go this route, remember to keep it short, keep it simple, and keep it friendly. There's no reason to beat up on potential bidders. Don't give them reasons not to buy from you.

Learning from Others

Don't let the warnings about copyright and fair use earlier in this chapter dissuade you from looking at how others do things and from patterning what you do after the sellers you admire for doing things the right way. ▶▶**The ability to see how others have built their success is one of the aspects to doing business on eBay that draws so many people to it, and what has made many of these individuals successful as well.** Just remember the above guidelines. If you ever have questions regarding fair use or copyright, either do what's necessary to put your fears to rest, or err on the side of caution and find another way to say it or show it.

When you're gleaning information about doing business on eBay, don't forget the site's discussion boards. There can be a lot of idle chatter here, but, even among the silliest, most off-topic conversations, you can find fantastic kernels of information that can go a long way to launching your selling career on the right foot.

It's a good idea to spend some time on the boards, either as a lurker or a poster, both before you start selling and as a new seller. Focus on the boards that can give your selling career the fastest start, such as these:

- ➲ **Category-specific boards:** They're a great way to get to know the real nitty-gritty about the categories you want to sell in.
- ➲ **Community help boards:** PayPal, Auction Listings, and Photo and HTML are just some of the boards that are worth your time.

As you read the various discussions, note the subjects that seem to come up over and over again, and note what participants have to say about them. This knowledge will come in handy in innumerable ways, especially when you're writing up your terms and conditions of service. If you know what issues you're going to deal with on the front end, you can fashion your TOS to head off problems at the pass.

▶▶ Test Drive

If you haven't already put together an auction listing, now's the time to do it. Using the information from this chapter, go to eBay's Sell an Item form and put together a dummy auction. There are plenty of fail-safes in place to prevent you from inadvertently launching it, so don't worry about that.

Fill in every field when you're prompted to do so. Be sure to include your TOS information—you can write it out before you start the process or simply enter it in the appropriate fields.

Crafting Clear Descriptions

Pictures do speak a thousand words, and while they're absolutely necessary for selling success, you should still never underestimate the power of good, clear descriptions. Along with great photos and killer titles, descriptions pack the one-two-three punch for success on eBay.

The vast majority of items offered for sale on eBay typically have to compete against numerous others that are similar, if not exactly like them. Even if you're selling something that's somewhat unusual or even unique, chances are very good there is something listed somewhere on eBay that gives buyers the chance to make a choice between items.

For these reasons, descriptions, advertising copy, or sales copy—call it what you will—have to work harder in the online environment than they do in traditional print media like newspapers and magazines. Not only do the words you put together in your listing copy have to do a good job of providing the details on the items being sold, they also have to create desire and convince people who are browsing through listings to take action and bid. Ideally, you want to convince them to choose the things you're selling over what the competition has to offer.

This is an extraordinarily big order to fill, and it takes a lot of skill to do it well and right. If you're not an experienced writer, writing up your listings might seem daunting. At first, it might be. But here's the good news: The more you do it, the easier it gets. What's more, once you figure out what you need to say and how you need to say it, you can save your descriptions and reuse them for the same or similar items. This can not only save you a lot of time, it allows you to build on past successes.

Can They Find You?

There's no denying that eBay gets bigger and more competitive by the day, but there's good news about that, too. It isn't just sellers flocking to the site—tons of new buyers are signing on, too. For this reason alone, it's critical to learn how to put together auctions that not only stand out from the competition but that can also be found via various search techniques. Buyers tend to learn one search approach, and once they do, they stick with it. If your descriptions are too narrow, you run the risk of the site's search engines not grabbing your listings, and this will significantly limit your potential audience.

Elements of a Good Description

Simply put, a good description follows the KISS model—keep it short and simple—while including enough detail so buyers have the information they need to make a purchasing decision. At a minimum, this includes the following information:

➲ Manufacturer and/or brand
➲ Style name (if there is one)
➲ Dimensions or measurements
➲ Technical specifications on things like electronics
➲ Color, texture, and finish
➲ Year manufactured, or a solid estimate of manufacture date
➲ Condition

Descriptions also need to include any other information that buyers need to know about the item, especially if there's something unique or special about it. However, it's important to keep the terms "unique" and "special" in perspective. Most things don't call for using either term, and if you use them too often you'll fall prey to the Chicken Little syndrome—people will get so used to seeing these words in your descriptions that when you list items that really warrant them, buyers will ignore them. Reserve superlatives for items that truly deserve them.

Good, Better, Best, and Overkill

It's one thing to talk about what goes into a good description, but showing is definitely better than telling. So let's take a look at a typical eBay description. The one used for this example was taken directly from an auction. For privacy reasons, some specifics have been changed, but the overall wording is nearly identical to the actual description. It's an okay effort, and definitely not the worst you'll see, especially since the accompanying picture, although somewhat blurry, contained some of the information that the description missed. That said, there's plenty of room for improvement:

WOMEN'S SIZE 8 NICE DRESS SHORTS? GOLF SHORTS? BY LIZS-PORT. THE RED WHITE AND BLUE STRIPES YOU SEE ON THE SIDES

IS ELASTIC WITH BUTTON. HAS 2 FRONT POCKETS AND 2 BACK
POCKETS. INSEAM ON THESE SHORTS ARE 6 INCHES. SHORTS ARE
LIKE NEW!! HAVE NEVER BEEN WORN. I ACCEPT PAYPAL OR POSTLE
MONEY ORDER. THANK YOU FOR LOOKING.

Here's what's wrong with this description:

1. **It's all in capital letters.** Not only are all-cap listings extremely
   hard to read, writing in all caps online connotes shouting. Not
   the greatest way to induce shoppers to buy.
2. **Question marks following "dress shorts" and "golf shorts."**
   Including both terms was a good idea, as the listing would turn
   up for buyers searching for dress shorts and/or golf shorts if
   they did a title and description search (the seller didn't include
   the terms "dress" or "golf" in the title). However, descriptions
   without question marks have far more credibility than ones
   that do. If you're not sure what you have, use a more general
   term in your description, and suggest ways the item could be
   used or worn. In this particular case, simply describing the
   items as "shorts" would have been a lot better. They didn't
   look at all dressy in the picture, and golf shorts typically have
   little loops on a pocket or the waistband for stashing golf tees,
   or a small accessory pocket for the same. These didn't.
3. **It's missing detail.** It's hard to tell, but it looks like only one
   pair is described. Actually, the auction is for two pair of the
   same shorts, in different colors. See how the lack of detail is
   misleading and confusing here? Also, no mention is made of
   the color of each pair, or whether colors are true in the picture
   (they often aren't). Fabric content is also missing.
4. **The details are confusing.** "The red whate and blue stripes you
   see on the sides is elastic with button." White is clearly misspelled as *whate* here, but the overall wording is unclear and
   it's difficult to understand what the seller is getting at.
5. **Measurements are missing.** Stating they're a size 8 and giving
   an inseam length isn't enough.

6. Listing was poorly proofread. As mentioned, white was misspelled as *whate*. Postal was also misspelled as *postle*. Errors like these might seem insignificant, but they aren't. Misspelling keywords in titles can result in items selling for less—sometimes far less—than they should, simply because buyers couldn't find them.

Here's a better description:

TWO PAIR OF BRAND-NEW WOMEN'S SHORTS FROM LIZSPORT. NEVER WORN, IN A MISSES' SIZE 8. BOTH FEATURE ELASTIC SIDE INSERTS FOR EASE OF MOVEMENT, AND POCKETS FRONT AND BACK. MEASUREMENTS ARE AS FOLLOWS: WAIST 29", HIP 37", INSEAM 7", LENGTH FROM WAISTBAND TO HEM OF LEG 19". 100% COTTON, ONE PAIR IS LIGHT CREAM OR BEIGE, THE OTHER IS DARKER CREAM OR A BROWN KHAKI. COLORS ARE TRUE IN THE PICTURE.

What this description has that the other doesn't:

➲ Better description of the side inserts, basically telling you what they're there for.
➲ Measurements. Measuring the rise (the distance from front waistband to back waistband) would also be a nice touch.
➲ Fabric content.
➲ Better detail on the colors.

Now, here's the best description (at least when compared to the others):

JUST IN TIME FOR THE HOTTEST SUMMER DAYS, THESE BREEZY WOMEN'S SHORTS FROM LIZSPORT WILL TAKE YOU FROM GOLF COURSE TO CASUAL DINNER IN STYLE. IN 100%● EASY CARE POLISHED COTTON, THEY FEATURE:

● FRONT PLEATS
● METAL ZIPPER

- SIDE-SEAM AND REAR POCKETS (PERFECT FOR STASHING GOLF GLOVES, TEES, AND MORE!)
- ELASTICIZED WAIST FOR MOVING COMFORT

BRAND NEW, NEVER WORN, LABELED WARM WATER WASH, TUMBLE DRY. MARKED A SIZE 8, BUT PLEASE GO BY THE FOLLOWING MEASUREMENTS FOR THE BEST FIT:

- WAIST 29"
- HIP 37"
- THIGH 24"
- INSEAM 7"
- LENGTH FROM WAISTBAND TO HEM OF LEG 19"

FROM A NO SMOKING, NO PET-HAIR HOME. PLEASE CHECK MY OTHER LISTINGS AND MY STORE FOR MORE HOT-WEATHER BARGAINS!

This description has several features that the others lack:

1. It shows you, rather than tells you, why you'd want these shorts. The writer took the time to think about the benefits of owning these shorts—it's hot, it's summertime, and the shorts are versatile enough to wear just about anywhere. Describing how the buyer can use the pockets is better than simply saying "pockets front and back."
2. It contains essential details, including information on the zipper. The fact that it is metal would be important to anyone wanting to wear them as golf shorts—metal holds up better than plastic does in sports.
3. It presents important details in the form of bulleted lists. Not only does this break up the copy and make it easier on the eye, it also directs buyers to the most important information in the listing.

4. It tells buyers the conditions in which the item was stored.

5. It tells buyers you have other things to look at. Be sure you do, by the way, if you include this line.

And, finally, here's an overkill description.

L@@K! L@@K!! L@@K!! YOU KNOW YOU WANT THEM, YOU KNOW YOU GOTTA HAVE THEM. ABSOLUTELY GREAT FANTASTIC SUMMER SHORTS BY LIZSPORT. SUCH A GREAT DESIGNER, YOU KNOW YOU HAVE TO HAVE THESE IN YOUR CLOSET. AND, WHAT'S MORE, YOU GET TWO PAIRS FOR THE PRICE OF ONE!!!!! CAN YOU BEAT THIS???? I LOVE THE SHORTS, I REALLY DO, BUT I HAVE WAY TOO MUCH STUFF IN MY CLOSET AND MY DH SAYS I HAVE TO SELL SOME OFF LOL!!!!! PLUS, I'VE LOST SOME WEIGHT AND THEY DON'T FIT ANYMORE. SO MY LOSS IS YOUR GAIN . . .LOL!!!!! I'M ONLY OFFERING THESE SHORTS FOR FIVE DAYS; AFTER THAT THEY'LL BE GONE. SO OIL UP THAT BIDDING FINGER AND HIT THE BUY BUTTON NOW!!!!!

Had enough? Before going any further, stop and think about how you felt as you read through this description. Did it tire you out? Make you angry? Did it include anything that made you want to buy?

▶▶**Overkill descriptions are exactly that—they work too hard.** They're typically characterized by lots of exclamation points, all caps, and run-on sentences, all trying to draw the viewer's eye by exchanging the o's in look for the "at" sign, long paragraphs, and more. Plus, they include lots of detail—often at the expense of detail that should be included, but isn't—that simply isn't necessary for buyers to know, such as:

➲ **Wording that tells potential bidders that they have to own the item:** In a nutshell, they don't. No one really *has* to have anything. This description is a classic example of telling instead of showing to try to build desire.

➲ **How the seller feels about the item:** Most buyers couldn't care less.

⮩ **Why the seller is offering the item for sale:** Again, telling the world that your dear husband (that's what DH stands for) said you have to clear out your closet or that the item no longer fits you isn't necessary.

⮩ **Wording that tells buyers they'd better bid now in an effort to spur immediate action:** Again, buyers usually don't care. They can check auction durations for themselves. Telling them they'd better buy now or the item won't be available only works for things that truly are unique or rare, and often not very well even for these items. Buyers typically know if they need to bid right away or not. If you're selling a commodity item, they'll simply find someone else to buy from if their time frame doesn't match yours.

This listing also illustrates improper tone at the end. The writer was trying to strike a conversational tone with "Oil up that bidding finger," but it's trite and corny and a bit condescending. Maybe it wouldn't be in conversation, but transferring the spoken word to the computer screen can be difficult even for seasoned writers. If you're not one, it's best to develop a style that fits you and works well for you, at least for the most part. Every so often, it's not a bad idea to venture out and do something different, but it's best to test-drive your efforts offline before throwing them out there for everyone to see.

Writing to Length

One of the biggest differences between writing ad copy for traditional media—newspapers, magazines, and the like—and writing eBay auction listings is that you really aren't constrained by length. When you place retail ads, you're typically limited by space or word count. Not so on eBay. You can write your heart out if you want to and make your listing copy as long as you want. You can also make it blessedly brief, as long as you include enough details.

It's your choice; however, it's best to avoid extremes on either side. Descriptions that are too short often read like they've been tossed together on the fly and like you don't care enough about appealing to potential buyers to put much effort into them. Copy that's too long is hard to plow through, especially if the details are buried deep within. Buyers will give up long before they reach what they need to know.

Where you are limited to length is on titles. You only get fifty-five characters, which is pretty short, so it's imperative that you make the best use of those characters. This is where keywords—yes, that word again—can make or break you.

Is There an Ideal Length?

The best listings use the appropriate amount of words to tell you what you need to know. They neither ramble nor are so short that they come off as abrupt or curt. When writing your descriptions, read them out loud before you put them up and see how they sound to you. If you have to stop and catch your breath before you finish a sentence, or you lose your place before you finish a paragraph, they're too long.

Titles That Attract Buyers

The titles, or headlines, that you give your auctions are the primary way in which buyers find your items. For this reason, they are the most important part of your listings. Although it's never a good idea, you can get away with so-so descriptions to a certain extent as some items will sell in spite of them. However, if buyers can't find you, you won't sell anything.

Unlike print ads, where you can change typefaces, fonts, the size of the letters, or run them in bold, you can't do much with your titles visually to make them stand out. Nor is it really all that important to do so. In the online world, good keywords—the words that describe the item—are critical to selling success. Working on the wording in your titles to make them the best they can be is a far better approach. It will save you lots of money on the front end and pay off better for you in the long run.

Analyze the following titles. Which do you think will do the best job in attracting "eyes"—that is, potential bidders:

Eames Era Pop Mod Vintage Do It Yourself Décor 60s 70s

Fab Pop Era BHG Decorating Book Lots of Pics No Reserve

The second title might make more sense, but the first one is the winner. Here's why:

⮑ It makes extensive use of highly searched keywords—Eames Era, Pop, Mod, Vintage, Do It Yourself.

⮑ It includes key eras for those who search on them.

⮑ It sacrifices specific item attributes for keywords. If you have to choose between keywords and attributes, keywords are the better choice. This is a title for a book listing, although you wouldn't know it from the title. But the item was listed in the book category, so people searching the category would find it. Using precious space title space for keywords instead of attributes also broadens the market for this listing. Bidders browsing for listings of items other than books that contain similar keywords might also come across this one and be interested in buying it.

The second title, while seemingly more descriptive, is actually light years away from the first in terms of its effectiveness. Fab is a throwaway word as it doesn't describe a thing. It simply wastes space. Other space-wasters are Lots of Pics No Reserve. None of these words come anywhere close to the list of most-searched keywords. BHG, which stands for Better Homes and Gardens, the publisher of the book, is meaningless to most people. So, we're down to Pop, Decorating, and Book. They're okay keywords but not overly effective.

This exercise proves an important point: The best headlines, at least when it comes to keywords, may not read very well, but they are extremely effective. There are certain things that should be included in titles, for instance:

⮕ Words that describe the type of product you're selling. Include combinations to grab the most eyes. As an example, if you're selling a fishing reel, say it. Don't just call it a reel. In the first title above—Eames Era Pop Mod Vintage Do It Yourself Décor 60s 70s—every keyword relates to an element of the book. In the second, only Pop, Decorating, Book, and Pics do.
⮕ Brand name, if there is one.
⮕ Model number, again if there is one.
⮕ Specific attributes, such as size and color, included after the keywords.

Here are a few more tips for creating effective titles:

1. If you're doing multiple listings of similar items, changing the keywords on your titles can draw more viewers to all of your auctions. As an example, if you're selling purses, use "hand-bag" in one title and "bag" in another.

2. If you're selling items that people often misspell, include some of the misspellings in your titles.

3. Use abbreviations or acronyms where they make sense, and if you're not sacrificing meaning when you do. As an example, the acronym DIY, which is fairly common, could have been substituted for "Do It Yourself" in the first title example above.

4. Sacrifice punctuation for letters, if you have to make a choice between the two. Commas and apostrophes are rarely necessary; if there's space left over after you're done composing a title, see if you can squeeze another word in instead of filling it with !!!!!!!s.

It Doesn't Have to Make Sense to Sell

The best titles aren't grammatically correct. Nor should correctness be the goal. This is something that Sylvia Petras, aka swedishdrama, knows well. She's written a good number of exceptionally fine titles in her six years as an eBay seller. They don't always make a lot of sense. But they've made her a PowerSeller.

Here are some of her top tips for writing effective titles and copy and for making your listings stand out from the pack:

"Know your product! I've collected these kinds of books myself for years, so I know them well and I like them. No matter what you're selling, if you know the product and like it yourself, it tends to come across in what you write about it.

"Do your research. When I first got involved in eBay, I was buying as much as I was selling, so I knew what attracted me. Also, I just researched, I looked at what other sellers were doing, who was doing the best and what seemed to work, and I tried to incorporate what seemed to make sense for them.

"Develop your own style. Some sellers in my category have very distinctive styles that work for them. I've tried to imitate them from time to time, but it doesn't work as well for me. Every time I try it, my books just bomb. Find what you're comfortable with; it has to be true for you or it won't come off right."

Auction Descriptions That Sell

Like advertisements in the brick-and-mortar world, descriptions for items listed on eBay not only need to describe what's being sold, they also have to incite people to buy. As one eBay seller put it, "You need to romance things, love them up and tell us why we need to buy them."

Look back at the best description above. As previously discussed, this description includes some wording that gets buyers thinking about the benefits of owning the item—how it will fit into their lives, how they can use it.

When you write a description, take some time to think about why someone would want to buy the product. Will it enhance her life? Solve a problem? Make her feel more secure? Prettier? More satisfied? If so, how?

There's an old saying in the advertising world that goes like this: Sell the sizzle, not the steak. It's easier said than done, but if you can learn how to sell the sizzle—the benefits of the product, what it can do for the buyer—instead of simply presenting the features, your listing copy will be much more effective.

Unsure of the difference between a feature and a benefit? Basically, features are the characteristics of the item; benefits are what the item can do for the owner. Benefits tie features to needs.

The following chart lists the features and benefits of a Nikon Coolpix 770 camera.

Feature	Benefit
3x optical zoom	Brings far-away items close up
Macro mode	Lets you focus on items just inches away.
2.1 megapixels	Good resolution for online pictures
Small size	Easy to hold, easy to stash. You can take it anywhere.
Eight shooting modes	Easy scene modes for better pictures.

See the difference?

When writing a listing, always make sure to include the item's features. They're the nuts and bolts, the things buyers need to know to make a decision. Enhancing the listing by including the benefits of the item can help sell it, but if this type of writing doesn't come naturally to you, don't spend hours trying to do it. Practice it, and try to include more of it over time. Doing so will also add a friendlier tone to your copy.

Using Keywords Effectively

As discussed previously, not only do you have to write descriptions that sell buyers on the benefits of owning the goods, you also have to use the right words so that potential buyers can find you, no matter what method they use for their searches.

The following is an example of a well-written auction listing that fits the bill in both areas. It contains good keywords and sells buyers on the benefits of the item.

Eames Era Pop Mod Vintage Do It Yourself Décor 60s 70s

Weird, Wild, GROOVY, Mod Decor – and You Can Have It!

Description

Better Homes and Gardens Creative Decorating on a Budget, Better Homes and Gardens Books, Don Dooley Editorial Director, New York/Des Moines, 1970, 128 pages of decorating for the fab young modern, with lotsa color photos

Feel the need to jazz up your Thonet chairs? Upholster them in hot pink and lime green. Need an inexpensive "Mediterranean" headboard? Find an old iron fence at the junkyard, paint it, and bolt *that* to your bed. Or cover your old scarred wall with oak parquet flooring tiles for a "kicky" look. Lots of weird and/or interesting ideas for a true vintage look, plus photos of Lucite furniture, Snoopy pillows (nestled on a bed covered in faux leopard), Parsons tables, wall systems, Knoll furniture, unfinished furniture covered with adhesive-backed plastic (in a yellow/orange/pink flower design!), weird lamps, fake Rya rugs, and outrageous color combos. Too much fun!

Condition of this 9x11 hardback book is good. Corners of the pictorial hard boards are a bit bumped/rubbed, a small scar on fc near spine, top of spine has a small piece missing, first fly has a name and address inked out, otherwise interior is clean and nice—and ready to help you redecorate your groovy pad!

Shipping & Payment Terms

We accept PayPal, cashier's checks, money orders or personal checks (we wait 7 days to clear), US dollars only. Payment must be in our hands by noon EDT on Friday, August 5, or items will not ship until after August 18. Please factor in time for money orders and checks to reach us in the mail and clear. If payment is not received within 2 weeks of end of auction, the item will be relisted. Optional insurance is $1.30 for the first $49.99—however, if you elect not to take insurance we will not be responsible for any item damaged in shipping or shipped and not received. New Jersey residents please add 6% sales tax to winning bid. Please e-mail us with any questions. We welcome international bidders, but please e-mail for rates and shipping times if you're not an experienced overseas buyer!

Thanks for bidding and thanks for being a fellow book lover. See our other auctions for more great books.

Let's go through the details on it. First, the headline makes effective use of keywords, so much so that the title doesn't actually state what's being sold—it's a book, but you don't find that out until you read on.

The seller then includes a keyword-heavy subtitle—"Weird, Wild, Groovy, Mod"—that again will pull prospective buyers to the listing. On the actual listing page, this is followed with some scans of images from the book. Then comes a strong description, which both gives detail and includes action copy. She gives bidders reasons to want the book—"Feel the need to jazz up your Thonet chairs? Upholster them in hot pink and lime green. Need an inexpensive 'Mediterranean' headboard? Find an old iron fence at the junkyard, paint it, and bolt *that* to your bed. Or cover your old scarred wall with oak parquet flooring tiles for a 'kicky' look."

What Not to Say

With all the emphasis on what you should include in your listings, you also need to know what you can't do. ▶▶**The biggest no-no is keyword spamming, or KWS, which is including words in titles and/or descriptions that don't relate to the item being offered.** If you've ever done a search and come up with listings that don't match what you're looking for, you've seen the work of keyword spammers. eBay frowns heavily on the practice and will shut down auctions that contain it. Continuing the practice can lead to more severe sanctions, including account suspension.

It can be fairly easy to keyword spam when you're a new seller and you're still learning how to write title and listing copy, so it's a good idea to get to know eBay's policies on this thoroughly to avoid problems. The last thing you want to do is have your auctions shut down for this practice. That said, you'll see many other sellers, including PowerSellers, who get away with it. This doesn't mean you should follow suit.

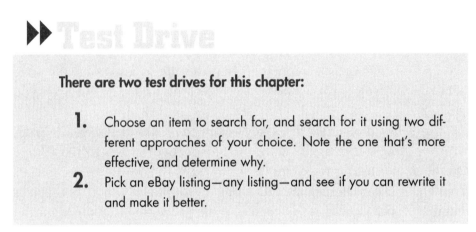

There are two test drives for this chapter:

1. Choose an item to search for, and search for it using two different approaches of your choice. Note the one that's more effective, and determine why.

2. Pick an eBay listing—any listing—and see if you can rewrite it and make it better.

Taking Photos That Sell

In eBay's early days, it was possible to list and sell items without pictures. Many sellers did, and with great success. But those days are long gone. Today's online buyers want to know as much as possible about the items they're interested in, just as they would if they were shopping in brick-and-mortar stores.

Since it's impossible to "reach out and touch someone" in cyberspace, the best auctions contain descriptions and pictures that give potential buyers the information they need to make their buying decisions. Both factors can significantly affect how much your items will sell for and how many of them you'll sell. But the old saying about images still rings true—a picture is worth a thousand words.

Characteristics of Good Pictures

Good auction shots share some basic elements. They're well focused and well lit. They're put together right, meaning that they're composed to put the emphasis on the item, not on what's around it. They're clean, not cluttered. They show detail, such as color, texture, construction methods, and so on.

Image size is also important. If your images are too large, they'll take too long to download, which can irritate people with slow connections. And for selling on eBay, detail shots can be critical.

Focusing In

As mentioned, crisp, clear photos are a necessity. Getting clear photos involves two things: focusing correctly and holding your camera still when you snap the shutter. Most digital cameras have auto-focus features, so the first factor shouldn't be an issue unless your camera isn't working properly.

Camera movement is more often the culprit behind fuzzy shots, especially if you're shooting in low light. The less light that's available, the longer the camera's shutter has to stay open. The longer it stays open, the greater the chances of the camera's sensors recording even the slightest movement.

Even if you think you have the steadiest hands on Earth, your camera will catch some movement as your finger snaps the shutter if you're taking hand-held shots. This doesn't matter that much when you're shooting with a lot of light, as the shutter doesn't have to stay open as long, but it does matter when you're shooting in low light, and it's especially problematic with digital cameras, which often require more light than film cameras do. You have several options for eliminating camera movement: adding light, putting your shutter on time-release (if your camera has this option), or using a tripod or another object to steady your camera.

Images can also get blurry if you're taking close-up shots and you're inside or outside of your camera's macro range. If you're selling things that require lots of detail shots, like jewelry, coins, gemstones, and so on, you'll need a camera that will let you get within a couple of inches or so of the objects. Good lighting and keeping the camera steady are essential for these shots. Even if you're shooting other images of the object in available light, you'll want to increase the lighting for these images to avoid blurring.

Household Help for Making Shots Better

Getting good pictures doesn't necessarily require investing in a bunch of accessory items. If you don't have a tripod, there are lots of other things you can use to keep your camera steady, and there's a good chance that you already have them in your house. One of them might even be in your pantry. Bags of beans can work just fine in a pinch. Just nuzzle the camera into the beans and snap away. If your camera's macro function doesn't let you get as close as you'd like, try shooting through a magnifying glass. You'll have to play with this a little bit to eliminate reflections, and using a flash is out of the question, but even a 10x magnifier can bring images into better focus when you're shooting up close.

Staging Your Shots

Images should be well composed and clutter-free. When people look at them, there should be no question about what you're selling.

There are two basic ways to get these shots: filling the lens with the object, and eliminating clutter. The first couldn't be easier: Simply crop your images through the lens by getting close to what you're shooting.

Don't stand any farther away than you have to. If necessary, use your camera's zoom feature. Make sure your camera is focused on the item you're selling, not in front of or behind it. Again, filling your lens with the image will help ensure this.

The best way to unclutter your shots is to shoot objects against a plain background. Lots of sellers use walls for this, but unless your walls are white or awfully close to it and there are no other colors in the room, you run the risk of the other colors throwing off the hues in the objects you're shooting. Wood trim and floors are other big culprits when it comes to altering colors—the warmth of the wood tends to turn everything a little yellow.

A better approach is to invest in some backdrops. You don't have to spend a lot of money on them. Some people use plain old sheets; others invest in muslin drops like professional photographers use. If you're shooting small objects, a piece of poster board is a great option. If you can set up your shooting area so you can curve the poster board under the object, you'll have a perfectly smooth, flawless background that will make the object look like it is floating in front of it.

Most people think that shooting everything against a light backdrop is the way to go, but it really isn't. In fact, light backdrops can wreak havoc with the tones of what you're shooting. A better option is a medium blue backdrop for high-contrast objects—black, white, or black and white. A darker blue or black background typically works well for lower-contrast items. You'll also have to rig up something to hang your backdrops from. This can range from cup holders screwed into a wall to a freestanding frame made from PVC pipe. Another option is to drape the drop over an adjustable shower curtain rod positioned in a door frame. When you're done with the shoot, simply take down the rod and roll the backdrop around it for storage. The neat thing about backdrops is that they don't have to be perfect—they can have some wrinkles in them or not hang perfectly flat and they'll still look okay.

Here's one last tip on staging. Most items look better if they're not shot head-on—that is, squarely facing the camera lens. This is especially true if you're displaying clothing on forms or mannequins. Position whatever you're shooting at a slight angle to the camera lens—about a quarter turn should do it.

Ditching the Background?

Many sellers eliminate clutter by dropping out backgrounds with their image editing software. Not only can this take a lot of time, it might not show your images to their best advantage. Viewing objects in context helps the eye determine true colors. If you don't color-correct your images, this determination can be lost when backgrounds are chopped out. Also, dropping out backgrounds tends to make images lose depth and look flat due to the lack of background shadows. You can correct this by adding some shadows back in when you edit your images, but that also takes time. The better option is to shoot your images against a simple backdrop that you don't have to edit out when you're preparing your images.

All about Lighting

Digital cameras, especially older ones, tend to be less forgiving in low light, which means your automatic flash will come on more often than you might like. This is one camera feature that you want to avoid using if at all possible—in fact, you should turn it off completely if you can—as the built-in flash is almost always positioned too close to the lens. When it goes off, the intensity of the light washes out details and colors, and it can throw a harsh shadow behind what you're shooting.

One of the best ways of telling if you have enough light is to watch your camera's flash indicator or exposure meter when you're setting up your shots. If it goes on when you press the shutter down partway, you'll know you need to either change your auto-exposure setting or add more light.

Working with Natural Light

Just about everything looks best in natural light, but it can be difficult to control indoors and out. However, if you have some flexibility over where you can shoot, try going natural first. Indoors, the directional light that comes in through windows can really pop details, but it can also throw some harsh shadows. You might have to add some additional light, maybe in the form of a clamp light or a simple reflector (a piece of poster board can work well for this) on the other side of the item, to diminish the shadows. Another approach to try is placing a sheer white drape over the window. This will filter the light and make it softer.

If you're shooting outdoors, and it's a sunny day, keep your back to the sun if at all possible. Even better is shooting in the shade. You'll want to avoid times and days when the sun is so bright and direct that it casts hard shadows. When the light is this strong, it will also wash out the colors and details of what you're shooting. If you have to shoot in these conditions, and your camera has a fill-flash setting, try using it. This setting adds flash to harsh light situations, thus balancing things out and softening sharp shadows. Again, positioning a reflector to one side of the item you're shooting can also help balance harsh, unforgiving directional light.

Lightly overcast days can be your best friend. On these days, the sun can turn the sky into one huge reflector. This results in soft, nondirectional light, which is just about the best kind of light you can ask for. However, overall light levels might be low on days like these, so have a tripod or some other means of steadying your camera at hand as your shutter speeds will be slower.

Working with Artificial Light

Professional photographers like to work with artificial light for one big reason: They can control it. Your camera's flash is the easiest source of artificial light, but, as previously mentioned, it's also the worst. A better approach is setting up a lighting rig. This sounds expensive, but it doesn't have to be.

Many eBay sellers use clamp or work lights. These are reflector lamps equipped with a clamp on the end. They're inexpensive (typically less than $10), widely available (you can pick them up at just about any hardware or home improvement store), and practical. If one breaks, it's a simple matter to buy another one. You can also clamp them on to just about anything.

You can use clamp lights that just take incandescent bulbs—the light bulbs most commonly in use in most households. Just be sure the clamp light is rated for the bulbs you use. Or you can buy halogen clamp lights. They throw substantially more light, which can be good if you're shooting large items from a distance, but they're overkill for almost anything else. They also get very hot, so be careful if you go this route.

Dealing with Haunted Cameras

If you've ever come up with pictures that show spots where there aren't any, and the spots won't go away no matter how hard you try, you might think your camera is haunted.

Apparently, many eBay sellers own these critters, as you'll see lots of item descriptions with statements like "Any spots are from the camera, not on the item." Sometimes they'll refer to these spots as camera ghosts.

Are their cameras really haunted? Is yours? Probably not. But it can definitely seem like it, especially if it only happens on some shots and not others, and it keeps happening after you've cleaned and dusted your lens.

What they—and you—are dealing with is a problem that seems to be endemic with digital cameras, and especially today's popular mini and micro-mini cameras. Positioning an ultra-strong light, which a flash definitely is, near a camera lens can cause a whole slew of problems. On tiny digital cameras, the flash is almost right on top of the lens. When it goes off, the light bounces off any dust particles that are floating in front of the lens. The result is out-of-focus spots. Ghosts, if you will.

You'll typically see camera spots on long shots, not closeups, which has to do with technical things that you don't need to know about to fix the problem. The best way to avoid them is to quit using on-camera flash. If you have to use it, don't move around a lot before you take your pictures. That will give the dust a chance to settle down as much as possible before shooting.

Understanding Image Formats

Lots of sellers take great pictures. Or at least they look great on the camera screen and on the computer screen at home. Then they get uploaded to a server, and wham! Something happens. They look funny, like they've been all chopped up. The technical term for this is "pixilated." The reason this happens has a lot to do with image formats. If you can get the basics behind them down, it will go a long way toward making your images really great online.

There are two basic approaches to saving images: lossy and lossless. The technology behind them gets pretty complicated, but it boils down to this:

➲ Lossy image formats results in smaller image files, as they eliminate some digital information when you save images.

➲ Lossless image formats result in larger files as they retain all image information.

JPEG, which is one of the most common photograph image formats, is a lossy format. One of JPEG's biggest advantages is that it lets you adjust compression levels when you save images, which gives you some control over final image quality. With JPEG, you can compress images into very small file sizes and still have great-looking shots. But, they won't be the same as the original, as some of the information has been deleted. This results in pixilation, which can make images look fuzzy and ragged. Most people won't notice it, but it definitely gets more noticeable as compression levels go up.

For this reason, you'll want to save JPEG images at medium to high settings. The file sizes will be larger, but you'll lose less information and the images will look better.

For saving raw images—that is, ones you haven't edited—TIFF is a better format to use. This is a lossless format, but you can compress these images to about half their size. Doing so won't result in files as small as JPEGs, but you will retain all image quality, which means you can go back and edit them whenever you want.

Although it's not typically used for photos, GIF is another lossless format that you'll probably get to know. It's used for static and animated graphics.

Choosing an Image Host

To get your pictures to appear in your auctions, you have to make them available to eBay's servers. To do this, they must be "hosted," and for this, you need something called an image host.

An image host uses special software to move, or upload, digital images from computers to a remote Web server. Here, images are stored—"hosted"—which makes them available for anyone who wants to see them. There are a number of options when it comes to image hosting, ranging from free to moderately expensive.

eBay

eBay's basic auction format lets you display one image per auction free. After this, you'll be charged extra for multiple images. For this reason alone, it's a good idea to find another service. However, it's a good idea anyway. eBay's photo hosting service has never been anything to write home about, although it has improved some over time. Still, even the sharpest and best-exposed images can turn somewhat fuzzy and muddy when eBay hosts them.

If you're a rookie seller and you're also just getting your feet wet when it comes to the digital environment in general, using eBay's photo hosting service is better than having no images at all. But it's not much better. You'll be better off, and you'll realize better sales more quickly, if you take the time to learn more about photo hosting and find another service.

Your Own ISP

If your ISP offers storage space, this is going to be the cheapest way to go. Most offer at least 5 MB of storage; 10MB is also fairly common. This isn't enough for storing thousands of images, but you'll probably be able to squeeze a couple hundred reasonably sized ones in.

If you use your own ISP, you'll need a file transfer program to get the images to the server. Most ISPs require file transfer protocol (FTP) software, and many of them make it available free for their customers. If yours doesn't, there are freeware and shareware FTP programs available online.

Online Image Hosts

These range from free services like Photobucket to pay sites like Ink-frog and Spare Dollar that also offer various levels of auction management features. eBay also recently launched its own hosting service. Called Picture Manager, it's priced competitively and allows users to add as many images to auctions as they want for no extra fee. Many people use free hosting sites, but you tend to get what you pay for with these. Many limit the size and number of images they'll host for you. They seem to go down more often, and they sometimes just go away without notice. If you're running a lot of auctions, why take the chance of having your images disappear?

Editing Your Images

Professional photographers believe in making their images as good as they possibly can be "through the lens," which means while they're shooting. This is the best approach for you, too. However, if you're not a skilled photographer, or you're just starting out in the digital world, there will be some room for improvement in your images.

Image-editing software programs can do wonders with bad pictures and can make good pictures even better. However, a large portion of that success will depend on the software you choose and how well you learn to use it. You still want to make your images look as good as you can when you take them. If you're starting out with good pictures to begin with, all you'll have to do is tweak things a little. If you're not, making them better can take a lot of time.

Many digital cameras—computers, too—come with editing programs bundled as part of their software. Most of these programs are pretty good. They're usually easy to use and they deliver good results. Others might be good, but they may not have the functions and features you'll need.

▶▶**Before you invest money in a digital-image editing program, check to see what you might already have on hand.** If you already have one, take some time to run it through some basic tests. If it has the majority of the features you want and it's not impossible to use, you should be set. If it's lacking important features or you feel like you're spending way too much time for the results you're getting, it's probably a good idea to buy something else.

Look for software with the following features:

- ⮑ **Crop:** Used to cut out anything you don't want to show up in your pictures and to remove extraneous background.
- ⮑ **Resize image:** This is different from cropping, though newcomers to the digital world often confuse the two. Resizing lets you change the size of the entire image. You do it before you crop, unless you're cropping so much out of the image that you don't need it.
- ⮑ **Rotate image:** If you're shooting vertically, you'll need this feature to turn images so they're not lying on their side.
- ⮑ **Brightness and contrast adjustment:** Used to lighten or darken images and to decrease or increase contrast.

- ➲ **Color adjustment:** This feature can help balance the three colors—yellow, blue, and magenta—that all images are composed of.
- ➲ **Sharpness adjustment:** If your picture wasn't exactly in focus when you took it, this will make things look sharper. Use it judiciously; over-sharpening can distort images.
- ➲ **Insert text in image:** This feature lets you add text to your images. You can use it to add a digital watermark to protect images from being stolen by other sellers.
- ➲ **Lasso or magic wand:** This feature lets you drop out backgrounds by outlining what you want to keep and deleting the rest.

The gold standard when it comes to editing software is Adobe Photoshop. This is professional-grade software designed for use by graphic artists and professional photographers, and it has more features than you'll ever need. Because it's so feature-laden, it's expensive—more than $650 retail—and the learning curve is steep, but the results can be superlative. If you already have Photoshop, there's no need to buy another program. If you don't know how to use it, take some time and learn how. This might mean taking a class or two.

Other popular and less-expensive editing programs include the following:

- ➲ **Adobe Photoshop Elements:** This powerful program has many of Photoshop's best features but isn't as overwhelming to learn and use. Available for both PCs and Macs.
- ➲ **Jasc Paint Shop Photo:** It's packed with features found in some of the most expensive editing software but costs hundreds less. Users rave about its functionality and customizable editing features. Only available for PCs.
- ➲ **Corel Paint Shop Pro:** Corel has been around for a long time, and the company has built its reputation on making easy-to-use software at good prices.
- ➲ **Ulead PhotoImpact:** Another affordable, easy-to-use program, and you can try it before you buy it by downloading a free thirty-day trial version.

⮑ **ArcSoft PhotoImpression:** A basic photo-editing package that's pretty easy to learn and use. Available for both PCs and Macs.

If you're a beginner, you'll want software that will walk you through the most common editing functions and that doesn't sacrifice more advanced tools for ease of use. You'll have to go through a learning curve, but software that's too simplistic will frustrate you when you're ready to use higher-level tools and you don't have them at hand.

Storing Your Images

There are various opinions on image storage, but it's usually a good idea to keep your images until you know the transaction is complete. If for any reason a buyer isn't happy about the condition of an item or feels it's been misrepresented, having images on hand to check against can save you lots of grief and aggravation. Aside from this, it might not be necessary to store your images at all. If you're selling unique, individual pieces, it's really up to you. If you're selling multiples of the same items, then you'll want to store your images somewhere.

You have lots of options to choose from here. Copying images to CD-ROM or putting them on a thumb drive is cheap, easy, and convenient. What you probably won't want to do is store them online, especially if you're hosting your own images, as they'll clog up space that you'll want to keep open.

Using Stock Photos

If you're buying inventory from drop shippers, they might have images of the items you're selling already available so you don't have to take them yourself. All you'll have to do is pop the images into your listings, and you'll be set.

You can also create your own stock images. This might even be a better approach, especially if there are other people selling the same products. Setting up your own product shots can distinguish your items from the rest. Plus, buyers like seeing exactly what you're selling.

Some eBay sellers download thumbnail images of widely available consumer commodities—perfume, cameras, MP3 players, you name it—from manufacturer Web sites when they're selling these items. This is a no-no unless you have permission to do it. The images a manufacturer places on its Web site are its property. Yes, you'll see other sellers using them. They may or may not have received permission to do so. This might seem like it gives you license to do the same, but it doesn't. Maybe you won't run into problems, but you're better off not taking the risk to begin with. If you're ever wondering if it's okay to use an image, resist the temptation and take your own shots. You might end up being very glad that you did.

▶▶ Test Drive

Like most electronic equipment, digital cameras come loaded with features that go unused in normal day-to-day activity. However, these features could make your images substantially better, and some of them can help you override your camera's quirks. All cameras have a personality of their own. Some digital cameras are better than others at close-ups, some are better at registering classically nasty colors to shoot—black, red, and purple.

Get out your operating manual (if you don't have it, see if there's one available at the manufacturer's Web site). Pick one or two features you haven't used yet, set up an item to photograph—you can kill two birds with one stone if it's something you're going to sell—and take some test shots using these features.

PayPal and Other Online Payment Systems

If you're serious about doing business on eBay, and you want your business (and you) to be taken seriously, you have to offer your buyers the convenience of paying for their purchases online. Yes, there are sellers who don't. There are even PowerSellers who don't, or who do but restrict the types of online payments they'll take. They probably have justifiable reasons—to themselves, anyway—for what they're doing. Regardless, the arguments for offering online payment to your customers vastly outweigh the arguments against.

▶▶**The bottom line is this: If you're going to do business online, do it 100 percent.** This includes making it easy for your customers to pay you through the same technology they used to buy from you.

Of the various electronic payment options, PayPal is the leader for doing business on eBay, and for good reason—eBay owns PayPal and promotes the heck out of it. Plus, the service is fully integrated into the site—you can hardly go anywhere on eBay without seeing a PayPal logo—which makes it very easy for buyers and sellers to use.

Beyond this, PayPal is simply an exceptional electronic payment service. Among its leading assets are speed and convenience. But there are many more, including these:

1. Cheap to use: You'll see eBay sellers bellyache about their PayPal fees on discussion boards, but they really don't have much of a leg to stand on here. It's more expensive to set up merchant accounts for accepting credit cards; and other payment forms, like checks and money orders, are riskier.

2. Financial information stays secure and private: All PayPal transactions take place between e-mail addresses—yours and your buyers. Only PayPal sees the details.

3. Traceable payments: There's no "The check's in the mail" with PayPal. You see exactly when payments hit your account. Buyers know exactly when their payments get to you.

4. Higher buyer confidence levels: PayPal's Buyer Complaint program protects each purchase for up to $200 after a $25 deductible. Qualifying sellers can also choose to offer PayPal

Buyer Protection. This gives buyers up to $500 of free coverage should something go seriously wrong with a transaction, such as not receiving items or getting items that are clearly not what they were represented to be.

5. Flexibility: Buyers don't have to have PayPal accounts to make payments. All they need is a credit card or checking account and your e-mail address.

6. Fraud protection for sellers: Meet PayPal's requirements, such as shipping to confirmed addresses within seven days and using shipping methods that are trackable online, and PayPal will protect you from fraudulent charge backs and payment reversals by absorbing the charge back at no cost to you. Coverage is up to $5,000 on any fraudulent transaction involving tangible goods.

7. Buyer financing: You get your money right away on higher-ticket items; buyers make monthly payments to a finance company, not you. This program is only available on certain items.

8. Post-sale management: Both the U.S. Postal Service and UPS have teamed with PayPal. You can generate packing slips right from eBay or at the PayPal site, factor and pay for postage or shipping, track packages—you name it.

Another benefit to using PayPal? The PayPal debit card. It lets you access funds in your PayPal account for shopping, ATM withdrawals—basically anything you can do with any debit card. Even better, you earn 1.5 percent cash back on your purchases when you use the card as a credit card. Now those PayPal fees really don't seem that bad, do they?

You can apply for the card after you've been registered with PayPal for sixty days or after you've been an eBay seller for six months. You'll have to agree to run a blurb in your listings that says you prefer PayPal payments, and you have to agree not to promote any other online payment services, although you can continue to offer these services.

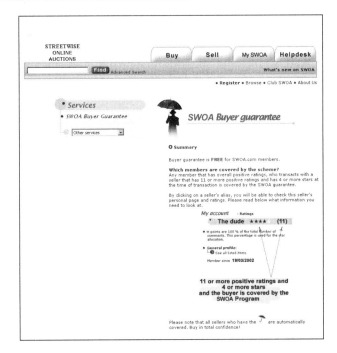

▲ This sample page describes a buyer guarantee program; on eBay, which doesn't use the word "guarantee," transactions are generally covered under the eBay Purchase Protection Program and under PayPal's Buyer Protection policy.

PayPal Service Levels

There are three different types of PayPal accounts:

- ⮕ **Personal:** This is the basic PayPal account. It's best for buyers and occasional sellers. Sending and receiving money is free, but you can't accept credit or debit card payments.
- ⮕ **Premier:** You can send payments for free, and you'll pay a small fee for each one you accept.
- ⮕ **Business or Merchant:** Like the other accounts, you can send money for free. Like the Premier account, you'll pay fees when you accept payments, but the fees are lower. You can also accept money in your business's name. If buyers use a credit or debit card, your business name will show up on their statements.

Premier accounts are for sellers with monthly sales volume under $3,000. You'll pay 2.9 percent and 30 cents per transaction. If your monthly sales volume is over $3,000, you can apply for a Business account. With this account, you'll always pay 30 cents per transaction, just like you do with a Premier account. You'll also pay 2.5 percent per transaction on sales volume of $3,000 to $20,000 per month and 1.9 percent on any amounts over this. There's an additional 1-percent charge for accepting payments from international buyers.

Some new sellers start with a Personal account and wait until their sales volume forces an upgrade. Or they keep their Personal account for their own purchases, and they open a business-level account for their business. The better approach is to upgrade or establish the second account before you start selling. Doing so will let you accept credit and debit cards right away in addition to bank account and PayPal account transfers.

Why Some Sellers Don't Offer PayPal

You will come across sellers who don't offer PayPal or who only offer the basic level. The most obvious reason behind this approach is that they don't want to pay the fees. Some sellers simply don't trust the service or have had problems with it. But here's another, less obvious reason: Sellers in the mature audiences category can't offer PayPal as an option on those auctions. If they're also selling in categories other than mature audiences, it's probably easier for them to just skip this payment option on all of their auctions.

Covering Your PayPal Fees

Are you simply out of luck when it comes to covering this cost of doing business? Not necessarily. Here's what eBay has to say about it:

❝ Sellers may not charge eBay buyers an additional fee for their use of ordinary forms of payment, including acceptance of checks, money orders, electronic transfers or credit cards. Such costs should be built into the price of the item. ❞

The operative words here are "costs should be built into the price of the item." There are two ways that you can do this. On the front end, you can set your starting price high enough to cover them. On the back end, you can charge a flat fee for shipping and handling. If you're going to take the latter approach, make sure you charge a reasonable fee. A dollar or two to cover your costs is reasonable, but $25 is not. What you also can't do is charge your buyers an additional fee for service as a percentage of the final price. It's against eBay's rules and regulations and against many state regulations as well. Try it, and you run the risk of incurring the standard triumvirate of eBay wrath: listing cancellation, limits on account privileges, or account suspension.

There are two exceptions to the no-additional-fees rule. If you accept payment in currencies other than those listed on eBay, you can pass along costs associated with currency exchange. Just be sure to disclose the costs in your auction or in your TOS. Your buyers also have to agree to the charges prior to finalizing the transaction.

Also, if you're an international seller and you trade on a site other than eBay U.S., the site on which you do business might permit certain types of payment surcharges.

Another way to keep PayPal costs down is to encourage buyers who win multiple auctions, or buy multiple items, to make one payment for everything. You'll only have to pay one 30-cent transaction fee on one consolidated purchase instead of the same fee for each item.

Other Online Payment Services

PayPal's dominance in the electronic payment marketplace makes it the top choice as a payment service.

At this writing, eBay does allow sellers to accept online payments through two other services. Certapay *(www.certapay.com)* facilitates e-mail money transfers from bank accounts. Propay *(www.propay.com)* lets small businesses accept credit card payments.

eBay has said that it will evaluate other payment services as they become available. For more information on eBay's current policies on approved services, go on its site to Home>Help>Rules and Policies>Rules for Sellers>Safe Payments Policy.

How PayPal Protects Buyers and Sellers

Imagine this scenario. You're getting ready to go to work, which now means going into your eBay room and powering up your computer (yay!). You go through your morning ritual, which includes checking your auctions and your e-mails. All's looking well, but wait . . . what's this? An e-mail from PayPal, and it doesn't look like spam. So you open it, and, horror of horrors, it says that one of your buyers has filed a complaint against you—a guy who bought something from you months ago—and has asked his credit card company to remove the charge for what he bought from you. PayPal is investigating, but for now these funds are frozen in your account.

Welcome to your first credit card charge back. Yes, they happen, and yes, they can happen to you. And you might not win the dispute.

While PayPal is far and away the most popular payment option on eBay, the service can seem more buyer than seller friendly, especially when buyers use credit cards to pay for auction wins. Stories abound about sellers who incur charge backs on their accounts without warning, and sometimes months after they thought transactions were complete. PayPal does offer protection against charge backs, but if sellers don't follow the rules—they don't ship to confirmed addresses or they can't provide tracking information on their shipments—buyers typically win these disputes.

There's one sure way to avoid charge backs: Don't offer PayPal. However, if you're serious about doing business on eBay, you'll want to think twice before taking this approach. Remember, it's difficult to do business without accepting electronic payments, which means you'd have to provide another service—and, most likely, a more costly one. And, making it convenient for buyers to pay you is one of the basics of good customer service.

The better approach? Do everything you can to follow PayPal's seller requirements to the letter. Doing so won't guarantee that you won't get any charge backs, but it will give you better standing in any disputes that do arise.

Taking Money Orders and Checks

Money orders are a fairly low-risk payment form. They're certified funds, and if lost, they can be traced and replaced. However, money orders can also be counterfeited, forged, or stolen. Incidences of all three problems are on the rise.

Personal and cashier's checks are equally problematic. Both can be counterfeited; personal checks can bounce. They're also inconvenient as heck. You have to wait for payment, and you can't send items out until after payments clear (well, you can but you shouldn't). Waiting for payment to arrive and clear can add as much as two weeks to the length of your transactions.

Many sellers take money orders and checks, and for the most part, they don't have problems with them. Whether you decide to or not, include wording that clearly states your policies on them in your TOS and your auction listings.

Electronic Checks Via PayPal

Instead of playing the waiting game on paper checks, you can tell your buyers that you'll take electronic checks though PayPal. This ensures that you'll get your money in a more timely fashion, and it protects against bounced checks. All the buyer has to do is give PayPal the necessary information for cutting an electronic check from her account. There's still a time lag involved—typically about three to four days—but it's faster than sending a check by mail, it eliminates the possibility of the check getting lost, and it guarantees that the check will be good.

Other Payment Options

Merchant credit card accounts, escrow services, and good old cash are other options for receiving payment from your buyers.

Merchant accounts are how brick-and-mortar businesses handle credit card payments. The fees for these accounts are less than what they used to be, but they're still typically higher than what PayPal charges. Also, depending on the service provider and the type of account, there might be a limit on the number of transactions they'll let you do each month. Escrow services protect both parties in a transaction by acting as an intermediary between the buyer and the seller. The buyer places funds in the escrow service's account, where they'll remain until he receives the item he's purchased. If he's satisfied with it, the escrow company releases the funds to the seller.

Escrow companies are typically used if there are large sums of money changing hands. If you're selling high-priced antiques or cars, for example, you'll want to look into them. eBay and eBay Motors have a standing relationship with Escrow.com *(www.escrow.com)*.

With so many different ways to pay, cash ranks at the bottom of the list. Many sellers have received cash payments without any problems. But this doesn't mean you should allow this option. Not only does cash have a way of "getting lost" in the mail, it's also very easy for buyers to short sellers—send less money than what's owed—and then try to pin the blame on the post office or even sellers themselves when the amount owed and the amount paid aren't the same. The bottom line is that you shouldn't accept cash payments unless there's no other way. Never encourage buyers to send large amounts of money through the mail, and never accept anything larger than a $10 bill. Counterfeiting typically begins with twenties. If you decide you won't accept cash under any circumstances, make sure your TOS clearly states this. While it's never a good idea to make your buyers angry, seriously consider canceling sales to anyone who doesn't follow your TOS.

eBay established new policies regarding payments in October 2005. Beginning in 2006, sellers may offer the following payment forms:

- PayPal
- Credit cards such as MasterCard, Visa, American Express, and Discover
- Debit cards and bank electronic payments
- Bank-to-bank transfers (also known as wire or cash transfers)
- Personal checks, money orders, cashier's checks, and certified checks

Also allowed are cash and cash on delivery (COD) payments for in-person transactions. However, sellers can't ask buyers to send cash through the mail, nor can they accept instant cash transfers through services like Western Union or Moneygram. Also not accepted are payments through any other online services.

eBay's payment forms policy is available at *http://pages.ebay.com/ help/policies/safe-payments-policy.html*.

Dealing with Overseas Buyers

As previously mentioned, most overseas buyers use PayPal, and there are rarely problems on either side of the equation. Cashier's checks and money orders are other options. But here's a little scam to keep an eye out for, and it seems to happen more often with international buyers. They'll send you a cashier's check or a money order for more than the amount of the purchase, and ask you to refund the difference. This is a sure sign of a fake or counterfeited financial instrument, and you simply don't want to go there.

Make the forms of payment that you'll accept from international buyers—for that matter, all buyers—very clear in your terms of service. Then stick to your guns. The one time you don't might be the time you get taken. If you don't bend your rules in the first place, the chances of getting gypped are greatly diminished.

▶▶ Test Drive

Sellers tend to get a little heavy-handed in their TOS when it comes to when and how they want to get paid. The better approach is a TOS that is firm, yet friendly. Review yours now to make sure it includes the following:

1. Payment forms that are clearly spelled out
2. Payment terms (when you expect to receive payment) that are clear and reasonable
3. Actions you'll take if buyers don't follow your TOS that are clearly stated but not threatening. Remember, you don't want to lecture buyers on their responsibilities to you. It's better to tell them what you'll do and when.

Make any necessary changes in your TOS. Be sure the information in your auction listings and your TOS match.

Using the Post Office

Many eBay sellers use the U.S. Postal Service (USPS) for shipping. Unless you're shipping certain types of items that you'll learn more about later in this chapter, you probably will too. For most sellers, and for the majority of items that are sold, USPS is a good choice. Here's why:

- ⮕ **Convenience:** Try to find a place where there isn't a post office or a USPS contract service station, typically within a few miles or so.
- ⮕ **Hours of operation:** Most USPS offices are open six days a week. Hours of operation vary, but you can almost always count on offices being open during normal business hours during the week and until around noon or 1 P.M. on Saturdays. Many locations now offer twenty-four-hour self-services, which you can use if you're shipping small parcels weighing less than a pound.
- ⮕ **Global delivery:** While there are certain restrictions on what you can ship to various countries, USPS delivers to virtually every possible place on the planet.
- ⮕ **Savings:** USPS rates are not only competitive with other services, they're often cheaper. Plus, USPS makes an amazing amount of packaging material available for free, including nine different sizes of boxes and several different sizes of Priority Mail envelopes. If your items can fit into them, you can save a lot of money on packaging supplies, and USPS will even deliver them to you.

Until fairly recently, you had to access USPS through the service's site, or through other online postage services. But no longer. USPS is one of two shipping services—UPS is the other—that eBay has partnered with and integrated at its own site.

This means you can do all of the following:

- ⮕ Print shipping labels directly from your My eBay or the Item page. If you're using PayPal to pay for postage, you can also print your shipping labels from there.

➲ Track delivery status on priority mail, first class, parcel post, and media mail shipments through eBay or PayPal (your buyers can, too).

➲ Get free delivery confirmation (DC) for priority mail packages instead of paying 45 cents for it at the post office.

➲ Purchase up to $200 in insurance. If you need more than this, you'll have to buy it at the post office.

You don't have to offer PayPal in your listings to use USPS through eBay, and there are no charges for the service.

USPS at Your Door

If there isn't a post office or contract service station near you, or if you just want to eliminate the hassles and inconvenience of hauling your packages to the post office and standing in line for service on your scheduled shipping days, you can call a toll-free number and USPS will come out and pick up your packages for free. You can also schedule a pickup through their Web site at *www.usps.com*. Pay an additional $12.50, and you can schedule a specific time for this service. Both options cover an unlimited number of packages as long as each package weighs less than seventy pounds.

The post office will also deliver packaging materials right to your door. All you have to do is file a request online at *www.usps.com*.

Using Other Delivery Services

UPS is the other shipping service that eBay has integrated into its site. As with USPS, both you and your buyers can track packages through eBay and PayPal, which cuts down on the number of "Have you shipped?" and "When will it get here?" questions from buyers. Another big plus is that shipping and tracking information is automatically e-mailed to your customers.

Like the post office, UPS will come to your home and pick up your packages.

FedEx

For items weighing more than four pounds, Federal Express is another good option. Once primarily noted for overnight shipping for businesses, the company now competes against USPS and UPS for ground shipping to residential addresses, and its rates are very competitive. Since FedEx isn't integrated into eBay's site, it's not as convenient to use as the others, but the company does maintain a good Web site where you can estimate shipping costs, pay for them, and arrange for package pickup.

Freight Companies

If you're selling items that fall outside of what the other shipping companies can handle in terms of size and/or weight, you'll have to find another way to get them there. Typically, this means using a freight or shipping company. Greyhound is another option. College students have used it for years to ship bikes and trunks to and from dorms to home.

Other Shipping Companies

You can use companies like Airborne and the like if you have good relationships with them, feel you get better service, and find them reliable.

Using eBay's Online Shipping Calculators

eBay makes available a free, optional shipping calculator that you can include in your listings. All you have to do is enter in the weight, package size, the type of service and any handling fees—such as packaging and so on—when you do your listings. Buyers simply enter their zip codes to see the shipping rates.

Rates are displayed both in a calculator on the listing page and in various parts of the payment process. You can choose up to three different shipping services, and you can include rates for international shipping.

Shipping Overseas

Some sellers shy away from selling internationally because they don't want to deal with shipping items overseas. They see it as a hassle they don't need, and they worry about items breaking in transit and having to fill out lengthy and complicated customs forms. In today's global economy, such concerns are, to be honest, a little dated. Once you do it a couple of times, you'll find that shipping to foreign countries is almost as easy as shipping domestically.

Determining Shipping Costs

Regardless of where the package is going and who handles it, international shipping costs are based on a variety of factors, including the weight and dimensions of the package, how it's traveling, and where you're shipping to and from. Costs can vary greatly, and the USPS Web site has actually taken a step backward on its most recent redesign and made it more difficult to figure out what these costs are.

Foreign shipping often costs more than what you think it will. To avoid having to cover the additional postage yourself, you might want to take foreign packages to the post office for assistance until you get the hang of things.

All about Customs

All shipments sent to a foreign country are subject to examination by the customs department in the destination country and must clear customs before they can enter the country. ▶▶**Shipping internationally typically requires filling out a customs form that declares the contents of the package and its value.** Keep some customs forms on hand, stored where you prepare items for shipping, so you can eliminate the hassle of having to fill them out at the post office. If you purchase and print USPS postage and labels through eBay or PayPal, the required customs forms will print out automatically as well.

Confirming Deliveries

USPS delivery confirmation is required if you're offering PayPal. If you can't prove that items were shipped and delivered, you'll lose your PayPal seller's protection. UPS and FedEx automatically provide tracking at all service levels.

Insurance

Some sellers include insurance costs in their shipping and handling fees and don't leave these costs open for discussion. That can be off-putting for buyers, especially on less expensive items. If you've only paid $5 for something, you're probably willing to take the risk of its arriving safely. A good approach is to offer it as an option on lower-priced goods, say anything under $50, and require it on anything higher.

If you ship with FedEx or UPS, you're automatically covered for the first $100 of value, which is another reason to consider using these services when you're shipping certain items.

Packing and Shipping Tips

All shipping services are automated, which means that anything you send through them is going to be handled more by machines than by human hands. It also means that you have to bundle up what you send through them in such a way to ensure that they'll get there in one piece.

The following tips are general best-practice approaches. For specific information on packing procedures or help with odd, unusual, or extremely fragile items, consult the Web site for the shipping company you're going to use. If the information you need isn't there, call them.

For non-fragile, non-breakable items, do the following:

1. Choose a sturdy outer container that comfortably fits the item being shipped. Don't try to cram items into containers that don't fit. This can strain the seams of the container and cause them to burst open. If you're recycling materials, remove or cross out any old address labels.

2. If the container is cardboard, consider wrapping the item in a plastic bag first to protect it from getting wet. If you're using a Tyvek envelope, you can skip this step, as Tyvek is waterproof.

3. Put photographs or other items that need to remain flat between two pieces of cardboard or a similar rigid material.

Tape the edges of the support material together to keep the items from sliding out during shipping.

4. If an item has sharp edges that could poke through its container, pad the edges with small bubble wrap.

5. Fill all voids in the container with material to prevent the items from moving around. Good choices are crumpled newspaper, packing peanuts, bubble wrap, or Styrofoam.

6. Include a copy of the paperwork for the sale—the PayPal invoice is a good choice here if PayPal was the payment method. If not, use eBay's buyer's invoice.

7. Seal the container with good-quality packing tape. Don't skimp on this stuff; you want the contents of your package to arrive at their destination safe and sound, and keeping box or bag flaps closed in transit is essential for this. Clear two- or three-inch-wide tape is the best choice as it's more versatile, but you can use brown if you want. Be sure to run a strip of tape over all seams and flaps. Don't use masking tape, kraft paper tape, cellophane tape, string, rope, or anything else to seal your packages.

8. Attach the shipping label to the top with packing tape. If you're not using crack-and-peel labels, tape over the addresses—both yours and the recipient's—to protect the ink from running should it get wet. Don't place the label over a seam or closure if you can avoid it. If you're doing postage online, don't tape over the bar code, as doing so will interfere with scanning equipment.

For fragile items, take the following steps:

1. Wrap the item in large bubble wrap. One layer should be fine for items that aren't too fragile; wrap two layers on more fragile items.

2. Choose a container that's at least two inches bigger than the wrapped item in every direction.

3. Place the item in the container.

4. Fill all voids with cushioning material. Here, packing peanuts will provide the best protection. If there's room to put additional cushioning material under the item, do so.

5. If you're shipping something that has glass over it, say a picture or a mirror, run two pieces of masking tape in an X pattern over the glass. If the glass shatters, this makes it easier to remove the shards.

6. Seal and label as before.

Double-boxing is the recommended approach for extremely fragile items. Here's how to do it:

1. Wrap each item individually, using at least two inches of bubble wrap.

2. Place the item or items in a corrugated cardboard box. Items should fit snugly if possible. If they don't, fill voids with cushioning material.

3. Choose a sturdy shipping box that's at least six inches bigger than the smaller box on all sides. Use a new box if you can; recycled boxes, since they've already been through the mill at least once, sometimes aren't as sturdy.

4. Put two to three inches of cushioning material in the bottom of the shipping box. Center the smaller box on top of the material, then fill all voids with additional cushioning material.

5. Seal and label as before.

Using Online Shipping Programs

eBay has made it extremely easy to use USPS and UPS by integrating both services at its Web site. There really isn't much reason to use the USPS or UPS proprietary online shipping programs—that is, the programs each makes available at its own site—as you can do it all through eBay and PayPal.

Inside UPS

Years ago, I owned a pack-and-ship franchise. As a new franchisee, I had to attend two weeks of training. They taught us a lot of things, but we spent the most time on two subjects. One of them was packing and shipping.

As part of our training, we spent an afternoon at a UPS center. If you've ever wondered why things sometimes arrive a bit roughed up, or even dented or punctured, going behind the scenes at one of these facilities will teach you everything you need to know about this, and more. It's amazing what boxes go through in transit. They fall off conveyor lines. They get dropped, sometimes from significant heights. This doesn't just happen at UPS. It happens anywhere where there are lots of packages being handled.

The biggest lesson I learned was that you can't control what happens with your packages once they leave your hands, but you can improve the odds on how well they'll travel by using high-quality packing materials. Doing so can go a long way toward ensuring that items get to where they're going in one piece.

Even so, there's lots of good information at both sites that can help you be a better shipper, so it's not a bad idea to take a look at them to see what's there. USPS is at *www.usps.com*. UPS is at *www.ups.com*.

If you're going to use another shipping company—FedEx or DHL, for example—it's a good idea to log onto their sites and familiarize yourself with their programs before you use them. Every shipping company is a little different, and knowing what those differences are can save you a lot of time and headaches, especially when you're rushing to get things sent.

▶▶ Test Drive

By now, you should know what you're going to sell on eBay or at least have a pretty good idea. Do you have the packing materials you need to ship these items? Make a list of what you need and start looking for places to buy the supplies you can't get through the post office or other shippers. Things you'll need include the following:

- ➲ Packing tape.
- ➲ A tape gun or dispenser. Make sure it's sturdy and sharp. If you have small children, buy one that has a guard over the cutting area.
- ➲ Masking tape.
- ➲ Cushioning materials. Besides bubble wrap, you shouldn't have to pay for it unless you want to. Companies that routinely receive shipments usually have tons of it on hand, and they're often more than happy to give it to someone who can use it.
- ➲ Boxes. Recycling used containers is perfectly okay if they're in good shape. Again, try to use free supplies from USPS and/or UPS as much as you can here. Think twice about recycling boxes with crushed corners, as this indicates damage to the structural integrity of the material.
- ➲ Tissue paper. Clothing should be tissue-wrapped if possible; it simply makes a nicer presentation. If you want to get really fancy, think about buying foil stickers to seal the top seam.
- ➲ Transparent tape. Use this to seal the seams on bubble wrap, tissue paper, and so on.
- ➲ Cardboard sheets to reinforce flat items.

Handling E-mail Inquiries

One of the things that has set eBay apart from other online selling sites from the beginning has been its emphasis on online communications. Buyers and sellers can contact each other by phone, or even by snail mail, and there are times when doing so makes some sense. But e-mail communication is far and away the preferred approach. Not only is it faster, it's a good way of keeping track of transactions and of who said what. E-mail can also prove a written record of transactions with your buyers, which is essential should something go wrong and you need proof of what you said or did.

Given the emphasis on e-mail as the preferred communications approach between buyers and sellers, it might be hard to believe there are sellers who don't respond to buyers' e-mails or who answer them too late to do buyers any good, but there definitely are. Log onto any eBay message board, and chances are good you'll see at least one recent thread complaining about a seller's (or a buyer's) lack of response.

Going Beyond E-mail

E-mail contact between buyers and sellers works about 99 percent of the time, but there are times when picking up the phone is more appropriate. Dealing with complex issues or problems is often easier when you use a medium that does a good job of conveying tone as well as content. For this, the telephone beats e-mail hands down.

eBay makes it easy for buyers and sellers to communicate at the site, so there's really no excuse for not responding to inquiries, and doing it relatively quickly. That said, unless the questions are about auctions that are ending soon, you usually don't need to jump on individual queries the second you get them.

Many eBay sellers develop a schedule for when they'll answer e-mails and set aside time every day for doing so. Two or three times a day—first thing in the morning, sometime in the evening, and possibly mid-afternoon—is fairly standard.

All about ASQ

ASQ, or Ask Seller a Question, is eBay's primary mechanism for facilitating communications between buyers and sellers regarding items offered for auction or sale.

Every listing page contains two ASQ links—the seller's User ID, and another at the end of the next line below the seller information—for buyers to use in contacting sellers.

When a buyer asks you a question, you receive an e-mail from eBay containing the question and the buyer's e-mail address. The ASQ system lets you decide whether you want to make your communications with the buyer private or public and whether you want to answer the question in eBay's system or through your own e-mail system. If you make your communications public, questions and answers will appear on the item listing. If the question and answer might benefit other potential buyers—for example, a potential bidder is asking for more details—it's usually a good idea to make your answer public. If not, then make it private.

eBay encourages sellers to keep their ASQ answers on-point—in other words, not to take advantage of the system by advertising other items for sale.

Using E-mail to Make Listings Better

You can always expect to get some questions from potential buyers when auctions are running, but if you're getting more questions than you think you should, analyze them to see if there's a pattern. If there is, take a closer look at your listings and look for the disconnect. Maybe you thought you included detail that you didn't, or maybe bidders can't find it because it's buried.

Answering in Bulk

When, or if, you get to the point where you're running a ton of auctions, handling e-mails individually can take up way too much time and energy. You'll always want to give personal attention to specific questions about your listings, but there are other aspects of e-mail communications that you can and should automate, including these:

⊃ First-contact auto responses. If you can't answer e-mails your-self right away, use these to let people know when you'll be in touch.

⊃ End-of-auction notices.

⊃ Shipping notices.

eBay offers two programs—Selling Manager and Selling Manager Pro—that you can use to e-mail your buyers individually or in bulk. Both programs also offer customizable templates that save you from having to type the same messages over and over. Bulk e-mail is also a function in many third-party auction management systems. It's a good feature to look for when you're shopping them.

Tips for More Effective E-mail

E-mail is so ubiquitous and so easy to use that we tend to take it for granted, and we also tend to assume that everyone knows how to use it appropriately. This definitely isn't the case. In fact, people who use e-mail incorrectly probably outnumber those who don't.

It takes time to do a good job with any writing project, and e-mails are no different. That said, lots of people clearly spend little time on their e-mail communications. They fire off poorly worded messages rife with spelling and punctuation errors.

▶▶In the digital age, e-mails are often the first line of communication. People form strong opinions from them, which is why it's essential that they be as good as they can be. While it's not necessary to make them as formal as business letters are, they should be well worded and clearly formatted.

The following tips should help you with your e-mails:

⊃ Match the tone to the situation. E-mails are typically less formal than letters are, although there are times when adopting a more formal tone is appropriate.

⊃ Put the most important information at the top. Don't make peo-ple scroll through a long e-mail to get to your answer. Along these lines, briefer is always better, but don't sacrifice meaning for brevity.

➲ DON'T TYPE IN ALL CAPS!!!! NOT ONLY ARE ALL-CAP E-MAILS HARD TO READ, ALL CAPS CONNOTE SHOUTING IN THE ONLINE WORLD.

➲ Use punctuation appropriately. Periods go at the end of sentences. Keep exclamation points under control.

➲ Use abbreviations sparingly, if at all. You might know what LOL, DH, DD, ROTFLMAO, and other online shorthand mean, but the person on the other side might not.

➲ Always include part or all of the original message below your response so the recipient has something to refer to.

➲ Develop and use a signature at the end of your messages. This serves as an online business card, as it tells people who you are, what you do, and how they can contact you. Be sure to include a clickable link to your eBay store or your Web site, if you have one. Don't miss the opportunity to tell others about your business.

➲ Don't say anything in an e-mail that you wouldn't want to be public knowledge. E-mails are not private communications.

➲ Never send e-mail when you're angry—it's almost guaranteed to make things worse. Plus, you might really regret what you said, and you won't be able to pull it back. Go ahead and write the e-mail, if it will make you feel better, but don't send it.

Finally, be a good communicator. If your writing skills aren't strong, don't just shrug it off—work on them. Read your e-mails out loud. If they sound right, they'll read right. Proofread before you send them. Ask yourself if you've left any questions unanswered. If you have, answer them.

The Value of a Rapid Response

Let's say you need new business cards. You've done your shopping online, and you've found two vendors you want to work with—for simplicity's sake, we'll call them Bob and Joe. Their offerings are virtually identical, but there are some pricing and service differences between them, and you want to ask some questions. You send an e-mail to both.

You hear back from both vendors almost right away. Joe's response is an auto responder that thanks you for your inquiry and says he'll be in touch within twenty-four hours to answer your questions.

Bob's response is tailored to your inquiry and is short and to the point. It answers your question, but the answer leads to another question, so you e-mail him back. Again, you get a rapid response and the answer to your question. You're pretty impressed, but Joe's offerings are a little lower in price than Bob's, and you're not in that much of a hurry, so you figure you can wait until he weighs in.

One day passes. Two days pass. Now you're getting impatient, and you begin to think that Bob's cards, while more expensive than Joe's, might be the way to go.

You finally hear from Joe late in the afternoon on day two. His response is as good as Bob's, but you still have a few questions, and you're wondering if it's going to take another two days to get them answered. What's more, you also wonder if his sluggish approach to answering your e-mail indicates how the transaction will go in general. Still, the pricing and service differences between the two don't make either of them a clear favorite.

Which company would you go with? Would you take a chance on Joe because his pricing is good, or would Bob's better communications win you over?

When you're selling on eBay, this is a decision you don't want to force potential buyers to make. However, many sellers do exactly that. They don't respond within the twenty-four-hour window in which 75 percent of e-mail users expect to receive a response. Their answers might be slipshod and address parts of the question or none of it. If you're a buyer, unless you really want what that seller is offering, it's simply easier to find something else from someone who seems to care a little more.

▶▶**On eBay, if you don't answer questions before auctions end, you're giving potential buyers reasons not to bid.** Beyond this, buyers tend to remember sellers who don't take the time to answer questions. If you're one of them, they might give you a second chance if they really want what you're selling. Then again, they might not.

Why put yourself in this position? Answer your e-mail inquiries! You'll be glad you did.

Paying Attention to the Details

Keeping track of where you are in transactions can be difficult if you're handling lots of them. At a minimum, you can expect to have the following communications with your buyers:

- Sending after-auction invoices
- Making second-chance offers
- Acknowledging when you receive payment
- Advising when you ship their merchandise
- Checking to see if their items have arrived if you don't hear from them or they don't leave you feedback

You can automate most of these communications, and you should plan to if you're managing a number of transactions at once. eBay's online systems can work to a certain extent, and they're a good place to start. If your needs grow beyond them, try to use one program to manage as many aspects of your automated responses as possible. Keeping things in one place is the best way to keep track of where you are in the transaction.

Is the Customer Always Right?

"The customer is always right" is an old saying in the retail world. However, more often than not, customers aren't right, and it's their own actions that put them in the wrong. Maybe they didn't read the fine print or follow your terms of service. Maybe they tried to pay you using a method you don't accept, or they didn't pay you in your stated timeframe.

It can be enough to make you scream, or at the very least say some nasty words to your computer screen, especially when you get e-mails blaming you for problems they create. (Both actions are more than okay, by the way, as long as you take things out privately.)

You can say goodbye to "The customer is always right." However, you can't ditch the philosophy behind it. Your customers may not always be right, but they're always in control, and for one simple reason—they've chosen you as the person they want to give their hard, cold cash to.

Putting Yourself in the Customer's Shoes

When you accept the fact that customers aren't always right, but they are in control, it puts a slightly different spin on your dealings with them. Instead of giving them the service you'd want to get, you focus on gaining a better understanding of what they want from you, and you match your responses and your actions accordingly.

Gaining a better understanding of your customers' needs can be difficult to do when all you have to go on are e-mail communications. They can provide some of the answers, but probably not all. To get them, you'll have to go beyond e-mail and do a little market research.

Going directly to your customers and asking them about their buying experiences with you is the fastest, most direct way to gather this information. You can do it in several different ways:

1. Via e-mail: After transactions are over, randomly select a few customers and send them a thank-you email that includes a short survey. Short is a key word here—if customers are willing to give their time to you, don't take advantage of them by sending them long, detailed surveys.

2. Via snail mail: Include a self-addressed, stamped postcard in packages to selected customers. Thank them first, and then ask them a few questions about their buying experience. Or send thank-you notes to some of your buyers separately from their shipments, and include your survey postcard. You'll want to do this fairly soon after they receive the merchandise—details fade quickly, and you want to make sure they remember who you are.

3. Via phone: Reserve this approach for transactions that go bad. While you might think that all you're going to get is a bunch of spew from the other side, you might be pleasantly surprised. Most people, even if they're really ticked off, like having their

opinions asked for. Ask the buyer what went wrong from his or her perspective, and be prepared to offer suggestions for how you can make things better. Don't apologize, but don't be defensive either. Say things like "I understand" and "I hear you."

From Gold to Platinum

You probably learned the Golden Rule—"Do unto others as you would have them do unto you"—when you were a kid. It's not a bad approach, but it has a "one size (mine) fits all" assumption that doesn't work well when it comes to providing great customer service. Business and communications expert Tony Alessandra suggests replacing the Golden Rule with his Platinum Rule—"Treat others the way they want to be treated." It's a subtle difference but an important one. Instead of imposing your belief system on your customers, you work at understanding their needs, and you shape your reactions and responses appropriately.

Dealing with the Bad Apples

Fortunately, the vast majority of your customers, even the ones who are in the wrong, will be worth your while to deal with. That said, all customers are definitely not created equal, and there will always be a few who will push your buttons no matter what. Regardless of how well you handle them and how much you're willing to offer them, they'll still be pains in the rear. They'll occupy way too much of your time, and you'll spend way too much emotional energy dealing with them. Thankfully, they're definitely in the minority, but you'll have to decide what you want to do with them.

As difficult and illogical as it may seem, you're almost always better off completing your business with these individuals as quickly as possible and moving on to transactions that will net more benefits for you in the long run. Yes, you'll run the risk of receiving negative feedback when you do, but even this is often better than the agony of allowing these transactions to drag on.

You'll find specific tips for handling these customers in Chapter 26.

In an article titled "Insanely Great Customer Service" that ran in the September 2000 issue of *Success* magazine, author Debbie Selinsky tells the story of a man who e-mailed the bakery company Sara Lee with a special request. He wanted to get his mother a cap like those worn by celebrity golfers in a Sara Lee–sponsored tournament that his mother had watched on television. Could the company help?

Sara Lee's customer service people searched high and low, but the company was out of the special caps. They were on order, however, and expected to arrive soon—in fact, the day before the woman's birthday.

Mom got her cap, along with a birthday card, by overnight delivery in time for her birthday. This example illustrates two core values of giving great customer service: treating customers like royalty, and making them feel appreciated. Sara Lee didn't have to go to the lengths that it did for this man and his mother. Someone could have said, "Sorry, not available." The company didn't even know if the two were loyal customers. But they did know that doing something special for his mother was important enough to warrant his contacting Sara Lee, and that was enough.

You don't have the kind of resources that Sara Lee has. But you can—and should—provide superlative customer service, including going above and beyond when the situation warrants it. Going the extra mile might cost you a little more, but it costs a lot more to woo new customers than it does to keep the ones you already have.

Earning (and Giving) Positive Feedback

On eBay, your customer service skills are out there for the world to see. All anyone has to do is check your feedback, both the comments left for you and those you left for others, to see how well you're faring in the customer service department. Unlike other retail settings, they can see for themselves the exact percentage of happy and unhappy buyers. What's more, they can read all about it. On eBay, feedback speaks volumes. The higher the score, the better.

Many eBay buyers and sellers get hung up on feedback for precisely these reasons. They strive for perfection to such a point that they'll avoid conflict with trading partners to protect their feedback scores. This works against the feedback principle and creates a false basis for trading in general, but they do it regardless.

While it can be a source of pride to maintain a perfect feedback score, and there are many sellers who have been able to do it even after thousands of transactions, the simple truth is this: The more transactions you have, the greater your chances are of receiving a few neutrals or negatives along the way. Most buyers realize this, and when they check feedback, they'll weigh what's been said against other things they know about the seller.

As a seller, you should do everything you can to earn positive feedback. This might mean going far above and beyond the call of duty to make things right for your buyers. But don't be afraid to sacrifice your rating in situations that justify it. If you're dealing with a terrible buyer and it's appropriate to leave a neutral or negative, do it. Yes, you might get one back, especially if you leave feedback first. You can respond to the feedback if you want, and if doing so will better explain your position. Or you can simply take the high road, do nothing, and move on to the next transaction.

eBay recently made some changes to the feedback system that address some of the feedback issues sellers (and buyers) have encountered over the years. They include the following:

➲ **De-scoring:** If members don't participate in issue resolution, and they leave feedback for the transaction, the feedback will remain but eBay will de-score it, which means it won't affect feedback scores.

➲ **Removing feedback left by certain users:** eBay will remove the feedback left by any user who's indefinitely suspended within ninety days of registering at the site.

➲ **Education:** New users are required to complete a tutorial before leaving neutral or negative feedback.

Exceeding Expectations

Successful businesses might have many things in common, but one factor takes the lead: They all treat their customers well. Good customer service makes first-class businesses stand out from the pack; great customer service that exceeds customers' expectations results in loyalty and attracts new business. You can offer the best merchandise at the best prices, but if you don't treat your customers well, it won't matter. They might buy from you once, but they might not come back.

▶▶**Customer service is the one thing that can make you shine in eBay's competitive selling arena.** Satisfying the minimums—answering e-mails promptly, shipping promptly, giving appropriate feedback—is good, but going beyond the minimums and exceeding customers' expectations will make you a far greater success in the long run and set you apart from your competition.

How do you exceed expectations as an eBay seller? Here are some thoughts and suggestions, straight from the people on the front line—buyers and sellers on eBay. You might disagree with some, such as offering a money-back guarantee regardless of the reason, but they're all tips worth looking at:

> "Outside packaging doesn't have to be fancy, but it does have to protect what's inside. Every so often, sellers should mail something to themselves, just to see how things arrive. They might be unpleasantly surprised."

> "I like getting an e-mail when the package ships."

> "When I first started, I put a penny in each vintage bag I sold, along with a notecard with a poem that basically was a wish for them to always have cash in their purse. I got lots of nice e-mails because of it."

> "I include a few peppermint hard candies (singly wrapped)."

> "Rain-proof items by wrapping them in a plastic bag before slipping into an envelope."

> "I offer a money-back guarantee on all items in case buyers are disappointed . . . don't want that! I also refund excess shipping charges if I've overstated."

"I always give repeat buyers shipping discounts. I always include a gift with the purchase—I go to a lot of auctions and buy little things just for this purpose."

"I never package in a bag, always in a box. I want it to be like a gift to the buyer."

"I answer all e-mails and questions, even if the answers are already in the listing (which they usually are) and even if the question is kind of weird. If the question seems kind of rude or critical, I just answer politely."

"I get a little miffed if I buy an item and it arrives without even a note, or at least a thank-you by e-mail. I don't like it when sellers say they're too busy to do little things like iron, send e-mail notices, or pay attention to packaging. You are running your own business; you control your own time, so you should make time to do these little things to make it a more personal experience."

"Ship promptly, and package well. Don't tape plastic—bubble wrap or bag—so much that it's impossible to open."

"If what an item sells for exceeds my expectations, I will ship for free and or pay for insurance—even to Europe! I ship promptly since I know that slow shipping is one of the biggest no-nos for buyers, and I don't charge any sort of outrageous "handling" fees. If I need packing materials, I'll charge an extra $2–$3 bucks, never more."

"When I first started buying here in 1999, I bought a few pieces from this one seller. She packaged everything in floral tissue, wrapped securely and tied with grosgrain ribbon. Then this tissued package went into a clean, new plastic bag, and then into a box. Attached was a simple, handwritten card saying "Thank you (my name)"—no mention of feedback and none of the usual "if you're disappointed, contact me first, blah blah blah . . ." I tell you, the first time I opened one of her packages, the *first* thing I did (after trying it on) was log-on and see what else she had listed. And of course I immediately left glowing feedback. Her packages were consistently wrapped this way. Her feedback givers were generous with the ALL CAPS and the exclamation points !!! and the A++++++'s."

"We always include a printed invoice, unless the buyer requests that we don't. We write a short thank-you sentiment at the bottom of the invoice. We don't do unconditional returns/refunds, but will usually do whatever it takes to make the bidder happy. If a mistake is ours, we refund the return shipping without question. If we ship a lot slower than we promised, we'll usually refund the shipping without question as well."

"For international shipping, we try to stay on top of shipping requirements/restrictions to different countries, and to be aware of the duties and taxes international bidders have to pay. We'll do as much as we can, while still being within the guidelines, to keep the cost of receiving the item down."

"We ship discreetly, with no mention of what is in the package, no "eBay" or eBay numbers, and no seller name on the outside of the package."

"When I ship, I send an e-mail saying so. All my messages include "Thank you for your business" notes. I include a packing slip with a copy of the auction and the ending price. I handwrite my thank-you note at the bottom. I include a colorful recipe card that I designed; on the back is my store address. I have had several people thank me for the recipe."

"If I see someone win something and they're bidding on something else of mine, I'll shoot them an e-mail to let them know I'm happy to wait until the other auction ends so they can take advantage of combined shipping and handling."

"For repeat bidders, I often have them choose an additional item or throw in something similar as a thanks. Or discount their shipping and handling as a surprise."

"I hate colored tissue paper and ribbon, and dryer sheets or smelly stuff, like potpourri. In my years on eBay, I have received three items that were damaged by color bleed from colored packing materials. One was also in a Ziploc—there must have been enough moisture in there to cause it to bleed when it got hot!"

"I like to get a business card or magnet—I really do keep them all!"

"I send a self-addressed return shipping label if I screw up on an order, or have it picked up if it's a major hassle for them to go to the post office."

"I have been known to make special trips to the post office, hold packages for people until they get back from vacation, mail to vacation destinations, mail to relatives, flex my TOS a bit, etc. That's all stuff I guess I don't have to do, but I'm happy to accommodate when I can, and people really appreciate it."

▶▶ Test Drive

Put together your own platinum customer-service plan using the tips in this chapter. Write down ideas for your standards and best practices in at least three areas. Here are some to consider:

E-mail response: How often? Daily? Twice a day?

Buyer notifications: How often do you plan on communicating with your buyers?

Packaging: What can you do to delight buyers when they open the box?

Maximizing Your eBay Selling Success

Using Keywords Effectively

By now, you should have received this message loud and clear: Keywords rule! In Chapter 12, the importance of good keywords is discussed in detail, but it deserves a second mention here.

If you're going to err on the side of anything in your auctions, don't make it poor keyword use. As mentioned, items with sloppy descriptions and fuzzy images can sell, but if your titles and descriptions don't include words that will direct buyers to them, no one will see them in the first place.

The effective use of keywords are crucial to separating okay sellers from really successful ones. If you're not realizing the sales figures you'd like to see, your keyword use is one of the first things to take another look at. Here are several approaches for doing it:

1. Pick two or three of your listings, and list all the keywords. Take a serious look at them. Are they the best picks? Could you find better ones to use? Are there keyword variations, even spelling variations, that would make sense to include in your listings?

2. Do a couple of searches in your selling category or categories, using different keyword combinations. Pick one or two sellers who seem to be doing well—check both current and completed auctions to make sure—and analyze their titles and listings. What are they doing that you aren't?

3. Run two different test auctions of your own—if possible, of two identical items—in which you use different keywords. Which one gets more hits? If they both sell, which one does better?

Hiring Keyword Help

If you're stuck on keyword use, think about having someone else take a look at your listings. Sometimes just having a fresh set of eyes can make all the difference in the world. You can also consider subscribing to an auction analysis service—ViewTracker is one—that can tell you how people are finding your auctions. Knowing the search terms they're using can help you fine-tune your use of them. More information on ViewTracker is available at *www.sellathon.com*, and you'll find other services to consider in Appendix Three.

Another way to fine-tune your keyword use is to check out a couple of areas on eBay that highlight how keywords are used. The eBay Keywords page indexes popular search terms used by eBay shoppers and makes them searchable alphabetically. If you're having trouble deciding which keywords to use, it can be source of inspiration.

eBay Pulse, a relatively new eBay feature, is a quick snapshot of what's hot and now across the marketplace. It indexes the most popular searches by keyword, both across the site and by category. If you're wondering what the hottest search terms are, you'll find them here. You'll also be able to see how well other sellers are using them, as eBay also lists the largest stores, by number of active listings, for each category. There's a link to eBay Pulse at the bottom of the site's home page.

And don't forget about eBay's discussion boards. If you're stuck, post there and let others weigh in on what they think will work best.

How Not to Use Keywords

We briefly touched on keyword spamming in Chapter 12. Now it's time to take a closer look at what this practice is all about. As mentioned, it can be a quick way to get your auctions cancelled. However, many new sellers are guilty of this practice without even knowing that they're doing it.

Take a look at the four following titles. They're from actual eBay auctions. Which of them, if any, violate the keyword spamming rules?

> 7 black cami *** GAP *** tank shirts size M bebe
>
> 512M Movie Player Photo Viewer MP4/MP3 VL535A Beat iPod
>
> JONATHAN STUART BABY BLUE SUIT JACKET SZ 6 SZ 4 P MISSE BFA, BEBE, LAUREN, POLO, BE, HILFIGER, ANN TAYLOR
>
> NWOT Due Per Due Yellow Black Santana Knit Tank M

If you answered all four, you're right on the money.

The first two are fairly obvious. In the first title, Gap and bebe are two completely different clothing lines, and there's no connection between them. That said, if you were a new seller and you had a Gap top that you thought looked exactly like a bebe top, this is one you might think would be okay. It's not. Interestingly, the word bebe didn't appear anywhere else in the auction description, just in the title, so the seller wasn't even making a comparison. He or she was simply including an unrelated keyword to attract more lookers.

The second one's a little more subtle, as the wording is a bit ambiguous. It could appear to be an attachment to an iPod, but it's not. This item popped up on an iPod search. In the item description, the seller did compare the features of his device to an iPod Shuffle in an embedded table, where search engines won't pick it up.

In the third title, the seller has keyword spammed by including a laundry list of unrelated names in her subtitle, which is also against eBay policies.

You'd have to know clothing terms to catch the last one. Santana is a trademark of the St. John Company, and it can only be used to describe certain knits that the company produces. This listing is for a top made by Due Per Due, which is not affiliated with St. John. In the listing copy for this item, the seller further violated keyword guidelines by calling the top a St. John Santana knit, which it is not, and by suggesting it be paired with other St. John pieces to spice them up.

Reporting the Offenders

Do a keyword search on certain hot items, and you might be astonished at what you get back. Keyword spamming is rampant on eBay, but eBay itself doesn't go through listings and yank them. Instead, the company relies on users at the site to report violations. Whether you report them or not is entirely up to you. Some eBayers routinely do it; others figure their time is better spent on other matters and simply ignore it.

What you'll also find is that some of eBay's biggest sellers are guilty of this practice. eBay has stated more than once that it plans on cracking down on these sellers in a big way, but it hasn't happened yet.

Keywords Versus Categories

eBay shoppers use two basic approaches to find items: by keyword search or by category. The vast majority of them search by keyword, but many shoppers like to browse categories first before doing keyword searches, especially if they're just window shopping or they're not sure which keywords to use.

While keywords are important, don't let your emphasis on them overshadow other things you need to do with your listings, including putting them in the right categories. The combination of effective keyword use with accurate category selection is one of the most powerful tools in your listings arsenal.

Understanding eBay's Keywords Program

Using the right keywords in your titles and listings is essential if you're going to participate in eBay's Keywords marketing program, which uses keyword-targeted advertising to direct buyers to your listings. The keywords you select in your advertising tie in directly with those you use in your auction listings, hence the importance of using and choosing the best keywords for your listings.

When buyers search for listings that contain your keywords, ads promoting your listings (along with ads for other sellers containing the same or similar keywords) appear at the top of the Search pages they get back. You bid on placement—the higher you bid, the greater the chances of your ad appearing. However, you're only charged for the ads when buyers click on them.

You can decide where you want buyers to go when they click. Possible choices include the following:

- Your eBay store
- A specific store category
- Search within your store
- All items listed
- Specific item list

Double the Category, Double the Profit?

Sellers sometimes list certain items in two categories (or more) at the same time in the hopes that doing so will attract bidders who depend more on category than keyword searches. Listing in multiple categories, they figure, will attract buyers in both categories who might not see auctions listed in only one of them.

This isn't a bad idea for some items. If yours fits the following criteria, you might want to consider it:

- ➲ If your item is slightly unusual, buyers might not know the keywords to use to search for it.
- ➲ The item truly merits listing in several distinct categories. As an example, say you're selling a pair of women's English riding boots. This boot style comes and goes as a must-have in the women's fashion arena, so it might make sense to list in the equestrian category and in clothing, shoes, and accessories to grab buyers in both sectors. Women wanting the look of riding boots might not think to search in equestrian for the real thing.

Keep in mind that when you list in multiple categories, you'll be charged the full listing amount for each one. Your fees can add up fast going this route.

The bottom line is that listing in multiple categories is a great way for eBay to make more money, but its effectiveness for sellers is debatable. If you're good with keywords in your titles and descriptions, you shouldn't have to take this approach very often. Reserve it only for those auctions that really call for it.

Using Gallery, Bold, and Other eBay Features

Unlike print ads, where you can change typefaces, fonts, and the size of the letters in headlines, you can't do much with your eBay titles visually to make them stand out. However, eBay does allow a small group of visual listing enhancements:

The Final Word on Keyword Spamming ▕ Inside Track

If you've ever been tempted to do a little keyword spamming to draw more attention to your auction listings, despite everything that says you shouldn't, the results of a recent study by Sellathon.com should definitely make you think twice. Not only is the practice a violation of eBay's policies, it's simply a waste of time.

According to Sellathon's research, shoppers spend an average of twenty-six seconds looking at an eBay item. However, that number drops to 2.9 seconds if they end up at auctions that don't accurately match the search terms they used.

The bottom line is that keyword spamming doesn't work, and it's a chintzy practice to get a reputation for doing. You might get more hits if you do it, but those hits won't turn into sales. Plus, the more hits you get, the more likely your chances of running afoul with eBay. Many, if not most, keyword violations are reported by eBay members.

Gallery: Gallery inserts a small picture of the item you're selling next to the title so buyers can get a glimpse of what you're offering right away. Most sellers believe that gallery is a necessity, not an option, and they make ample use of it. You should, too. Those little thumbnail shots are worth their weight in gold for directing people to your listings. The gallery option costs 25 cents per listing, but it's 25 cents that is well worth spending. According to research conducted by ChannelAdvisor, an auction management service, it's the most effective upgrade of all that are available. However, again according to ChannelAdvisor, it only makes sense on non-commodity items greater than $10.

Bold: The text of the headline appears in heavier type. According to eBay, adding this enhancement to your listings increases final prices realized by an average of 25 percent. Bold titles cost $1 per listing.

Highlight: These listings are displayed with a colored band that helps them stand out in search results. This enhancement costs $5.

Border: Bordered listings are enclosed in a bright purple border that appears on search results. Borders will run you $3 per listing.

Subtitle: This enhancement is exactly that—an additional line, like the subtitle on a book, that adds more information to the title. You can say anything you want—give more detail about the item, promote shipping specials, you name it. This in itself can be a neat feature, but the additional line itself also helps listings stand out. There's a drawback to this feature, however, in that subtitle text is only searchable if buyers use the "title and descriptions" search feature. It doesn't help you one bit if buyers just conduct a basic search. Subtitles cost 50 cents per listing.

The additional costs for listing enhancements can add up fast when you're running a lot of auctions. For this reason, it's best to reserve them for times when you really need them. Working on the wording in your titles to make them the best they can be is a far better approach. It will save you lots of money on the front end and pay off better for you in the long run.

Building Your Own Templates

Most beginning eBay sellers use the auction templates offered at the site. This is okay, especially when you're first starting out, but if you're like most sellers, sooner or later you'll be tempted to give your listings a custom look and feel. Should you? Maybe. It all depends on what you're trying to accomplish. If you're customizing as part of an overall branding program (as described in Chapter 19), adding some special touches to your auction layouts to support your branding efforts makes a lot of sense.

If you're doing it simply to make your listings stand out from your competition, think again. When buyers search for listings, they don't base their decisions on what listings look like. If they're lucky, they'll have a tiny thumbnail image to work from—if you decided to use one—but that's pretty much it.

That said, if you want to customize your auctions, you have some choices for going about it, including the following:

⮕ **Paying eBay a little extra for its Listing Designer service:** This is a fairly bare-bones service, but it is a step up from eBay's standard listing layout.

⮕ **Subscribing to an auction program that offers custom templates:** Many do, and some of the offerings are pretty nice. You can use the templates as is, or tweak them some more to personalize them to your own needs.

⮕ **Hiring someone to design a custom template for you:** There are eBay sellers who do this. If you're interested in seeing what they have to offer, do a search for auction templates, graphic design, logo design, or web design. Or, spend some time on eBay's Photos & HTML board; some of these sellers post regularly there.

⮕ **Doing it yourself:** Learn some HTML, and you can build your templates in the privacy of your own home.

If you're going to develop your own auction-listing format, stay away from the following "enhancements":

⮕ **Animation:** Things like animated cursors and moving logos are not only annoying and distracting, they make auction pages maddeningly slow to load for dial-up shoppers, and there are still lots of them out there. Many eBay buyers close auctions that feature these things as quickly as they open them. Avoid this stuff at all costs. There's nothing cute about this stuff. Nothing.

⮕ **Colored or animated backgrounds:** Undesirable, for the same reasons as above. Don't even be tempted.

⮕ **Fancy, frilly borders and frames:** Again, they're distracting and they diminish the effectiveness of your copy and photos.

⮕ **Music:** Music files can make page loads excruciatingly slow, and they can startle the heck out of your buyers, especially if they have the speakers on their computers turned up.

HTML Codes You Should Know

Even if you decide to stay with eBay's basic templates, you can take your listings beyond their somewhat Plain Jane appearance and give them a custom look. As mentioned, all you need to know is some basic HTML, which is the programming language used to create Web pages. With this set of codes, it's possible to do simple tweaks to your listings that both make them more user-friendly for buyers and help them stand out from the crowd. Most HTML coding requires tags at the beginning and end of each code string to indicate where the formatting begins and ends. A few do not.

Paragraph and Line Breaks

Want to break up your copy so it doesn't look like one big gray area? You can do it in several ways. To distinguish paragraphs, put a <p> in front of the first word of the paragraph. When you get to where you want paragraph breaks to end, use </p>.

Here's how to format a paragraph break:

<p>Like what you see?<p>Add me to your favorite sellers.</p>

And here's what it will look like:

Like what you see?

Add me to your favorite sellers.

Another way to break copy into more readable chunks is to insert a forced line break using the <br> tag. This makes lines break exactly where you want.

Here's how to format a break:

Like what you see?
Add me to your favorite sellers.

And what it looks like:

Like what you see?
Add me to your favorite sellers.

Finally, you can use the horizontal rule tag to separate blocks of copy by inserting lines between them. It looks like this:

Here's how to format a horizontal rule.</hr>See how easy it is?

And here's what it looks like:

Here's how to format a horizontal rule.

_____

See how easy it is?

Drawing Attention with Bold and Italic

These codes are a great way to emphasize key words in your descriptions. <b> is the symbol for bold. <i> is the symbol for italic. When using them, be sure to include the end tag; otherwise, whatever you've specified will go on ad infinitum.

Here's how to use them:

<b>Like what you see?</b><i>Add me to your favorite sellers.</i>

And here's what they will look like:

Like what you see? _Add me to your favorite sellers._

Centering Text

This is one of the most useful tags to know about. Without it, text in listings runs like you see it in this book. This isn't necessarily bad, but centered text often works better and just looks cooler.

Here's how to format centered text:

Like what you see?

Add me to your favorite sellers.

And here's how it looks:

Like what you see?

Add me to your favorite sellers.

Making Lists

You can make a variety of lists with HTML tags. Two of the most useful are bulleted lists and numbered lists.

For lists, it's necessary to insert tags that indicate the kind of list you're building and tags that delineate each item. As an example, <ul> is the code for bulleted lists; <ol> is the code for numbered lists; <li> is the tag for each line in the list.

Here's how to do them. Tags for bulleted lists look like this:

This item measures: <ul><li>10.5" long</li><li>5" wide</li><li>3" deep</li></ul>

Here's the end result:

This item measures:

- 10.5" long
- 5" wide
- 3" deep

Here's how to build a numbered list:

My checkout process is easy. All you have to do is:

<ol><li>Buy something.</li>

<li>Pay me.</li></ol>

Here's what it looks like:

My checkout process is easy. All you have to do is:

1. Buy something.
2. Pay me.

Inserting Images

The <img> tag inserts images directly from your image host into your auction listings. You can also use it to upload images to discussion board posts.

The complete tag line looks like this:

<img src=http://www.yourphotohost.com/images/yourpicturename
.jpg>

Your photo host is where the images are located.

Coloring Up

These codes change the color of your fonts. Use them judiciously to highlight important words in your auction copy. In the following example, the tags indicate the color red for the second and third sentences.

Terms & Conditions: <font color=red> Respond to my end of auction notice within 2 days. Online payments due within 3 days, money orders due within 8 days.</font>

Here's what the text will look like on the page:

Terms & Conditions: Respond to my end of auction notice within 2 days. Online payments due within 3 days, money orders due within 8 days.

Changing Title Sizes

These codes let you custom-tailor the size of titles in your listings. Here's what they look like:

<h1>Terms and Conditions</h1>

Terms and Conditions

<h2>Terms and Conditions</h2>

Terms and Conditions

<h3>Terms and Conditions</h3>

Terms and Conditions

<h4>Terms and Conditions</h4>

Terms and Conditions

If you're interested in learning more about formatting your own auctions, you'll find lots of information on eBay's Photos & HTML Discussion Board. As a fair warning, though, you'll also find information on things you've been warned against in this chapter, such as animations, colored backgrounds, and so on.

If you're looking for a place where you can practice your HTML skills and see how things will really look, you'll also find information on practice boards there. Be sure to check Tips & Links and Bob's Tip Pages, two excellent resources that appear near the top of the board.

▶▶ Test Drive

The way you put your auctions together as a new seller might have worked fine for you then, but do your auctions reflect what and where you are now? If you're not sure, spend some time analyzing how other sellers in your category present their auctions, and see how yours compare.

Developing a Customer Loyalty Program

If you're like most U.S. consumers—more than 75 percent of them, as a matter of fact—chances are good that you have at least one of the following in your purse or wallet:

- ⟳ A punch card from your favorite coffee shop
- ⟳ A discount card from a local or national retailer
- ⟳ A membership reward card from the airline you fly with most often, or the hotel or motel where you stay most frequently
- ⟳ A supermarket club card

These are all examples of customer loyalty programs, designed to—you guessed it—increase sales and boost corporate bottom lines by creating and/or strengthening customer loyalty. How well they work is up for some debate—well, more than some—but the belief that they do work on some level has put just about every major company on the customer loyalty program bandwagon.

It's common knowledge that it costs more to attract new customers than it does to retain current ones—an estimated six times more, as a matter of fact—so retention is what customer loyalty programs are all about. What's more, repeat customers spend an average of 33 percent more than new customers do. They're also a fantastic source of referrals, eclipsing non-customers by 107 percent.

Following this logic, it makes sense to put a certain amount of your time, effort, and money toward building a customer loyalty program of your own so you can retain your repeat customers. When you're building your business, and gearing much of your efforts toward capturing new customers, it can be difficult to take a step back and direct your attention toward what you're doing to meeting the needs of your existing customer base. However, it's essential to handle both. Doing so can be another important step toward guaranteeing your long-term success as an eBay seller.

Is Customer Loyalty All It's Cracked Up to Be?

According to the Gartner Group research firm, American businesses spent more than $1 billion on customer loyalty programs in 2003. Other research found that customer loyalty programs weren't necessarily effective at increasing how much loyal customers spent, but they were effective at helping companies build loyal customers who would continue to buy at their current spending levels.

Customer loyalty programs don't have to be fancy, and they don't have to cost a lot. But they do need to deliver on what they promise. They also have to offer something that your customers will find valuable. If they don't, they're a waste of everyone's time and a waste of your money.

Before embarking on a customer loyalty program of your own, be sure of the following:

1. You know who your best, most loyal customers are. They should be the primary focus of your attention. This means having a system in place that tracks who they are, how often they shop with you, what they buy and how much they spend.

2. You're providing superlative customer service to all of your buyers. A customer loyalty program will not make up for things like slow shipping and poor communications.

3. You can afford the costs of a customer loyalty program. You need to offer something of value, and this typically costs at least a little bit of money. Be sure your profit margins are strong enough to cover your expenses. You don't want to be caught short and unable to follow through on what you promised.

Showing You Care

Customer loyalty programs don't earn or build loyalty—they only enhance it. You have to earn your customer's loyalty yourself by doing things right. If you don't, even the best customer loyalty program won't repair the damage caused by your sloppy business practices.

Part of doing things right is showing your customers that you care. Not just telling them, showing them. This includes basic things like communicating with them well and mailing their merchandise quickly and securely. It also means paying attention to the finer points of your transactions with them. Doing so will help you learn more about the people who buy from you and help you tailor your offerings to them.

This last point is crucial. While it's possible to have a one-size-fits-all customer loyalty program to a certain extent—you can offer everyone things like free shipping, shipping upgrades, or discounts on purchases over a certain amount—targeting your offerings to your customers' individual likes and/or needs will add a personal dimension that can set your programs apart from the others.

Targeting your offerings will add significant value to your customer loyalty program. You won't be wasting your time and resources on perks and benefits your customers aren't interested in. Instead, you'll be spending them on things they do value. In so doing, you'll be showing them that you cared enough to take the time to find out what they're all about.

How can you get this information? Some of it comes through analyzing your sales. This sounds complex, but it doesn't have to be. Chances are you can pull this information from the systems you already have in place.

The following examples compare the customer loyalty programs of two eBay sellers. One took the time to analyze buying patterns to build his customer loyalty program; the other didn't. The examples are from the front line—the buyer's perspective. Some details have been changed for privacy reasons.

❝I've bought incense from Seller #1 for about four years now. There are many sellers who offer the same products for about the same price, maybe a little more or less, but I've never found a reason for switching, even though he ships a little slow sometimes. After I had bought from him for about a year, he started including an extra box of my favorite incense with some of my orders, even if I didn't order it that time. The first time he did it, I thought he had made a mistake, but no, he continues to send a box along now and again. Every so often he includes a sample or

The Importance of Really Getting to Know Your Customers

In the May 2000 issue *Inc.* magazine, John J. Kilcullen, the creator of the popular series of *Dummies* how-to books, discussed how even large companies like his can make major missteps when it comes to knowing what their customers like and want. Kilcullen told the author of the article that the biggest mistake they made was not collecting relevant data about the company's customers from the beginning. They collected data from using mail-in cards bound in the books, but the cards didn't ask for much beyond the basics. As Kilcullen put it, the company didn't ask buyers how they felt about buying books that described them as "dummies." As a result, some of the company's earliest efforts failed. Had he collected this kind of data, "we might have developed new products more efficiently and achieved more cost-effective and targeted direct marketing."

two of something he thinks I'd like. Sometimes he's wrong, but I've ordered a few things off those samples. He also sends me a flyer in each shipment with information on new products and sales, and he always handwrites 'namaste' at the bottom. 🙙

This seller might not know a lot about this particular customer, but he does know that she likes a particular type of incense and that she buys it enough to make it worth his while to send her a complimentary box of it every so often. But he waited a year before sending the first box. By that time, her buying patterns were well established, which told him she was pleased and would probably continue with him.

He also knows enough about her to send her samples of other types of incense. His selections aren't always a hit, but they have resulted in increased orders.

If this seller has a formal program, he hasn't pitched it as such. Maybe his research has shown him that programs like this turn his customers off. But he clearly has some sort of an incentive-based customer loyalty program that kicked in after this buyer reached a certain purchase level, and it's paying off.

Now for Seller #2:

❝**A few years ago, I** was the buyer in an eBay transaction that, sadly, looked great on the front end but turned bad the second the auction ended. For starters, the seller didn't respond to any of my e-mails after the sale. Just sent me your basic invoice. However, that didn't worry me too much, as I was dealing with a PowerSeller who had hundreds of transactions weekly, so I went ahead and sent payment via PayPal.

"A week passed. No word from the seller. No package. Then I notice the seller is starting to rack up negs. Still, I'm not that worried. I didn't spend much on the item—a couple of bucks. If the transaction went bad, so be it.

"Finally, on the tenth day after the auction ended, I got the item. It came in packaging so torn and beat up that it looked like it had been around the world and back. I checked the mailing date—just a couple of days previous, so much for shipping in three days, like his auctions promise—and opened it up to find that they had sent the wrong thing.

"I e-mail the seller. Another week passes. Then, out of the blue, I received another package with the item I had bought. Also in the package was a flyer, poorly worded and riddled with misspellings, welcoming me to the seller's frequent buyer program and offering me free shipping on my next order.

"As if! At that point, I'd do anything in my power to find someone else to buy from, even though his prices are good and he sells other things I can use. ❞

While you could give this seller the benefit of the doubt, as everyone's entitled to a bad day or two (or more), so many things are wrong here that it's hard not to conclude that this is standard operating procedure for this individual. For starters, communications were poor throughout the transaction. The buyer didn't receive his win until days after it should have arrived, and when he finally received the merchandise, it wasn't what he ordered.

On the plus side, the seller acted appropriately by immediately sending the correct item without asking for the other one back (reimbursing shipping both ways outweighed the profit he would make on such an inexpensive item), but again, there were no communications between seller and buyer to let the buyer know what was happening. Finally, the seller showed no knowledge of the buyer's purchasing habits by sending him a promotion for a frequent buyer program—it was the buyer's first purchase, and it wasn't for all that much to begin with. The seller probably did it to help make up for all the missteps along the way, but, as you can see, it had far from the desired effect.

Keeping in Contact

One of the best ways to keep in contact with your client base is through an e-mail marketing campaign. Setting one up will let you send updates about sales, store promotions, new items—you name it.

Doing an e-mail marketing campaign requires the following:

➲ Putting together mailings with value. The best combine a special offer—maybe a shipping incentive or a discount on purchases—with news and information of interest to your customers.

➲ Letting your customers know about your program.

➲ Giving them a chance to say yes or no. This step, called "opting-in," is required by law.

You can accomplish the second and third bullets on this list by promoting your mailings in your after-sale e-mails to your buyers and including a link at the end of the message where they can ask to be put on your mailing list.

If you decide to open an eBay Store, you can use eBay's E-mail Marketing Program, which takes care of most of this for you. However, you'll trade ease of use and convenience for personalization. The e-mails will show featured items with pictures, lists of what's in your store, personalized messages, articles, and other elements of your choosing. You can target your mailings to a certain extent, as the system will let you customize up to five different messages. However, since the program is eBay's, the overall message is also strongly eBay oriented. If you sell on other sites, this might not be to your liking, but it might be a way to get a program started, especially if you're short on time and resources.

"Have I Got a Deal for You"

Reward programs are the oldest and best-known customer loyalty programs. They've lasted because they work, but some are definitely better than others. The best programs do the following:

- Provide an incentive for signing up
- Tell customers what they'll earn if they make repeat purchases
- Offer rewards customers want
- Make rewards easy to earn
- Give customers the chance to earn more rewards as they buy more
- Offer customers rewards for referring new customers

Whatever program you put together, make sure you think it through carefully and base it on what you know about your customer base. Pick rewards that match their wants and needs. Make your program clear and easy to understand. Stay away from concepts based on surprises or that try to build suspense or excitement. They're hard to manage well, and they're usually anticlimactic.

Finally, test-drive the program before you launch it. Ask friends for feedback, or throw it up for discussion on one of eBay's Discussion Boards.

Warranty Programs

Standing behind your products is a great way to build customer loyalty, but it can be tough to do when you're a small business with limited resources. It can be really tough to do if you're selling one-of-a-kind items, which are bread and butter for many eBay sellers. On items like these, you're pretty much limited to value replacement warranties—if there's a problem, you either reimburse the buyer a certain amount or try to find the same or similar item as a replacement.

▶▶If you sell in certain categories—computers, photography, consumer electronics, or musical instruments—you can offer warranties through eBay's Service Plan protection program. This program, which is administered by N.E.W. Customer Service Companies, Inc., covers new, used, and refurbished products for one year after purchase. The latter items must be less than five years old and in working condition when sold.

There are two different plans—the Standard Service plan or the Extended Service Plan. It's a free program for sellers; the cost to buyers is based on how much they pay for the items they buy.

Participating in the program can be a good thing for your buyers, and it can put some extra money in your bank account, too. Program participants get paid when their buyers opt for a service plan, and receive 25 or 50 percent of the final value fee, depending on how much items sell for.

Managing Customer Lists

Whether you use eBay's e-mail marketing program or you put together your own, you should build your own customer list. Some auction management programs offer this function, and it's worth looking for when you're shopping these programs. You can also build it yourself by capturing buyer information and entering it into a simple spreadsheet program or a contact management program such as ACT!

Using Lists to Bring Customers Back

If you have a fair number of inactive customers on your list, try doing a special e-mail to them to see if you can bring them back into the fold. Target your message specifically to these buyers. Tell them you've noticed that they haven't bought anything from you for a while. Ask them if there's a reason. Maybe you're not meeting their needs. Maybe you did something that displeased them. Give them a chance to vent.

> ## Keeping Little Problems from Becoming Big Ones
>
> Business owners sometimes shy away from the negatives of doing business, and dealing with unhappy customers is definitely one of them. Sometimes they simply don't want to face reality. Sometimes they're not sure how to handle the information once they get it, and they don't know how to get the help they need, so they keep putting it off. Or they figure their disgruntled customers are in the minority, so they don't have to worry about them. Whatever the reason, not tackling problems as they arise can lead to minor concerns becoming major ones, and they can seriously undermine your success. Addressing issues like disgruntled customers head on is the best course of action. Yes, it can be painful, but here's the truth: Problems never go away on their own. And they usually get worse over time.

Most customers don't bother to complain. They just go somewhere else, and when they do, they're often more than happy to tell their friends and family why they did. When it happens, you're not only losing those customers, you're losing all the business they could have referred to you.

Asking customers about their experiences dealing with you and being prepared for hearing things that could be upsetting is one of the best ways to show that you care. Most businesses don't take the time to find out why they lose customers. Doing so can leave a lasting impression with your customers that money simply can't buy.

When Good Addresses Go Bad

When you're dealing with e-mail mailing lists, it can be difficult to tell when good addresses go bad. Some e-mails might bounce back to you as undeliverable, but most will simply go into abandoned e-mail accounts. Every so often, go through your list and cull out the addresses you know are bad. But don't give up on the others. Assume that your mailings are going through unless you know for sure that they aren't.

▶▶ Test Drive

As you operate your business, consider the following questions:

1. Are you doing everything you can to show your customers that you care? What ideas from this chapter and from the comments of eBayers in Chapter 16 could you incorporate into your practices?

2. Think about how you handle your communications. Is there room for improvement?

3. How about shipping? Are you getting auction wins into the hands of your customers when you say you will?

Communications and shipping are two key areas where a lack of attention can quickly erode your customer base. If you're offering the same goods and you're not getting repeat business, it's time to take a look at what you might be doing to keep it away.

Selling "You"

Branding is something that you might associate more with what major corporations do when they launch new products. But the same approach they take—stamping their identity on their products so indelibly that you forever equate the product with the company, and vice versa—can be applied to your eBay business and result in increased sales and a healthier bottom line.

Branding is hardly a new concept, but it's one whose power many eBay sellers either don't realize or don't know how to harness. It's not all that difficult, but it does take some time and effort to learn how to do it right. When you do, you can use branding to define who you are and why buyers should seek you out.

In the online world, and especially if you're competing against a bunch of other people who are more or less doing the same thing you are, branding is more about building a name for yourself and showcasing what sets you apart from the others. In other words, the product you're branding is you. Your brand describes the added value that you bring to the equation, which is the reason why people would want to pick you over someone else. Through branding—or perhaps better put, self-branding—you can transform who you are and what you are into a valuable commodity that is yours and yours alone.

Getting Past "I Can't Market Myself"

Some people—maybe you're one of them—think self-branding is egocentric. Others see it as phony or manipulative. Taken to the extreme, branding can be all of this. To avoid it becoming so, it's important to get a feel for the boundaries—the lines between doing enough self-promotion and too much of it, and to work within these boundaries at whatever level is comfortable for you.

Most people err on the side of doing too little self-promotion, not too much. This happens for a number of reasons. They might think it's prideful or that they'll alienate people if they're too boastful. Some people are simply uncomfortable about drawing more attention to themselves. But here's a good reason why you shouldn't follow suit: If you don't brand yourself, others will do it for you, and you might not like what they come up with. So why not take matters into your own hands and establish your brand exactly the way you want it to be?

You As a Brand

Many people don't realize that who they are—how they look, talk, their skills, their experience, the entire package—not only distinguishes them from others but is also their greatest asset. When you realize the inherent value in what you are as a person, you can use that value to benefit both yourself and your business.

Branding Versus Identity

Many business people equate branding with identity, but the two concepts are different. Identity is the set of characteristics that are recognized as belonging uniquely to a certain thing—a person, a product, a company. As an example, your identity is your name, what you look like, the way you talk, the color of your hair and eyes, what you do for a living, and so on. Online, things like your logo, your auction layout, your description on your "About Me" page, and your product photos, among others, are what will establish your identity.

In contrast, your brand is your expertise, your reputation, what you bring to the table, and what people value about you. Your identity is used to build your brand, but your brand is not used to build your identity.

Identity comes first; brand follows. Identity is the "what." Brand is the "how." Branding speaks to what people think of when they see or hear your name.

This can be a difficult concept to grasp at first, and the difference between the two concepts can seem fairly narrow. But there definitely is a difference. Once you get the feel for it, you'll start to identify branding when you see it, and you'll start thinking more along the lines of branding than identity. When you do, your marketing efforts will be brand based rather than product based—in other words, you'll be selling people on why they should choose you, not just on the products you offer—which is the key to long-term success as an eBay seller.

The following chart illustrates the difference between identity and brand:

Product or Company	Identity	Brand
Lexus	Car manufacturer	High-end luxury vehicles
McDonald's	Fast-food vendor	"You deserve a break today"
Microsoft	Software developer	Ruler of the world
Liz Claiborne	Clothing manufacturer	Office and casual attire
You	eBay seller	??????

To further illustrate this concept, try this simple test: Pick three eBay sellers whom you've bought from in the past or whom you simply admire for how they run their businesses. What's the first thing that comes to mind when you think about them? Chances are, it's going to be what you bought and how the transaction went, not the wording in their e-mails to you. In other words, the brand comes first. If it's one they've worked to establish, that's what will come to mind. If they haven't established a brand, then you're going to assign them one based on your beliefs and experiences with them.

Branding Challenges

On eBay, it can be difficult to establish a brand based on the specific items you sell, especially if you're a generalist who lists in a variety of categories and your offerings are never quite the same from one week to the next. Thus, your branding will be based less on what you sell and more on the value you bring to your transactions—your expertise, your customer service skills, and so on.

Branding as a Promise

Some marketing experts describe branding as what the product promises to deliver—its intangible value based on tangible characteristics. In other words, it's what people stand to gain should they use the product and what would drive them to choose the product over its competition. To be successful, the product must deliver on the promise.

Setting Yourself Apart from Other Sellers

Branding is one of the best ways to give yourself an edge over other sellers. This is true regardless of the categories you sell in, but it's especially important if you're selling in highly competitive categories that are flooded with merchandise. Even if you're offering items that might be a little different from the others, you're still competing with the other sellers around you who are selling the same or similar products.

Just about anyone can sell on eBay, but can they do it quite like you? Absolutely not, and that's what branding reinforces. There's a huge difference between just selling and bringing the something extra to the table that makes buyers pick you.

Building Your Brand

Everything you do to establish your identity as an eBay seller should be geared toward establishing your brand. When you think and act like your brand, you'll create and maintain the demand for your most important product—you.

The most effective branding campaigns are based on two basic factors: the conditions of the market you're in or wish to enter, and what you'll do to become a player in it. Marketing experts recommend conducting a market analysis as the first step in launching your branding campaign. This calls for taking a close look at the market to determine what opportunities and challenges lie ahead. Doing so can help you tailor your branding more closely to market needs, but it isn't 100 percent necessary. However, if you do, it can help you create a market niche that, once again, distinguishes you from other sellers and that buyers identify with you. (More on this later.)

If you do take this approach, you'll want to focus on the following factors:

- The market's current conditions
- What you think might happen to it in the future
- Market needs that aren't being met
- Problems that need solving

Next, conduct a self-review and consider the following:

➲ Your past accomplishments. These are the foundation of your brand, and they're part of what you'll use to position yourself strategically in the marketplace.

➲ Your strengths

➲ Your weaknesses

➲ How you think you measure up against your competition in general

▶▶**Don't keep your analysis in your head; write it down. Seeing, as they say, is believing!**

When you're done with this analysis, you should have a list of your key attributes and resources. Zero in on the ones that you think set you apart from the others and that you can use to distinguish yourself in the marketplace. These are what you'll use to build your personal brand identity, the unique identity that sets you apart but that also adds value to the marketplace.

The following is an example of this process. It's based on a seller in the collectibles category who feels she has a good personal brand but hasn't capitalized on it well in the past.

Here's her market analysis:

Current conditions: Very competitive, have been for years. Competition has driven down prices in some areas; inexperienced sellers have further diluted value in the marketplace.

What the future might hold: More of the same, unfortunately. However, based on talks with antiques dealers at trade shows, meetings of a local collector's group, what I've read, etc., I think that mid-century modern pieces, which are hot now, will continue to gain in popularity and value.

Needs that aren't being met: There's a whole category of buyers out there who like the looks of these pieces but don't know the first thing about them. They need educating to understand value, what to look for, etc. There are also a bunch of sellers who are throwing anything that looks to be of this era up at auction and calling it such. Buyers need to know what's real and what's not so they can avoid these sellers.

Problems that need solving: Educating the uneducated. Meeting the demands of the collecting audience in this category.

And here's her personal analysis:

Strengths: I've collected mid-century modern items for years. I know it and I like it. I'm an established expert in certain collectibles categories, and I have a loyal following in them. Some of my clientele are trend-watchers and are always looking for the next great thing.

Weaknesses: Don't have a lot of inventory to sell at this point; haven't established myself as an expert in this category as well as I could have.

How I measure up: Other sellers in this category often don't specialize in this era and are listing items without really knowing what they're doing. That said, there are a few sellers who have been at it for a while, are good, and have a loyal following.

This seller's next step, should she choose to go further, is to develop a branding plan. Similar to a business plan, this is a map of goals and objectives and how she'll achieve them. Once again, it should be written down. Not only does doing so often help bring new creative options to light, it also sets personal brand goals with a specific time frame and plan of action for achieving the goals. Here are some elements of a branding plan, based on this seller's analysis:

- **New business name:** Something that incorporates the area I want to focus on.
- **New logo:** Something that incorporates the mid-century theme.
- **New business cards:** Same reason.
- **Teach some classes on collecting mid-century modern pieces.**

- **Wear it:** Mid-century design is fun and funky. Wear it, and develop a reputation for wearing it. People will ask questions, one thing leads to another, etc., etc.
- **Live it:** Time to redecorate anyway. Time to pull out all the fun mid-century modern furniture I have.
- **Post to mid-century design boards:** eBay has one, need to see if there are others.

Over time, as this seller's branding program comes together, she'll come to be recognized as an expert, and others will seek out her expertise.

Are Two Brands Better than One?

Can you lead a dual existence and have two brands? Yes, but before you establish the new one, be sure you can devote the energy and resources to making it as good as your established one. This might mean boosting your knowledge and/or experience through additional studying; it might even mean taking some classes. Try not to rush the process. It's better to take your time and do it right, even if it means delaying the launch of your new brand for a while.

Using Words and Images to Develop a Strong Online Identity

Branding is often easiest if you gear your efforts toward establishing one from the get-go. That said, not all sellers have the kind of vision that allows them to cast their efforts out into what the future might hold. If you're the latter, don't feel like you've missed the boat when it comes to defining and establishing your brand. Branding can also be an evolutionary process.

When you do start the branding process, focus on the following:

1. Your seller ID: Does it define what you do, give buyers an idea of what you do? Or is it something you chose in haste because you were anxious to get going? Did it fit you at one time but

Making the Case for Branding

Branding is such a key element in establishing a lasting presence on eBay that at least one eBay seller has made a business of providing branding services to other sellers.

Lesley Feeney, a self-described "computer freak," has been offering her graphics services to sellers wishing to establish a recognizable Web presence since 2002. While she says she can't imagine why anyone would not want to do build a strong brand, she makes a strong case for why it's so essential. "Especially on eBay, when people are hearing horrible things about fraud, about being ripped off. When you have every single page branded with your logo, everything is familiar, people start to recognize you, they begin to get more comfortable with you. Even if people are just casually shopping and browsing categories, if they do it consistently, they'll say 'I recognize that person,' and they'll be more comfortable spending money with you."

Feeney, who has lost count of how many pages she's done, starts by asking clients a slew of questions—"kind of like getting a pop quiz in the mail. If they want a storefront, I ask them what kind of a logo, their favorite colors, graphics they already want to use. Most already have a store open, and have already selected their colors, so we work within that."

Contrary to what others might recommend, Feeney doesn't believe in spending money on a broad-based branding campaign right away. "I wouldn't waste my money unless I was sure I had a viable eBay business. There's so much competition out there. Before spending money branding, get into selling, make sure you know what you want to do, be sure you have a niche. I had someone e-mail me just yesterday wanting me to help build his site. He has ten feedbacks, five items in his store, and no selling experience. No one's going to go there; I told him he needs to get selling some things, get your feedback up, don't waste your money if you don't need to."

not now? You can change your User ID. Many sellers have done so without any loss of business.

2. Your store name: Ideally it should fit in well with your User ID, but not necessarily be identical. Think about the fit, and think about choosing a name that's an extension of your User ID and that will further define your brand identity. You'll find more information on choosing a store name in Chapter 20.

3. The look and feel of your auction listings: Images and copy should match your branding approach throughout.

4. Your "About Me" page: Many sellers overlook or forget about their "Me" pages for various reasons. Remember, buyers don't have that many ways to learn what you're all about. "Me" pages are prime real estate for building your brand, as you can say just about anything you want to on them. It's okay to do some bragging here, even if it embarrasses you a little (or a lot). Remember, you're doing it for the brand!

The most important point here is the need to keep branding. When people see your eBay store, your Web site, or your "About Me" page, they should immediately be able to get a sense of who you are, what you are, and why they should care.

Creating a Market Niche

One of the things that branding can do for you is help you establish a market niche that can possibly be uniquely your own. Instead of being a generalist, you instead hone your appeal to a very specific group of buyers who come to you and no one else when they need things.

Taking the mid-century design seller as an example, it's possible that the category she wants to sell in might be flooded with other sellers offering similar merchandise by the time she jumps in. However, if she enters the arena with a solid branding plan that revolves around a specific facet of the category, she might be able to dominate this market segment to such an extent that it becomes hers.

The research you did on the front end might help you develop a niche, too. Did you discover clusters of buyers whose needs could be met more fully or served more effectively? Are you one of these buyers? Are your needs being fully met? If they aren't, there's a good chance there are others like you.

Networking with Other eBay Sellers

Putting yourself out there as an expert is a key element of branding. Participating on eBay's Discussion Boards, where you can both help others and learn from them yourself, is an ideal way to do this. Actively contributing to boards like these by posting informative and useful information spotlights you and your expertise. Do it consistently, and people will associate you with the information you offer. What's more, you'll leave behind a positive impression that enhances your brand.

You don't have to stop at eBay, either. Find other online forums that relate to what you sell. Build more relationships on them by being visible, offering up good information, and being helpful to other posters.

Making a Contribution

Active participation in groups, both online and offline, is one of the best things you can do to build your brand. Look for arenas where your contributions will pay off the most and where you can freely put your expertise and your experience to use. Be sure to offer helpful information; don't just use these forums for sales pitches. It's okay to talk about your accomplishments, too, but don't do so at the expense of contributing good information that's of value to others.

▶▶ Test Drive

Put together your own branding program using the tips in this chapter. Write down a few ideas for building your brand, such as these:

➲ Your logo.
➲ Your seller name. Does it support your brand or the brand you want to establish? If not, how can you fit it into your branding?
➲ Your offline efforts, such as print materials, networking, etc.

Advantages and Disadvantages

eBay puts a great deal of time and effort into making sure its new product offerings are going to be successful before launching them. It clearly did so prior to introducing eBay Stores in June 2001, as it was a genius move for a company noted for making many of them.

This selling format answered the needs of many sellers who wanted to make their eBay businesses seem more like, well, businesses, with a place buyers could go whenever they wanted, find things to buy, and not be constrained by the auction format. It also answered the needs of many sellers who wanted to establish their own selling sites online but lacked the time and resources to do so, and it also gave eBay itself an amazing ongoing revenue source. (More about this later.)

In a nutshell, eBay Stores are online selling sites just like any other. **▶▶In fact, if you set up your store right, your offerings will show up in search results just like those from other online shops.** This means that when people search on keywords that match what you sell, they'll be directed right to your listings. Not just to eBay, but *to your little (or maybe not so little) spot on eBay.*

This is one huge advantage over auction and fixed-price listings, which almost always expire before search engines can pick them up. Even better, you don't have to pay a penny more for this kind of visibility—your storefront, custom pages, store inventory listings, and your "About Me" page will come up in the search engines' unpaid search results, not as paid advertising links.

The big difference between eBay Stores and other online stores, of course, is that the former are under eBay's wing. As such, sellers who want to operate them have to play by eBay's rules. Also, they have to pay eBay's store fees, which are charged every month that the store is in operation. (At this writing, eBay does give sellers a one-month free trial so they can test-drive the store concept.)

Some eBay sellers view both factors as drawbacks, and they've been especially vocal about the monthly subscription fee, which was hiked from $9.95 to $15.95 for basic stores in early 2005. In the broader scheme of things, however, neither eBay ownership nor fees is that big an issue.

Dollar for dollar, there's no place on the Web where you can get an online commerce site up and running as quickly and cheaply and have the potential for drawing as many eyes as you can with an eBay store.

Spend enough time on eBay's discussion boards, and you'll see the "Should I or shouldn't I open a store?" discussion come up fairly often. To be honest, there's really no right or wrong answer to the question. It's more a matter of whether a store fits into your business plan.

Why You'd Want to Open an eBay Store

For many eBay sellers, the advantages to having an eBay store far outweigh the disadvantages. The following are just some of the pluses:

1. **Bigger profits:** According to eBay's research, store sellers realize an incremental increase in sales of 25 percent (on average) in three months after opening their store.

2. **Lower listing fees:** Individual item listing fees are less expensive than what you pay when selling items at auction. eBay charges just 2 cents a month for each store item, regardless of the selling price. Adding a Gallery image costs just a penny more. What's more, since insertion fees are based on listing duration, not on quantity, you can offer as many of the same items as you'd like in one listing and pay just the single insertion fee.

3. **Longer listings:** Listings last anywhere from a month to indefinitely. The "Good 'Til Cancelled" option lets you leave items in your store as long as you want for the same 2 cents per month insertion fee.

4. **Time savings:** Unlike auction, BIN, and fixed-price listings, you don't have to keep relisting unsold items in eBay Stores. The Good 'Til Cancelled option automatically renews listings every thirty days until items sell or you cancel the listings.

5. **Selling in the off-season:** If you carry seasonal items, why eliminate a potential source of revenues by yanking them off your shelves in the off-season? There's a reason why mega-retailers have Christmas-in-July sales and why department stores in cold climates carry things like swim suits year round. With eBay

stores, you can follow their lead and make it easy for shoppers to find products no matter what season it is.

6. **Parking the odd and unusual, or simply the unsold:** eBay stores are a little like stockrooms in retail stores, with one big difference—people can see inside them. If you've offered certain widgets a couple of times at auction and they haven't sold, you can keep them in your eBay Store for as long as it takes to sell them.

7. **Stocking fixed-price merchandise:** If it doesn't make sense to offer certain items at auction—the fees don't justify it or the competition's too steep—list them in your store instead. The fact that there's a ton of other widgets just like yours doesn't mean yours won't sell; someone browsing through your store might buy on impulse because they're there.

8. **More promotional opportunities:** As mentioned, eBay Stores can be found and indexed by search engines like Google, MSN, Yahoo, and others. This not only can drive more buyers to your store listings, it also puts your auction listings at their fingertips, as everything you list shows up in your store. Also, you can link your eBay store to other selling sites.

9. **Better sales analysis tools:** eBay includes Sales Reports Plus, which is a step up from the site's Sales Reports service that's free to any seller who subscribes to it, and to all store sellers as part of their monthly fees—it costs $4.99 a month if you don't have a store. Traffic Reports, which offer real-time reporting on things like page views and keywords used by buyers, is also free with a basic store subscription.

Finally, eBay offers Accounting Assistant, a QuickBooks-compatible accounting program, to all stores sellers. If you use QuickBooks for your business accounting, eBay's program will let you export eBay and PayPal transactions data directly to QuickBooks.

Why You Might Want to Think Twice

Surprisingly, a fair number of big sellers on eBay don't have stores, although more of them are adding this feature. Like other things eBay, once the ball gets rolling, it's hard not to want to jump on the bandwagon yourself. That said, ▶▶**eBay Stores are definitely not for everyone, and they might not be right for you.**

The biggest drawback to the eBay Stores concept is eBay's origin as an auction venue. It started out as one, it continues to be one, and research shows that this is the format that continues to attract the majority of shoppers to the site. This isn't to say that these individuals won't shop in eBay stores, but it's not their primary reason for being there. Since they're not drawn to the site to shop in the stores to begin with, chances are strong that they won't even know where or how to look for store listings. This one factor makes it imperative to run auctions when you have a store. If you don't, the chances of shoppers finding your store listings are significantly diminished.

Other drawbacks to eBay stores include these:

1. **The monthly fee:** Monthly fees eat into profit margins. If yours aren't where they should be, the hit might be more than you can afford. At the time of this writing, the fee for a basic eBay store subscription is $15.95 per month. This is next to nothing when you consider how much it can cost to design, build, and maintain an online commerce site. However, it does represent a fairly significant increase from the price that eBay charged when Stores was first launched, and there's no reason to think that it won't go up in the future.

2. **Higher final value fees:** Once again, you only pay these on the things you sell, but the fees are higher than what you'd pay on regular listings. However, promoting your eBay store in e-mails, print materials, and other Web sites can knock these fees down quite a bit—75 percent, in fact—when your promotions result in store sales. There are a bunch of technicalities to this program, which makes it difficult to discuss here; for more information, go to Seller Central>Stores>Stores Referral Credit.

3. **Not enough merchandise:** It doesn't make sense to open an eBay store unless you have enough product to stock it appropriately. While there's no magic number for the amount of items stores should carry, you should have enough inventory in your

store to make it worthwhile for people to shop with you, and your supply streams should be strong enough to keep your inventory levels steady over the long run.

4. Not enough experience: As mentioned, eBay doesn't require much to open a store. It makes sense for the site to set its requirements low—the fees are a nice long-term source of income for the company, and when it comes to fee income, numbers rule and the more the merrier. That said, if you haven't been selling on eBay long enough to really have it nailed, and you're not doing well with your regular auctions, there's no reason to believe you'll do any better when you stick stuff in a store. As eBay itself puts it: "We have found that higher volume and more experienced eBay users tend to get the best results from their eBay store."

5. Poor organization: You can't just dump a bunch of inventory into an eBay store and expect it to sell. You'll have to spend some time setting up your store, establishing your product categories—ideally, by keywords that will grab potential buyers when they're surfing the Internet—and then sort your merchandise in these categories. You can just put everything into the stores default category—Everything Else—but buyers aren't going to paw through hundreds of listings unless they really want what you have.

6. Goes against eBay's basic structure: As previously mentioned, eBay Stores are still fairly new, and lots of shoppers haven't figured out how to access them separately from auctions to shop for store inventory items. They will over time—eBay will make sure of that—but making eBay Stores an integral part of the eBay experience for these shoppers will take some time.

7. Less visibility for your items unless you do things right: eBay Stores merchandise typically won't show up when buyers do keyword or category searches. If you don't have auctions or fixed-price listings running to direct buyers to your store, they won't be able to find store items unless they know how to do store searches.

8. Can take more of your time: Again, just having an eBay store isn't the ticket to Easy Street. You have to spend some time on managing your store, marketing your store, and so on. You can't just take the "build it and they will come" approach. You have to show them—your current and potential customers—the way, and when they get there, you have to give them reasons for staying.

As mentioned, eBay's requirements for opening a store are fairly low, which also works against them to a certain extent. You'd like to think that having an eBay Store was a measure of one's success. But it's really not. All you have to have is a feedback score of at least twenty, ID verification, or a PayPal account in good standing, which just about lets everyone in, including a bunch of people who, to be completely frank, have no reason for being there. Looking at it from the buyer's perspective, how many poor excuses for a store would you want to wade through in hopes of finding a good one?

So you're not necessarily operating among the elite when you open an eBay Store. It's not a feather in your cap, a measure of your success, or of how good a seller you are. At the most basic level, it says you're willing to pony up the monthly fee. It's up to you to go beyond the basics.

When Plenty Becomes Too Much

While the table-of-plenty philosophy is definitely key to operating a successful eBay store, it's also possible to overwhelm shoppers with too much merchandise. It's okay to offer hundreds of items, but if you're going to do so, be sure to make it easy for shoppers to find things by keeping everything neatly organized. Separate items into categories the moment you open your store. Edit and add categories as necessary, always with an eye to making the shopping experience as enjoyable as possible for your customers. They might not come right out and thank you for it, but they'll appreciate it.

Why Thinking Like a Retailer Make Sense for eBay

Over the years, eBay has definitely tried to embrace more of an online retailer approach, which is what eBay Stores fits into. Why? While auctions are fun, and eBay wouldn't be the same without them, there's more money to be made from stores.

The monthly fees are a good ongoing revenue source for the company, and they provide it with a fairly predictable cash flow. While the basic store fee isn't that much, multiply it by 299,000—the approximate number of eBay stores the company said were in operation in the middle of 2005. That's nice cash flow. And that's just considering the basic store subscription fees. They go up from there—Featured Stores, which offers more exposure and branding opportunities, costs $49.95 a month; Anchor Stores, the venue for high-volume sellers who want maximum exposure, costs $499.99 a month. Add the listing fees, and the final value fees . . . you get the idea.

According to industry analysts, fixed-price sales in eBay stores, Half.com, and the Buy It Now auction format account for a little over a quarter of eBay's gross merchandise volume. They have nowhere to go but up, which is a good thing for eBay Stores sellers. With eBay Stores being such a huge economic driver for the company, it only stands to reason that eBay will continue to develop more incentives for sellers to operate them, and more tools to make it easier for them to do so. Still, it's hardly music to the ears of eBay's traditional constituency—collectibles sellers and others who are dead loyal to the auction format—since they're being left more and more behind as eBay puts more of its resources toward its retail concept.

Thinking Like a Retailer

Running an eBay store requires a shift in focus. Instead of thinking like an auctioneer, you'll have to think like a retailer. If you haven't worked retail before, this might not come easily. For starters, instead of researching appropriate starting prices and letting the auction process take over from there, you have to determine set prices for your items, as fixed pricing is the only option in eBay stores. Unlike auctions, there's no chance of items going up in price. If anything, you'll end up marking them down if they don't sell.

Second, you have to make sure your store is well stocked. As an auctioneer, it's okay to run just a few auctions at a time. It might not be the best approach, but it can and does work for many sellers. With retailing, on the other hand, the table-of-plenty philosophy is key. People simply prefer shopping in stores that are well stocked to those that aren't. This is so true, in fact, that when merchants have going-out-of-business sales, they often bring in merchandise from other sources to replenish their inventory until the doors close forever.

Finally, while it's always important to promote your eBay business, you absolutely have to invest time in marketing if you're going to operate an eBay store, as just opening one won't bring you more business. You have to drive buyers to it. Fortunately, eBay provides a number of tools for this, including the Stores E-mail Marketing program discussed in Chapter 18.

Choosing a Store Name

eBay's guidelines for store names follow many of the same guidelines and restrictions as eBay User IDs—for instance, they can contain letters, numbers, and some symbols, have to be at least two but no more than thirty-five characters long, can't be obscene or profane, and can't be an e-mail address or URL. However, eBay does allow a little more flexibility with store names. They can contain spaces and symbols like the ampersand ("&").

Many sellers simply use their User ID or a close variation of it as their store name. This is an acceptable approach, especially if they've had the name for a while and it's closely associated with them. But the better approach is to come up with a store name that extends your brand, and it's definitely the preferred approach if your User ID is more about you than it is about what you sell. Here's why. Your store name is searchable and will show up if it includes keywords that describe what you sell.

As an example, let's go back to barkandmew, our eBay seller from Chapter 6. Opening an eBay store is part of her business plan, so she needs to come up with a name for it. As User IDs go, hers isn't a bad one. It speaks (pardon the pun) to the market for what she sells—dogs bark, cats mew (well, okay, they meow, but she chose mew because it looked better). This

ID would work just fine as a store name, too. But does it do everything it can? Does it really tell people what she's all about? Is it flexible enough to allow for future growth if she decided she wanted to expand her offerings at some point in the future? Will it drive people to her store? Probably not.

Keeping these thoughts at hand, let's see if there are some better names to be had. How about these:

Barkandmews Spot: Frankly, this one doesn't tell anyone much more than her name does. Let's keep going . . .

Barkandmews Pet Treat Place: This is better than the first one, thanks to the alliteration—"pet" and "place"—but still not there. However, it would show up on pet-treat searches. Let's keep going . . .

Barkandmews Pet Treat Emporium: This name also tells shoppers what she's offering—pet treats. The use of the word "emporium" alludes to there being more than this in her store, but it's a hokey, somewhat cutesy word that tends to be a bit overused in general. Plus, it's a throwaway word—people don't search on it.

Barkandmews Pet Treat Store & More: Another nice name, with good swing—"store" and "more" rhyme. Again, it speaks to what she's offering, but this time she's coming right out and telling buyers she goes beyond pet treats. Store is another throwaway word, but people are more likely to search on it than they are on emporium.

Barkandmews Pet Toys Treats & Chews: This one's keyword heavy, so doesn't look as good, but does contain four good keywords—pet, toys, treats, and chews.

Remember to follow eBay's policies on keyword spamming when coming up with your store name, and only use keywords that reflect what you're selling. And, finally, keep the name as simple as you can without sacrificing keywords. You only get thirty-five characters, so you won't be able to go on for too long anyway. It's still best to do what you need to do concisely and simply, for one important reason: The name you come up with, minus punctuation and spaces, will become part of the URL that eBay will assign to your store, and it's always a good idea to keep URLs fairly simple.

Setting Up Your Store

As is the case with virtually every other part of the site, eBay has done most of the work involved in setting up an eBay store, which makes them extremely easy to get up and running. To get started, all you have to do is go to go to *www.ebaystores.com*. You can opt to take an audio tour that explains the process and walks you through it, or you can simply click on "Open Your Store Now" and follow the directions there. You'll be asked for the basics—payment information, business address, phone number, and the like. You'll also be asked for the following:

- **Business summary:** Basically, this is 250 characters on what you're all about that will tell shoppers why they want to buy from you. If you've done a business or branding plan, you should be able to draw this information from there if you don't want to start from scratch. That said, you can enter this information at any time; if you don't have words ready to go, you can come back to it later.

- **Store specialties:** Again, you won't get much space for this—200 characters—but it's more space for telling shoppers what you're all about. Be sure to include keywords that describe what you're selling.

- **Store categories:** Similar to standard eBay categories, categories here are what organize your store. However, you get to call the shots on the categories in your store. You can create your own categories and name them however you want. Since stores are searchable, you'll want to use keywords in your category titles that search engines will grab.

You'll also be able to choose from some basic store layouts and colors. Many sellers start with the basics and stay there, but eBay does allow a certain amount of customizing. If you've developed a unique look, you can—and should—pull it through to your store so you can make it a part of your brand.

Managing Store Categories

As mentioned, you can decide what you want your categories to be. Once you do, you'll sort your inventory into these categories to make it easier for buyers to find what they want.

When you set up your categories, include product keywords that will bring buyers in. Using our pet-treats-and-more seller as an example, here are some possible categories for her shop:

Pet Treats

Cat Treats

Dog Treats

Catnip Treats

Liver Treats

Puppy Treats

Kitty Treats

The names are a little repetitive and they overlap, but they also contain the keywords that buyers are most likely to search on. ▶▶**Store categories can be changed and updated whenever you want, and it's a good idea to keep an eye on them to make sure that they're doing all they can to bring buyers in.**

Promoting Your Store

By now you should have received this message loud and clear: Promotion is essential for success with eBay Stores. Fortunately, there are tons of ways to do this, both on and off the Internet. eBay provides a significant amount of help in this category as well, including cross promotion links on all Item, Bid Confirmation and Purchase Confirmation pages, and a link to eBay Stores on sellers' "About Me" pages.

On eBay, the following promotional approaches are key:

➲ **Always running regular auctions:** Auction listings include links to stores, which increases the chances of buyers finding them. Plus, you can use auction listings to cross-sell and up-sell additional items in your store. You can include up to four store items on item listing, Bid Confirm, and Purchase Confirm pages.

➲ **Including links in your e-mails to all buyers:** E-mail is the primary communication mode, remember?

➲ **Including a link to your store in your "About Me" page:** If you don't have one, you'll definitely want to build one if you open an eBay Store. Like other store elements, they're searchable.

Off eBay, don't forget these promotional approaches:

➲ If you have your own selling site, you can link to your eBay store.

➲ If you participate in other message boards, see if you can add your eBay store URL to your signature.

➲ Add your eBay URL to all e-mails, even those not related to eBay. You never know where your next buyer will come from.

Exchanging Links

Participating in a link-exchange program is another way to get your store in front of more eyes. While keywords are important, links rule. The more high-quality links you have, the greater the chances of your listings being picked up by search engines and of ranking well with them.

Several selling areas on eBay have link-exchange cooperatives. If you're not familiar with these, the place to start is the eBay Stores Discussion Board, which is also a great place for information on just about everything related to opening and running an eBay store.

Links In and Out

It's important to have links directing people to your store from other Internet sites and directing people from your store to other sites, too. Here's why: If you don't have any inbound links, search engines won't pick you up at all. What's more, if you have just a few in-bound links, and they're from low-ranking pages, you might get indexed, but you'll rank lower than you would if you had better-quality links.

Setting up links and submitting your URL to search engines can take a lot of time, but it definitely pays off. As one eBay seller happily reported:

❝Since I got my "About Me" page up and added the link exchange and submitted to Google and Froogle, my store page views went up overnight by over 100 percent *and* my traffic reports say that over 40 percent of my views did not come from eBay, but from other search engines. This is so cool! **❞**

eBay Store Promotions off the Internet

It's important to promote your eBay store in the real world, too. Be sure to add your URL to all of your print materials—business cards, flyers, advertisements, and so on. If you really want to get aggressive, get a magnetic sign printed up for your car and display your store address when you're driving around town. Don't miss a chance to drive people to your store.

▶▶ Test Drive

If you're thinking about opening an eBay store, ask yourself if it makes sense for you to do it. Be sure you can answer the following questions in the affirmative:

- ⮕ Can you keep enough auctions going to drive customers to your store?
- ⮕ Can you consistently offer enough same or similar merchandise to entice them to stay and buy?
- ⮕ Do you have enough time to market your store appropriately?
- ⮕ Are your profit margins high enough to cover the monthly subscription fee?

Understanding the Trading Assistant Program

eBay's Trading Assistant Program is one of the company's newer ventures. As the name suggests, it's designed to connect people with items to sell, but who don't want to do it themselves, with experienced eBay sellers—Trading Assistants, or TAs—who will do it for them for a fee.

Selling on consignment isn't new to eBay. In fact, a good number of sellers have done it for a long time and have based most, if not all, of their business on it with excellent results. The basic advantage of this approach is pretty obvious—pocketing profits without investing in inventory. This is what auction houses and consignment shops have done for years as well.

In recent years, brick-and-mortar shops have sprung up that specialize in eBay consignment sales. The Trading Assistant program lets eBay sellers go head to head with these shops, either by operating as a Trading Assistant or as a Trading Post, which is the same program taken up a few notches.

Why would someone want to consign their items to someone else to sell instead of doing it themselves, especially when they have to give up a fairly large chunk of the money they could make doing so? You might enjoy selling on eBay, and doing it might seem second nature to you, but there are still many people to whom eBay is an absolute mystery and who want nothing to do with it. There are also people who are computer savvy enough to do eBay, but they don't have the time and/or the patience to manage auctions themselves, or they don't want to do the research or deal with the other aspects of selling on eBay.

Sellers Hiring Sellers

While it might seem like the Trading Assistant program is geared more toward meeting the needs of people who are not eBay users and have no interest in being such, this is far from the truth. You can also use the program to your advantage and hire TAs to sell merchandise you don't want to handle yourself.

Program Requirements

eBay states that the Trading Assistant program is for experienced sellers. However, the requirements for becoming a TA are fairly basic. All you have to do is the following:

➲ Sell at least four items in the month prior to joining the program
➲ Have a feedback score of at least fifty
➲ Have at least 97 percent positive feedback
➲ Be in good standing with eBay (in other words, current on your fees and not under suspension for some other infraction)

If you're a high-volume eBay seller, and you're willing to offer staffed drop-off locations or storefronts with regular hours, you might qualify as a Trading Post, which is basically the same program with a few enhancements. Prospective clients can search specifically for TAs that are Trading Posts, and Trading Posts can receive priority placement in search results. Plus, Trading Posts show up with a special Trading Post icon next to their User ID.

The requirements for being a Trading Post are more stringent than those for Trading Assistants, and include the following:

➲ Feedback greater than 500
➲ At least 98 percent positive feedback
➲ Monthly sales on eBay of at least $25,000

Most sellers—probably you, too—would consider the requirements for being a basic Trading Assistant far from reflecting the level of experience that would constitute a professional eBay seller. This is a concern that eBay has pondered as well, and there has been talk of raising the minimum feedback score to 100 and of requiring PowerSeller status for program participation. But it's important to look beyond the surface here.

Remember, you can have multiple seller accounts on eBay. While it's best to become a TA after you've been running your own auctions for a while and you feel comfortable doing them, the current guidelines definitely take into consideration seasoned sellers who might want to establish separate seller accounts specifically for their Trading Assistant business. As such, the guidelines as currently stated allow these sellers to get up and running fairly quickly.

There are some advantages to establishing separate seller accounts, with one of the biggest being able to protect your feedback on your other seller IDs. Even if the items you're selling aren't your own, you're the one selling them, and all feedback—good, bad, or indifferent—will go on your ID. This is something to consider carefully, especially since you might have less control over certain aspects of your TA transactions than you would with things you own.

If you feel you're ready to become a Trading Assistant, and you meet eBay's requirements for the program, you're good to go. All you have to do is go to the Trading Assistant area on eBay *(http://pages.ebay.com/ tradingassistants)* and follow the directions there, which include creating a profile in the Trading Assistants Directory. You'll find some tips on writing your Trading Assistant profile later in this chapter.

Program Fees

At this time, there are no charges for the Trading Assistant program beyond those for listing and selling. However, this could change in the future, as eBay states that it reserves the right to charge for listings in the Trading Assistants Directory. Like anything you sell on eBay, you'll still be responsible for listing and final value fees.

Advantages and Disadvantages

Some of the Trading Assistant program's biggest advantages are also its biggest drawbacks, making it imperative to carefully consider both sides before signing up.

One of the program's most obvious benefits is the ability it gives you to use your expertise as a seller to make money without having to buy inventory. Since inventory acquisition is often a large part of the cost of selling on eBay, this can eliminate a big chunk of your overhead and boost your bottom line in a hurry.

The flip side of this is one of the program's biggest drawbacks, or, better put, can be a big drawback. Since you're not buying the inventory yourself, you have to find people with items to sell or put systems in place that will help them find you. Yes, they can search the Trading Assistant Directory, but, to be honest, if they're not familiar with eBay to begin with, chances are slim they'll even know it exists or how to find it. ▶▶**When you become a Trading Assistant, you can add the TA logo to your own eBay listings,** which can be another way in which consignors might be able to find you. However, once again, they have to be at the site to do this.

Second, you'll have to deal with these people, and their expectations. They might be realistic. Then again, they might not be. If they've fallen prey to the Antiques Roadshow syndrome, they might think their possessions are worth a great deal more than they really are. Having to deliver a big reality check to these individuals might not be something you want to do, especially if they're convinced they know more about their goods than you do. It can be beyond frustrating, not to mention a waste of your time and money, to meet with a consignor who has wonderful pieces but unrealistic expectations of what they will bring on eBay.

These are just a couple of factors to think about. Let's take a look at some others, starting on the positive side of things with advantages:

1. **Increasing your visibility:** Becoming a TA is another way to promote your eBay business in general.

2. **Establishing yourself as an expert:** Ideally, you'll already have expertise in the areas you want to recruit clients in, but being a TA can help you spread the word that you are an expert in these areas.

3. **Partnering up:** If you want to work with someone else, consignment sales offer a great opportunity to do so. You can set this up any number of ways—by specialty, by area of expertise, you name it.

4. **Working with merchandise other than what you'd typically come across:** Kind of like real estate agents who get to show properties they'd never be able to afford themselves, you might get the opportunity to sell things that you wouldn't have the resources to acquire on your own. If you've always dreamed of

being in the same room with a piece of California Impressionist art or a Regency tea service, you just might get the chance.

5. **Expanding your business:** If you're thinking about taking on additional selling categories, accepting consignments in these categories can be a great way to test the water.

And now for some disadvantages:

1. **Finding consignors:** On the face of it, the TA program might seem to be driven by buyers looking for people to sell for them. However, this is far from the truth. If people don't know how to sell for themselves on eBay, they probably don't know how to find TAs. It's a good idea to plan on finding most of your consignors yourself, not on getting them through eBay.

2. **Paying higher promotional costs:** To expand further on the previous point, just being listed in eBay's Trading Assistants Directory isn't enough. To really work the program so it delivers maximum benefits, you'll have to promote yourself. eBay provides some tools for this, including flyers, pre-built ads and direct mail pieces, but you'll have to pay for your promotions yourself, at least for the most part. eBay also makes available co-op advertising funds that can be used to offset up to 25 percent of ad placement costs, should you choose to go this route.

3. **Trading in uncharted waters:** You can and should specify your areas of expertise in your TA profile. Still, don't be surprised if you get requests from people asking you to sell items you're not familiar with. This could put you on the horns of a dilemma, especially if it's something you'd like to sell and you'll potentially make a nice profit selling it.

4. **Increased liability:** If you're going to physically take possession of other people's goods, it can increase your risks if something happens to them. To protect yourself, you can include language in your contract limiting your liability, but you might also have to do things like increase your

Minding the Law

If you're thinking about establishing an eBay Trading Assistant business, be sure your plans line up with the laws and statutes where you live. Many areas regulate consignment businesses, which the TA program definitely is. Some states are also considering legislation to require Trading Assistants to get auctioneer's licenses. If they don't, they'll have to stop selling on behalf of others.

Make sure your operation will be legal by checking local and state laws. If necessary, hire an attorney to work with you. It's also a good idea to have a legal expert review your basic contract to make sure you're covering all the bases for yourself and your consignors.

insurance coverage to really be safe. If you don't take possession of items when you sell them, you also open yourself up for liability if they're not as you describe them.

5. **Legal issues:** Consignors might try to foist stolen goods on you, which could cause significant problems for you, but probably not for the consignor, who will likely be long gone by the time people start flashing badges at you.

6. **A more complex business:** Selling for others requires keeping meticulous track of everything—their auctions, your communications with them, payments, and so on. If you end up with a good number of clients and lots of things to sell, you'll definitely need to use an auction-management program—either from eBay or a third-party developer—to keep everything in order.

Before you jump into the TA program, carefully weigh the advantages and disadvantages. If you're not good at dealing with the quirks and foibles of your fellow man, you're not all that organized, and marketing really isn't your thing, it might not be a good fit for you. But, as mentioned, you can even get around these factors if you want to. Partner up with someone with better customer relations or marketing skills. Let that person be your frontman—the individual in charge of finding and handling consignment customers and promoting the business in general. You do the rest.

Determining Fees and Terms

Selling for others requires a more formal approach than when you're just operating on your own behalf. You have to tell your clients what it's going to cost to have you sell for them, and you have to agree on the terms of your agreement. Both factors are essential elements of doing business as a TA and are necessary for protecting the interests of both parties.

What to Charge

There are two basic approaches for determining the fees to charge on consignment goods: percentage and flat rate. Many TAs choose one approach and basically stick to it. Others vary their fees based on what they're selling—the type of item, the size, the price, and so on. Typical percentage fee rates range from 10 to 50 percent, with the average being around 30 percent. Another percentage approach is a graduated scale where the percentages go down as the sale prices go up.

Flat-rate fees typically run between $10 to $20 per auction. Some sellers charge a fairly low flat rate—say $5—as a minimum fee plus a percentage of realized prices. Secondary fees for additional services are often added as well.

Fees can be based on the gross selling amount or on the net amount after eBay and other fees are deducted. For simplicity, many sellers base their fees on the former approach and pay eBay and other fees from their commissions.

Whatever approach you take, be sure you charge enough. Don't underestimate what you're bringing to the table. ▶▶**If you don't set your fees high enough to cover your time and expenses, what you'll make on your sales won't justify your efforts.**

Coming to Terms

Before taking anything on consignment, you'll need to have a consignment contract in place that spells out the details of the transaction and specifies the responsibilities of all parties involved. Contracts can be extremely complicated, but they don't have to be. They do need to include the following elements at a minimum:

➲ **The basics:** This includes the name, address, and phone number of the consignor and the seller. Some sellers ask for the consignor's driver's license number. This isn't a bad idea. Consignors should be willing to let you see positive identification. If they aren't, they might be trading in stolen goods.

➲ **Date:** This is more important than you might think. Signatures aren't enough for a valid contract. It must also be dated.

➲ **Terms:** How long the contract will be in effect.

It is also important to explain the specific details of the consignment and auction process, including these:

➲ What the consignor will do, including bringing items to the seller, authenticating items, cleaning, and so on.

➲ What the seller will do, including inspection, research, photography, writing listing copy, collecting payment, paying fees, and so on.

➲ What happens when items don't sell. Options include returning to the client, donating to a local charity, or relisting.

In general, it's a good idea to keep contracts as simple as possible while including enough detail to protect both sides of the agreement. But don't sacrifice detail for simplicity. Make sure all bases are covered. Again, if you need help, find someone with experience in writing contracts—preferably an attorney or a qualified business consultant—to review your contract before you start using it.

eBay has a Trading Assistant Discussion Board that you should read through thoroughly before signing up for the program. Questions about contracts are frequently posted there. At the time of this writing, there's also a thread tacked to the top on contracts where some TAs have graciously posted their own contracts for others to use. There's tons of useful information here, directly from the front lines—the TAs themselves. Make it your second home, both when you're just looking into the program and when you join it, if you decide to.

Writing Effective Profile Copy

eBay provides a standard format for Trading Assistant profiles that includes the following:

- ⮑ Seller information, including user ID, feedback score, positive feedback, and how long a member
- ⮑ Contact information
- ⮑ Specialties and services, including drop-off hours (if offered), item pick-up information, and selling categories
- ⮑ Service description
- ⮑ Fees
- ⮑ Terms and conditions

Much of this information is boilerplate. But not all of it is, and you can—and should—use the parts that aren't to set yourself apart from the others if you're to participate in this program.

Anyone can sell on eBay, and just about anyone can be a Trading Assistant. However, your goal, if you want to really be successful at it, is to convince people to choose you over the others. To do this, you have to sell yourself, which means giving people reasons why they should pay you to sell their stuff.

To illustrate this point, let's say you're looking for someone to sell a roomful of old, possibly antique furniture that you recently inherited from your great aunt. You think you might have some pieces of value, but you're not entirely sure. After going through the Trading Assistant Directory, you've found two TAs who live in your area and handle the kind of items you have to sell.

Both of the following are real profiles, with some details changed for privacy.

Trading Assistant A

Service Description:

Trading Assistant A accepts consignments of new and used merchandise to sell at auction on eBay. Trading Assistant A photographs your items, writes a detailed description, posts your auction on eBay, and stores your merchandise in a secure area. Additionally, Trading Assistant A tracks your auction, answers all bidder inquiries, collects payment from the winning bidder, and then ships the item. After the auction, you will receive a check from us in the mail minus applicable fees.

Fees

Fees vary depending upon the quantity and price of the goods I will be selling for you.

Terms and Conditions

I have a standard contract that we will agree to, which will clarify our roles as Trading Partners.

This is an okay profile. It covers some basic points. But it leaves a lot to be desired, including these details:

- ⮌ **Specific expertise:** There's nothing to tell you why you'd want to choose this seller.
- ⮌ **Details on fees:** It isn't necessary to go into great detail here, but not including any information at all is a great excuse for consignors to go to the next person on the list.
- ⮌ **Details on terms and conditions:** Having a standard contract is to be expected. Again, the lack of detail here is good reason to go to the next TA.
- ⮌ **Lack of attention given to copy:** The copy switches midstream from third person (Trading Assistant A) to second person ("you") to first person ("I"). Makes you wonder how the listing copy will read, doesn't it?

Trading Assistant B

Service Description:

I am a retired retail antiques dealer and member of the American Society of Appraisers, with 20-plus years of experience in evaluating and marketing antiques and collectibles. I have a broad knowledge of antiques with an emphasis on porcelain. A member of the eBay community since 1998 with a 100-percent positive feedback rating, I will attend to every detail of your transaction from beginning to end!

Fees

I charge a flat rate of 30 percent of final sales price, and pay eBay and PayPal fees from this unless items fail to sell. If so, consignor will be charged eBay-related fees and a $25 handling fee. I do not accept consignments valued under $300. If reserve prices are desired, I will set them. Consignor will be issued a check or payment to PayPal account for the final sales price minus 30 percent within 1 day of receipt of payment by Assistant.

Terms and Conditions

Whether you have one item or an entire estate, please contact me by telephone or e-mail for an initial evaluation. A personal appointment can then be scheduled for a more thorough inspection. Upon agreement by all parties, I will provide a written contract outlining all terms and fees listed here. Formal written appraisals are also available.

This profile is heads above the other. Here's why:

- ➲ **Details on experience:** You know right away that you're dealing with a pro who knows the category well. Including information on membership in a professional organization relevant to what you're selling is always a good idea.
- ➲ **Details on fees:** Excellent description of fees. You know what to expect right away.
- ➲ **Details on terms and conditions:** Again, this TA has provided enough information for potential clients to make a valid decision.
- ➲ **Offers multiple payment options:** Your choice, check or PayPal.

In general, this profile is well written and professional, yet warm and reassuring in tone. Wouldn't you feel comfortable hiring this person?

That said, both of these profiles are missing a few key elements that you should include in yours if you sign up for the TA program:

➲ Whether you sell internationally
➲ Other venues you sell on, if any
➲ Storage and protection information for items you warehouse, if any
➲ Experience as an eBay seller, if you've sold on consignment before, and so on

As mentioned, your profile is just part of the battle. You'll also have to find consignors. However, this might not be as hard as you think. Here are some approaches to consider:

1. Placing ads in free shoppers, Thrifty Nickel publications, community newspapers.
2. Speaking to community groups, civic groups, and similar organizations about selling on eBay.
3. Sending out a press release announcing you're open for business.
4. Contacting local businesses to see if they have inventory they'd like to consign.
5. Making up special eBay TA cards. If you do this, make sure you carry them with you wherever you go. You never know when you'll run into someone who will want to learn more about your services.
6. Posting flyers with tear-off contact information on community bulletin boards, grocery bulletin boards, and other high-visibility areas.
7. Contacting senior centers, retirement homes, storage facilities, moving companies, and so on. They often need to dispose of items left behind due to changes in life circumstances.
8. Including a TA business card or flyer in auction wins.
9. Adding a line about your TA business to your e-mail signature.

Managing Trading Assistant Clients

If you're selling for a number of different consignment clients, it is imperative that you keep them separate and track their transactions separately.
This definitely calls for auction-management software. If you don't use it,
the chances of making mistakes on your client accounts are significant.

If you aren't already using an auction-management program, look into
programs like eBay's Turbo Lister and Selling Manager; the latter tracks all
stages of every auction as well as eBay and PayPal fees. There are a number of applications available from third-party developers to choose from
as well. You'll find a list of products to consider in Appendix Three.

▶▶ Test Drive

**As discussed in this chapter, becoming a Trading Assistant can
put a significant burden on your business.** Before you take this step,
take a serious look at the following:

1. Your business setup: Make sure your new venture will comply
with local and state laws.

2. Insurance: You might need more coverage if you're going to
take possession of and warehouse items.

3. Contracts: Make sure yours is iron-clad to protect both you and
the consignor.

4. Systems: If you're not already doing a good job of keeping
track of everything, put systems into place now and test drive
them for at lest three months before you become a TA. When
you're selling on behalf of others, you can't take the "tomorrow
is another day" approach. You have to stay on top of things.

Setting Up Your Own Web Site

Developing your own selling Web site might seem like the last thing you need to do if things are going well for you on eBay, but it's not. Doing so can be one of the best ways to improve your bottom line and ensure long-term success for your business.

Many eBay sellers own and operate e-commerce sites separately from eBay. They do so for two basic reasons. First, having a separate Web site is a great way to increase the visibility of their eBay business on the Internet. Second, sellers can use such a site to drive business to their eBay listings, and vice versa. What's more, they don't have to pay eBay's fees on anything they sell on their own sites.

Diversity Is a Good Thing

The old saying "Never put all your eggs in one basket" is another thing to think about here. While there's no reason to believe that eBay will ever be anything other than the predominant online commerce site that it is now, things do happen. If for some reason something catastrophic happened to eBay and the site went down for an extended period of time, your buyers could find you somewhere else.

Your eBay business might always be at the center of what you do online. Then again, it might not be. At some point, it might make sense to make it a part of your overall business plan, not the factor around which your business plan rotates.

Done right, there's a synergy between selling on eBay and selling on your own Web site that works extremely well for bolstering an online business. The key to this success, of course, is building your Web site right. Web sites—good ones, anyway—don't come easy. What's more, while Web sites do make sense for most businesses, they aren't for everyone. It's definitely not necessary to jump on the Web site bandwagon because "everyone has one."

Setting up a Web site and keeping it running can take a lot of time and money, especially if you don't know what you're doing. Not having a clear idea of what you want to accomplish with your site can also stall you out in a hurry. You can't just dump a bunch of inventory on a site. You have to manage it and market it just like you do with your eBay sales. Nor does it make sense to have a site if you can't stock it adequately. Remember, no one likes to shop in an empty store.

So spend some time thinking about why you want a Web site and whether it makes sense for you to have one before you jump in. If you're doing well on eBay, chances are that having another online spot to sell from will be a good idea at some point along the way, and most likely sooner than later.

The technical aspects of putting together a Web site are beyond the scope of this book. If you're interested in learning more about them, you'll find some information in Appendix Three. What's here are some basic strategies, things to think about, and points to keep in mind as you go through the process.

Setup Strategies

One of the most important decisions you'll need to make about your Web site is your level of involvement in it, both during the development phase and in the long run. Technology-savvy sellers with some Web-site design experience often like handling a lot of the nuts and bolts themselves, and you might want to do so as well. However, the better approach is to hire someone to do it for you unless you really know what you're doing and you like doing it. You're not in the "building and maintaining Web-site business," remember? Let someone who is handle this side of your business while you focus on doing the things you do well. You'll be glad you did.

Many people build their own sites—or try to—because they think they can't afford the money to have one professionally designed. Nothing could be further from the truth. Simple, entry-level Web sites from turnkey creation services can be very affordable. They provide basic layout and graphics options, you pop in your pictures and text, and away you go.

You will have to shell out a decent amount of money for a Web site that's custom-tailored to meet your needs, but most business owners will tell you that expense is worth it in the long run. If you're doing well, you'll outgrow turnkey solutions in a hurry, and it can cost you more money to move everything to a new site than it would have if you had started out with one with all the features you needed from the start.

Finding a Web-Site Design Company

If you've never had your own Web site, just finding a company to design it for you can seem daunting. Resist the temptation to go with the first company you find just to get things rolling. ▶▶**Do some shopping around, and talk to several companies before deciding.** Ask others for referrals to companies they've used. When you have a list, review their portfolios to see if you like their work. Talk to their clients—they should be more than happy to provide you with a client list. Check out their history—how long they've been in operation, if they've won any design awards, and so on. Finally, make sure that their fee includes ownership rights to the completed site. In other words, when the work is done, you own it, not them.

Your Responsibilities

What you will need to do, at a minimum, is direct whoever puts together your site. In other words, you'll have to tell them what you want, and you'll have to stay involved in the process at some level until its complete. You'll also have to provide content—the text and images for your offerings, along with whatever else you decide to include on your site.

While the designer should come to the table with some ideas on how your Web site should be put together, the overall look and feel of your site and its content are your responsibility. It all needs to be geared toward the wants and needs of your buyers—both the ones you have now and the ones you hope to attract—and no one should know more about what they want and like than you.

By the time you find someone to design your site, you should be able to answer the following questions:

1. What do you want to do with your Web site? Most sites are set up to accomplish one or both of the following purposes—educating and selling. Since your primary business is selling, educating might not seem to fit here, but it does. When you're selling people on your items, you're also educating them. You're teaching them why they want to buy from you.

2. Who is your target audience? This includes both your current customers and people you want to turn into customers.

3. What kind of content should you include? This includes sales-oriented and educational images and copy.

4. What is your vision of your overall look and feel? Put yourself in your customers' shoes, and imagine your site from their perspective. What would they expect to see? Will a sleek, sophisticated approach work? Would down-home and homespun be better? Funky and fun? What might you be able to offer that your competition doesn't?

Regardless of the approach you take—do it yourself or hire out—your Web site needs to have the following elements at a minimum:

➲ **A well-designed, welcoming home page:** What buyers see here will determine their relationship with you from the get-go. You only get one chance to make a first impression; this page has to be as good as it gets.

➲ **Clear, easy-to-use site navigation:** Make sure that site navigation is on every page, ideally in the same place. It should look the same on every page, too.

➲ **Graphics that grab the eye but don't kill the connection:** Sites don't have to be graphically dense to be effective. Keep Flash and other animation elements to a minimum. Lots of people don't have high-speed connections. If pages take too long to load, buyers will go somewhere else.

➲ **Good, clear pictures and descriptions:** Your standards for your eBay listings should be no different for your own site.

➲ **Terms and conditions:** They're just as important here as they are on eBay. Don't go on for pages and pages, but do make sure you include what buyers need to know about payment, shipping, return policies, etc.

➲ **Well-organized product pages:** Think about how your buyers like to shop, and arrange things accordingly.

➲ **A little bit about you:** Like your eBay "About Me" page, telling buyers a little bit about yourself and your business is a great way to market yourself, build relationships with buyers, and build their confidence in you too.

➲ **Contact information:** At a minimum, include an e-mail address for buyer e-mails.

➲ **An easy-to-use shopping cart or checkout area:** Any snags in this area will quickly discourage buyers unless they really need what you want.

➲ **An opt-in area:** Not everyone who visits your site will buy something right away, but they might be interested enough in what you have to offer to sign up for your e-mail list so they can keep up with your product offerings. Put an opt-in link on every page.

Checking Out the Competition

One of the best ways to get a feeling for what you want your Web site to look like is to research what other online sellers are doing. Analyze their site design, functionality, look and feel, and content. Choose an item and walk through the buying process. Is the order form functional and easy to fill out? Does the shopping cart work correctly? Does the site make it easy to go back and revise orders, or do you have to start over every time you make a change?

Solo Versus Mall

Another decision to make is whether you want to have a completely freestanding site or if it makes more sense to set up a presence as part of an online mall. It typically costs more to develop stand-alone sites, as online malls usually have a footprint that you have to work with. There's no one best answer here; the approach you take needs to make sense for you and fit into your overall business plan. For sellers in certain categories, online malls—Ruby Lane is a well-known one, and there are others—can make a great deal of sense.

Maximizing Your Online Presence

The most successful Web sites are designed and operated in such a way that they garner top-dog position in the top search engines. This process is called optimizing, and again, it's something you can do yourself, but it can be a good idea to pay someone else to do it for you. To do it well, you have to keep on top of developments in the search engine industry, and you have to commit to spending a certain amount of time on it regularly.

Whether you optimize your site or have someone else do it, be sure to focus on the following:

Exchanging links: Keywords are used to drive search engines, and they're still important, but Web-site optimization today is based more on links. The quantity of links counts, but quality is important, too, as the search engines take both into consideration. Inappropriate links, or links to sites with weak content, will work against you rather than for you.

Keyword selection and placement: As mentioned, keywords are still important. If possible, your main keyword phrase should be part of your domain name. Don't include keywords that aren't relevant to what's on your site. It's keyword spamming, just like it is on eBay, and the search engines can penalize you for it by lowering your ranking.

Content-rich copy that includes your most important keywords: Make sure you include as many relevant keywords as you can in the details on the items you're selling as well as on all general content pages. Include as many variations of your keywords as you can think of. As an example, if you're selling baby blankets, "infant," "toddler," "pregnancy," and "twins" are just some of the keywords that people might search on. If you don't include them in your sales copy, you lessen the chances of grabbing these buyers.

Submitting your site to online directories like the Open Directory Project, Yahoo, and About.com should also be part of your optimizing strategy. Doing so will improve your rankings with the major search engines.

Using eBay's Web Store Services

One of eBay's newest service offerings is designed to help eBay sellers create their own Web-based stores. Called ProStores, the service, according to eBay, "allows eBay sellers and other small- to medium-sized businesses to create a customized e-commerce storefront, independent of the eBay marketplace."

Sellers can customize their sites with their own branding, select their own categories, and operate under their own unique Internet address. They can also share listings and inventory between their ProStore and their eBay store.

This is a canny move for eBay and one that reflects the company's marketing research efforts. Sales that take place on Web sites other than eBay represent revenues that eBay would rather have in its coffers. Offering sellers an e-commerce solution that integrates with their existing business or allows them to expand to their own Web site is a way for the company to recapture those lost revenues. ProStore operators pay a monthly fee to eBay for the privilege of using the company's e-commerce solution. They also pay fees ranging from 0.5 to 1.5 percent on each successful transaction.

Choosing Your Domain Name

It's been said that you should select your domain name as carefully as you would a spouse. Ideally, you're going to be tied to the name for a long time—it's a bad idea to change names once your site is established—so it needs to be a good fit.

There are two basic approaches to choosing a domain name. One is to use your existing business name if at all possible. The other is to use a keyword phrase that reflects what your site and your business are all about.

Whichever approach you take, make sure you choose a name that you can register as a dot.com. Yes, there are other extensions. No, they're not a good choice, no matter what anyone says. We live in a dot.com world, not a dot.biz or a dot.net world. Stick to dot.com. If you don't register your domain name with this extension, you open yourself up to the possibility of someone else doing it.

All about the Blog
Inside Track

Back in the day, it was considered good form to keep your innermost thoughts to yourself. But no longer. Today, Web logs, usually called blogs, are all the rage. It seems like everyone is revealing their observations—important and not-so—to others online. If you're not, you might want to think about doing so, as it can also be a way to boost your business.

According to Microsoft's online small-business forum, blogs can complement Web-based commerce sites by exposing buyers to new or little-known products or ideas. Blogs with a public comment area can improve search engine rankings, as each comment constitutes another Web page with searchable keywords. Establishing a blog and regularly posting to it can also help build your reputation and image—both key aspects to branding.

If you're not familiar with blogging, spend some time researching it—including reading other people's blogs—and see if it's something that fits into your business plan. If it does, and you want to try it yourself, there's software that will let you add a blog to your selling site, or you can establish it on a blog hosting site with links to yours.

Once you choose a domain name, you'll have to register it. This used to be fairly expensive, but prices have dropped significantly over the years. You can register the name yourself through any of a number of companies that offer this service. Web hosting and design companies typically offer this service as well.

Finding a Site Host

Site hosting is what makes your Web site available on the Internet. It's done in two basic ways: you do it yourself from your home computer, or you contract with a Web hosting company. Hosting your own Web site is okay if all you're doing is putting a page or two on the Internet for fun. Anything else should be handled by a Web hosting company that has the requisite equipment for making your site work the way it should.

There are tons of Web hosts to choose from, ranging from free and shared hosts that require all sites to share bandwidth, disk space, and so on, to dedicated and co-location services that assign your Web site to its own server. You don't necessarily have to make the choice yourself. The company you use to do your Web site development might offer hosting services or be partnered with a company that does. If so, simply going with who they suggest isn't a bad approach.

If you do decide to look for your own Web hosting service, pick one that fits your needs based on the following:

- Size of your site
- Anticipated traffic to your site
- How much storage space you think you'll need
- Other offered features, such as e-mail, databases, and extra domains

Your Web host can be located anywhere you like. You can choose to work with a local company for convenience or you can choose a company halfway around the world. More important than location is dependability. It doesn't do you any good to have a Web site if the company hosting it is down half the time. Scalability and flexibility are also important—the site should be able to handle your company's future growth—as are service and support. When things go wrong, you want to be able to get them fixed right away.

Linking to Your eBay Listings

Linking your store to your eBay business, and vice versa, is essential for building the synergy between your site and your eBay sales. eBay only allows one link to a an outside site that offers goods for sale, and you can only put it on your "About Me" page. However, you can include as many links to eBay as you want on your own Web site.

Becoming an eBay Affiliate

Having your own piece of real estate on the Internet will also make you eligible for eBay's Affiliate program, which will increase your profits without you having to do anything more than include an eBay banner ad or link on your Web site. You'll get paid for anyone who goes to eBay from your site, registers as a new user, and places a bid on an item or does a BIN within thirty days of registering. At this time, eBay pays up to $45 for each of these referrals, which they call Active Confirmed Registered Users, or ACRUs. You'll also receive up to 25 cents for each bid or BIN placed by buyers coming from your site.

eBay's Affiliate program is one of the most popular on the Web, and for good reason—it pays well! As of this writing, some eBay affiliates are earning more than $100,000 a month. The top 100 affiliates average almost $25,000 a month.

▶▶ Test Drive

Do a Web search, and identify three e-commerce sites that you've never visited before. Spend some time on each site, and then analyze each on the following:

- What attracted you to the site
- If your interest in the site changed any after you explored the site
- The site's best feature
- The site's worst feature

Teaching Others How to Sell on eBay

Once you develop a certain level of expertise as an eBay seller, what you do might seem second nature to you, but it won't to others. There are tons of people to whom eBay is an absolute mystery. They don't know the first thing about buying or selling there, but they're fascinated by it and want to learn more. Or they "know someone" who does. What's more, if they find out that you're an eBay seller, they'll want to learn more about it from you, either for their own benefit or for the "someone they know." You've got a few choices when this happens, and rest assured, if it hasn't happened to you yet, it will. Here are a few potential courses of action:

1. Simply answer their questions. When you do, you're going to give them a business card, of course.
2. Ask them if they have items they'd like to consign to you. Again, have a card handy so they know how to contact you.
3. Teach them how to sell on eBay. Again, leave them with your business card so they know how to reach you.

One approach isn't necessarily better than the others, but the way you handle inquiries like these illustrates a key ingredient to success as an eBay seller: Never turn down an opportunity to market yourself and your business. Oh, and always carry your business cards with you. You never know when one of those opportunities will come up, and you should always take advantage of the opportunity to market your business when they do.

The third option—teaching others how to sell on eBay—might seem counterproductive to your own efforts as an eBay seller. However, it can be one of the most effective ways to improve your bottom line.

For starters, sharing what you know is an essential element of building your own brand. Secondly, sharing your knowledge with others doesn't necessarily mean that they're going to run with what they learned from you. Lots of people take classes just for the sake of taking them. They want to learn more about a subject, but their inquiry ends when they're done with the class. Or they learn enough about the subject to convince them that they don't want to go any further with it. But they'll be impressed with you—probably even more so after they've learned how hard selling on eBay really is—and they'll be more likely to pass your name along to others as an eBay expert.

When it comes to eBay, not wanting to become a seller is a fairly common response when a teacher presents the real lowdown on what being a seller entails. People think it looks easy. When they take a class on the subject, they find out that being a good eBay seller is anything but. Even if you present the information at its basic, most simple level, the sheer amount of details and steps involved in even the simplest auctions are too much for some people to want to deal with.

Finally, there's an unlimited supply of inventory in the universe, certainly more than enough for you and everyone you'd ever want to teach. So why not help other people do their own selling? Do an Internet search, and you'll see a ton of people already making good use of the model of teaching others how to sell on eBay. Lots of them offer some fancy-looking and expensive products—books, CDs, DVDs and the like—that people can buy and study on their own.

This can all seem pretty daunting, but don't for a minute assume there isn't room for you in the "teaching others how to eBay" marketplace. ▶▶**The demand for knowledge never ends. Nor does the demand for people to impart it.** What's more, you might bring something different to the table, based on your experience, that's different from everyone else.

Teaching can turn into a source of sustainable income for you. If you want, you can even develop your own set of materials and sell them—on eBay, in your classes, and/or on your own site.

Finding Teaching Venues

Where can you teach? Really, anywhere you want. Again, once word gets out that you're an eBay expert and you're willing to teach others, you probably won't want for opportunities to spread your wisdom.

Possible venues include community colleges, continuing education classes, community centers, senior centers, and so on. You can rent space and market your classes on your own. You can even hold them in your own home if doing so isn't against rules and regulations where you live.

Promoting Your Classes

Hooking up with a local school or community ed program removes most of the promotional burden, as they'll spread the word through their own promotions. If you decide to offer classes on your own, you'll have to promote them, too. The following approaches are fairly inexpensive, but effective:

- Posting flyers on community bulletin boards, grocery bulletin boards, and similar public places.
- Sending out a press release to the local media. This approach tends to be most effective away from major metropolitan areas, but you should do it even if you live in the big city. As long as your release is well-written, contains the information it needs to have, and is sent to the right person, it has as much chance of making print or being aired as anyone else's does.
- Placing ads in local newspapers, free shoppers, church bulletins, and so on. Don't waste time or money on display ads. Go directly to the classifieds section and place small ads. Choose categories that people are most likely to see them in, such as antiques and collectibles, housewares, furniture, or electronics.
- Spreading word of mouth. Tell everyone you know that you're offering classes on how to sell on eBay.
- Putting class schedules on the back of your business cards.

The Who, What, When, Where, and Why

Press releases are almost embarrassingly easy to write once you know the formula behind them. Known as the five Ws, this formula determines how basic news stories are structured, and it's how press releases are structured, too. In fact, some of the best press releases simply present this information in bullet form. Whether you take this approach or write a more detailed press release, be sure all the information is correct. Put your name and phone number somewhere on the release as a contact for more information.

Putting Together Your Classes

Another decision you'll have to make is the format you want to teach in. Do you want to do a series, or would you rather present as much as you can in a stand-alone seminar? Do you want to take a formal classroom approach, or does a more informal setting fit your style better?

After you've figured out your general approach, you'll need to put together an outline for what you're going to cover. How brief or detailed your presentation will be largely depends on the kind of classes you're going to offer. If you're doing a one- or two-hour seminar, you won't have enough time to do much more than an overview of what it's like to sell on eBay and answer a few questions at the end (have those business cards available, too!). If you're teaching a couple of hours once a week for four to six weeks, you'll be able to present much more detail.

Dealing with Visuals and Handouts

If possible—that is, if you have the necessary time and resources—give your students something to look at while you're talking. Options here range from notes on a chalkboard or simple flip charts to PowerPoint presentations.

People always like to come away from classes with something tangible. Again, if possible, provide written materials they can take with them when the class is over. It doesn't take much time or money to do handouts that outline what you've presented. Providing handouts also eliminates much of the need for taking notes and lets students focus on what you're saying.

Becoming an eBay Education Specialist

Going through special training and becoming an eBay Education Specialist is another approach to teaching people about selling on eBay and to marketing your services as an instructor. This is an online program specifically developed to meet the demand for eBay teachers. When you complete the course, you get a certificate, a logo that identifies you as an official "Education Specialist Trained by eBay," and you can list your class offerings in eBay's Education Specialist online directory. The eBay Education Specialist training costs $149, which includes an instructor manual and an eBay University CD. eBay also makes student materials available to eBay Education Specialists to use in their classes.

Overcoming "Front of the Crowd" Jitters

If the idea of getting up in front of a bunch of people and telling them what you know about eBay is far from your idea of fun, you might come down with a big case of performance anxiety when it comes time to do so. One of the best ways to overcome this is practicing what you're going to say beforehand. Bullet-point your presentation on index cards and carry it with you. Run through it as often as you can—in the car when you're stuck in traffic, when you're standing in line at the grocery store, when you're getting dressed in the morning—you name it. The more familiar you can get with what you're going to say, the easier it is to say it.

Selling Yourself as an eBay Expert

As mentioned, teaching is a great way to sell yourself as an eBay expert, and doing so is a great way to promote your business in general. But it's far from the only way to attach expert status to your brand.

Once again, some of these approaches might seem egotistical, and they might embarrass you. Don't let that happen. As discussed in Chapter 19, people tend to err on the side of not promoting themselves instead of doing it too much. If you don't beat your own drum, who's going to do it for you?

- **Send out press releases when you have a reason to do so.** These reasons include opening your business, expanding your business, or if you win any awards. Do this right, do it regularly, and the local media will think of you when they need a local quote on some aspect of eBay.
- **Offer to speak at civic groups.** Organizations like the Optimists and so on are always looking for interesting speakers at their meetings. Once again, have those business cards on hand.
- **Donate your services to a local charity.** More and more charities are adding eBay to their fundraising activities.
- **Offer your services as a prize in a charity auction.** There are a couple of ways to go here—you can teach others how to sell or sell for them.

The Power of Business Cards　　　　　　　　　

Business cards might seem like a modern-day invention, but they're actually far from it. Tradecards, which were similar to business cards, were part of doing business in Europe during the seventeenth century. They were fanciful and colorful, and they functioned more as advertising than as ways to exchange contact information, but this soon changed. By the nineteenth century, elaborate illustrations and colors had given way to simpler cards that provided contact information as well as directions to the merchant's place of business.

Many predicted that electronic communications would spell the end of business cards or at least diminish their use, but this hasn't been the case. As long as people meet face to face, there will always be the need for the exchange of contact information, and business cards are still a great way to do it.

People who use business cards effectively will tell you to never leave home without them. You never know what might happen, and you never know when you might meet someone who could make a big difference in your business and your life.

"Here's My Card"

This chapter has poked a little—well, maybe more than a little—fun at business cards, but it did so to illustrate an important point. Business cards are a big part of the business world. Sadly, many eBay sellers don't get the importance of this and overlook this simple, yet very effective tool. Maybe it's because of how they began. If they weren't geared up for business from the get-go, they might not be approaching it as a business now.

Business cards are, hands down, the easiest and most effective way to get your name out. But here's what's even greater about them when you're an eBay seller—the hype and mystique surrounding eBay works in your favor. You won't have to foist your cards on people. They'll want to take them from you. So arm yourself with a ton of cards, and get busy handing them out.

If you've avoided buying cards because you don't think you can afford them, think again. You can even get free cards if you don't mind ones that carry discreet advertising for the company that makes them on the back. For more information on these cards, go to *www.vistaprint.com*.

Exploring Business-to-Business Opportunities

One way to market your own business is to connect to other like-minded individuals. It might seem old-fashioned and corny, but it's really amazing what getting out and networking with people can do for your business. Join the small-business associations in your area. Join the chamber of commerce. Volunteer at local social service agencies. Make an effort to meet someone new who you can talk to about your business on a regular basis—at least once a week.

Getting out and networking with people is not only a great way to make your work less solitary, it's one of the best approaches for spreading the word about your business that you could ask for. Yes, it can take time—probably more time than you'll want to spend at it at times—but the payoffs are more than worth it.

Using Co-op Advertising Funds

eBay's Co-op Advertising Program isn't available to all sellers, but if you qualify for it, it's something to seriously consider. This program pays for a percentage of your print advertising and is a great way to offset some of your promotional costs.

You can participate if you're a PowerSeller and you operate an eBay store, or if you're a PowerSeller who's also a Trading Assistant. Your eBay account must also be in good standing, of course.

Follow eBay's guidelines, and the company will reimburse 25 percent of your advertising insertion fees. Advertising placed in general circulation newspapers, magazines, or Yellow Pages are all approved venues for this program, as long as the publication has a circulation of 10,000 or more. Catalogs, newsletters, and other printed materials might also qualify if they're preapproved by eBay.

▶▶ Test Drive

Consider what you are doing to market yourself and your eBay business in the real world. Are you leaving no stone unturned, or are you living under a rock, hoping people will somehow find their way to you? Think of three offline ways you could employ to make your business more visible and successful.

5

Keeping Your
eBay Business
Running Smoothly

The Value of Market Research

Knowing what your customers like to buy and tailoring your offerings accordingly is a key aspect of doing business no matter where you are—online or not—and it's definitely a critical component of building a long-term operating strategy for your eBay business. Gaining this knowledge is what market research is all about.

As discussed in Chapter 5, doing your research on the front end—exploring categories, seeing what other sellers offer, figuring out how and where you fit in—is an effort that can not only make the difference between success and failure, it can help you become successful faster and avoid many of the typical problems that beset beginning sellers. But market research activities shouldn't—in fact, can't—stop there. It's also important to keep them going throughout your time as an eBay seller.

No business has ever been successful by simply studying its potential markets on the front end and stopping there, for one basic reason: Nothing ever stays the same. To be competitive and keep up with the marketplace and the competition, a certain amount of ongoing market research is an absolute necessity. It can be done by using easily attainable and readily available information to get to know your buyers better, understand their buying habits better, and to better gear your efforts toward them. Or, resources permitting, you can go deeper than this.

How Do the Joneses Do It?

There are always a few sellers who seem to never make a misstep when it comes to satisfying customer needs. Not only do they have solid product line-ups, they always seem to be on the cutting edge of trends. How do they do it? In the old days, their success might have been the result of intuition, marketplace knowledge, and good old-fashioned common sense. Today, these factors might account for some of their success, but the rest of it comes from cold hard analysis of market trends.

The best business people are always tweaking, analyzing, and looking for ways to do it better. Even when things are going well, they don't rest on their laurels. If things go wrong, they analyze why, and they learn from their mistakes.

This might seem a bit obsessive or paranoid, but it really isn't. Ask any business owner and they'll tell you that if there's anything they'd like to do more of, and think they need to do more of, it's market research.

You can never know too much about your customers, but you can definitely know too little about them. Knowing too much rarely, if ever, results in missteps. Knowing too little definitely can.

Market Research Approaches

The best business people admit to having a somewhat intuitive feel for what works and what doesn't work for them—it's what often sets them apart from others who lack this intuitive sense or who don't know how to tap into it as well as others do—but they don't rely on their intuitions alone. Instead, they back up their feelings with as much information as they can gather, both on their markets and on how well they serve them.

If you're like many eBay sellers, you don't have the resources for conducting in-depth, far-reaching market-research studies of your own, or for analyzing your own selling effectiveness. But this doesn't mean you have to fly in the dark when it comes to knowing your audience and satisfying their needs. Nor does it mean that you have to rely on gut feelings alone. There are other ways to gather the information you need without having to crunch lines and lines of data or run analysis programs that, when all is said and done, sometimes don't deliver the kind of information you're looking for.

These approaches might not be as exacting as you'd like or deliver exactly the kind of detail you want, but they can point you in the right direction and give you a feel for what you need to do.

Automated Analysis Software

The need for good market research on eBay has driven the development of a fairly large pool of software developers who are aiming to deliver research tools that do exactly this. As such, as the eBay marketplace has expanded, a number of products have become available that are designed to help sellers be better at what they do and grow their businesses. Such research comes at a price, of course, and the price can be pretty steep depending on the product, but what you pay can be more than worth it if it results in better business and a healthier bottom line.

Here are a few data analysis programs to take a look at:

Andale's Research and Reporting Tools: This is a suite of products that gathers information from closed eBay auctions to track marketplace trends. Data can be broken down into reports on prices, popularity, and success strategies. Detailed reports on your specific sales performance are also available when you sign up for the service.

HammerTap: Another product suite that uses closed auction data to analyze sales performance for products and categories, HammerTap also combines this information with, according to the developers "the experience of expert market research specialists . . . the combination provides buyers and sellers the best research results available." This research tool can deliver information on things like the best auction types, the best times to list specific items, optimal auction lengths, and more. The entire suite is pricey, but you can pick and choose the applications that best suit your needs and bring the price down a bit. That said, Deep Analysis, which is the research tool that's at the heart of HammerTap, is what you'll want, and it's the most expensive at $179 for a year's subscription. Available through Bright Builders, Inc. and Wise Research.

Terapeak: This is a newer program that's creating a bit of a buzz for its combination of robust analysis of live auctions and a low price—less than $10 for the basic service. It analyzes current auctions on factors including category performance, trends, buying habits, and more.

More information on these and other research tools is available at eBay's Solutions Directory. The directory also features links to the specific products.

eBay debuted its own marketplace research service in late 2005. Fees range from $2.99 for a two-day peak at 60 days worth of market information to $24.99 a month for a Pro subscription that provides 90 days of historical data. For more information, go to *http://pages.ebay.com/ marketplace_research/index.html.*

Doing It Yourself

This approach can take the most time, and it might not be the most scientific way to go about things, but it can yield good results if you configure your research right. It's also the cheapest way to go. Many eBay sellers rely on this approach and employ more sophisticated data-analysis approaches when and as needed.

Here's how to go about it:

- **Browse eBay's categories regularly.** The more time you spend "getting your hands dirty" at the site, the better feel you'll get for the dynamics of the marketplace. Do it enough, and you should be able to get a feel for marketplace trends and for where certain products are in their "must have" cycle.
- **Analyze completed auctions.** This is something you'll also have to do fairly often, as eBay deletes auction details two weeks or so after auctions end.
- **Keep up with industry trends in your selling categories.** Read general business publications as well as category and product-specific publications regularly.
- **Participate in online discussion boards and newsgroups.**
- **Attend trade shows.**
- **Join professional organizations.**

You can also go right to the horse's mouth—your customers themselves—and ask them what they'd like to see you sell. Doing so will involve putting together a survey that you can either mail or e-mail, which takes some knowledge of how to construct marketing surveys and how to do it right. People like to be asked for their opinions, and eBay buyers tend to be pretty loyal to sellers they like; however, neither factor guarantees a good turnout for this approach. Try offering an incentive—a free gift, a discount on a store item, or free shipping on their next purchase—as an incentive for participating in your survey.

Getting to Know Seller Central

eBay is constantly tweaking its site to offer increased value to its users and to better organize its various efforts so people can find them more easily. One of the latest site tweaks resulted in a new area called Seller Central.

▶▶**When it comes to learning more about the eBay marketplace, eBay's Seller Central is a treasure trove of information and definitely a place to get to know.** Here, gathered together in one place, is a ton of information about what other eBay sellers are doing and what works for them. It's also a place that can both keep you abreast of what's going on in various selling categories and assist your marketing and your market-research efforts in general.

Some of the information at Seller Central is fairly elementary—for instance, this is where you'll find the site's getting-started guides—but there's lots more here as well. Yes, it is all from eBay's perspective, which makes it a bit rah-rah and propagandistic in nature, but don't let the general tone and approach deter you. There is a lot to be learned here for sellers at almost every level.

Seller Central consists of the following areas:

Getting Started: This spot contains the aforementioned getting-started guides, but don't neglect them if you're new to eBay. There are guides here for individual sellers conducting virtual garage sales all the way up to enterprise solutions for large corporations.

Best Practices: This area details the eBay selling process and offers solid tips and suggestions in all areas—research, pricing, choosing selling formats, using eBay's promotional tools, and so on.

Advanced Selling: Designed for sellers with some time and experience under their belts, this area contains information on eBay

Sales Reports, Stores, Seller Tools, the PowerSeller Program, the Trading Assistant program, and more. Also here are links to information on keyword advertising, international trading, buying wholesale lots, and more.

Category Tips: This area contains category-specific selling strategies and resources for many of the hottest categories on eBay. Digging through it can take some time, but the results can be worth it. While some of the information is basic knowledge, and a lot of it repeats across categories, there are some gems to be mined here. Also, it's not a bad area to explore if you're thinking about taking on a new category that you haven't traded in before.

What's Hot: You'll find eBay's merchandising calendar here, which is a good way of keeping track of the site's seasonal promotions. It also lists the categories that are spotlighted on eBay's home page, which can be good to know about if you sell in any of them. Also here are Hot Items by Category, aka "The Hot List," a monthly update on eBay's biggest selling categories, and eBay Pulse, a very kicky area that tracks trends and hot picks by category, and tells you who the biggest stores are in each. This is also the place to go if you want to check out the latest stupid eBay auction. The title on one recent offering: "Advertise on my Teeth! Pulled but not Forgotten."

News and Updates: This area indexes eBay's *PowerUp* e-mail newsletter, a breezy, chatty offering that includes news on things like special seller promotions, category programs and changes, and other news of interest to eBay sellers. It also includes a seller's profile, which can be both interesting and inspiring to read. The *PowerUp* newsletter is also available free via e-mail to everyone who subscribes to it at the site.

Resources: Here, finally, in one spot is information on every seller program, product offering, and resource available on eBay. This is a page to bookmark, as you'll probably come back often.

One example of the kind of information you'll find at Seller Central is a report called "How Buyers Use eBay," which resides in Best Practices. This is an eBay usage report, gathered from the site's own data, which highlights how buyers use eBay. It's somewhat of a gloss-over, and doesn't present any deep analysis, but it does cover things like the following:

- Visit patterns, by day of week, category, and time spent
- Typical user paths as they travel through eBay
- Visitor demographics
- Market research on active eBay buyers

Using eBay's Data Analysis Services

As eBay continues to put its emphasis on attracting people who want to use eBay to establish and develop their businesses, it's also increasing its efforts to develop quality tools to keep sellers at the site and help them grow their businesses while they're there.

As eBay puts it, "Continuing to understand how your business changes and identifying new opportunities are the keys to your success! Our goal is to make this easier for you!" eBay's data analysis services aren't the most robust out there, but they can give you some good baseline information on how you're doing in the marketplace.

eBay's Sales Reports track your metrics, which is a fancy term for measuring how your business performs (also referred to as "business performance metrics" and/or "sales metrics"; eBay uses the term "key performance metrics") in such areas as sales, ended listings, the percentage of successful ended listings, average sale price, and what you pay in eBay and PayPal fees. You can measure your existing eBay sales against your sales goals, gain a clearer understanding of the factors that drive your business, determine areas of opportunity and of improvement, and more. The service is free—all you have to do is sign up for it at the site—and available to all sellers. Up to six months of reports are archived at the site for review.

Sales Reports Plus takes eBay's basic Sales Reports to the next level. It's more in-depth and gives category breakdowns, format, category and format, ending day or time, buyer counts, and more. It's available for $4.99 a month and is free if you have a store.

Taking on New Categories

In the retail world, there's always a next big thing. The problem is, how do you find it? If ongoing, effective market research is an Achilles' heel for big businesses, how can smaller ones do it, especially with limited resources? And if you do find the next big thing, how will you know if it's the right fit for you and your customers?

Once again, you can base your decisions on what other sellers seem to be doing as you scan eBay to spot trends. Or you can simply ask your customers. Doing so can be a great way to test your research and proof your conclusions. ▶▶**If you decide to take on new products and/or new categories, be sure it really makes sense to do so.** Ask the following questions:

➲ Are you really ready to take on something new?

➲ Are you doing it for the right reasons? It's not a good idea to branch out if you're doing it to distance yourself from a strategy that's not working.

➲ Can your existing business setup and systems handle the demands that offering new products might create?

➲ Can you continue to provide the same levels of service to your customers if the new products really take off?

➲ Do you have a plan for disposing of the merchandise if you misgauged the market for the product?

If you decide to go ahead with new product offerings, consider segregating them from other areas of your business by selling them under a different User ID until you know for sure that they'll work. Finally, consider taking on new products over tackling new categories. New products can reinforce your brand and further develop your market niche. Entering a new category can move you too far away from your core business and muddy your offerings in the marketplace.

Knowing When to Fold 'Em

If you conduct your market research right, and you depend on a blend of gut instinct, solid market research, and asking your clients what they want, chances are you won't have to come up with ways of disposing of your purchasing mistakes. But sometimes, no matter how hard you try or how solidly you research your buying options, things don't work out. You overestimate demand or come in too late on a trend. What you bought doesn't sell, or it doesn't sell anywhere near as well as you thought it would.

How do you know when it's really time to fold? The answer varies quite a bit, but the following are good indications:

- ➲ Average sales prices are falling below what you paid for the merchandise.
- ➲ Categories are flooded with same or similar products that aren't selling.
- ➲ New technology has made the items obsolete.
- ➲ You've put items up multiple times at auction, then put them in your store, and they still haven't sold.

Having unsold goods, whether it's a storage bin or a warehouse full, is simply not a good idea. You've got money tied up in merchandise taking up space that could be used for better merchandise that you can sell. Here's the bottom line. If you have merchandise that's been around too long, that demand has passed by, and that you sense won't be worth keeping around for another selling cycle, it's time to get rid of it before it further drains your resources.

Inventory Liquidation Strategies

Okay, so you've admitted that it's time to round 'em up and head 'em out. But how? Here are some tried and true approaches to getting rid of the stuff you just don't want to see hangin' 'round your door no more:

Everybody Flops, Even the Big Guys | Inside Track

Even companies renowned for launching great products can make missteps when it comes to gauging what their market likes and wants.

One of the greatest test-marketing failures was the April 1985 introduction of New Coke. Based on its marketing research, Coca-Cola determined that it was time to introduce a new product to the marketplace. However, instead of introducing the new product—called, of course, New Coke—as a new product, Coca-Cola, in its infinite wisdom, replaced the classic drink with a product that most people called "swill."

Customer protests brought back the old product, but not before Coca-Cola lost a lot of money, and, more important, eroded its reputation.

⊃ **Mark it down, way down.** If you sell at a loss, you might be able to use the losses to offset profits.

⊃ **Lot it up and sell it on eBay.** Okay, so maybe it didn't work for you, but another seller might appreciate having a go at it.

⊃ **Put it on your other selling Web site.** Some online sellers set up a special clearance section on their sites just for this purpose.

⊃ **See if the parts are worth more than the whole.** Sometimes the raw ingredients in items can be mined and reengineered into something that is sellable. As an example, let's say you bought a bunch of rhinestone pins and earrings that just didn't sell. Pluck out the rhinestones and offer them up.

⊃ **Donate the merchandise for a tax credit.** The rules and regulations on this vary quite a bit depending on your business structure. Before you do it, make sure it makes sense to do so by checking with your CPA or other tax professional.

As discussed in Chapter 21, hiring a Trading Assistant to sell unwanted merchandise for you might be another approach, especially if you really don't want to put the effort into it yourself.

▶▶ Test Drive

How well do you really know your marketplace, your competition, and your customers? If the answer is "I'm not sure" or "Not very," start doing some market research right away. Get into the habit of studying your categories on a regular basis. Get to know your way around eBay's Seller Central and use information available to you there. Subscribe to seller reports, and take the time to read and study them.

Avoiding Burnout

For many people, being self-employed and/or working from home seems like a dream come true. No more commuting, no more keeping regular hours, being able to work in your pajamas if you want to—what could be better?

Being your own boss can definitely be a dream of a lifetime realized, but it can also have its disadvantages. What they are and how strongly they factor into your life depends on who you are, your work style, and your lifestyle.

For starters, running your own business can be, and probably will be, more work than you ever thought imaginable. If you're like most small-business owners, you'll probably have to shoulder the lion's share of the responsibility for every aspect of your day-to-day operations, especially when you first start out. You'll have to wear many hats, ranging from business owner to advertising director, from bookkeeper to packing-and-shipping clerk. ▶▶**If you're not good at juggling responsibilities, you'll have to learn how to do it, and you'll have to get good at it in a hurry.** Not doing so can have a big effect on your profitability and can even shut you down fast.

Other factors about working for yourself that might wear on you include the following:

1. **Being alone:** If you're used to being around people, spending too many hours by yourself might drive you nuts until you get used to the solitude. Working on line, which is such a large part of running an eBay business, can be extremely isolating.

2. **Not being able to share what you're doing with others:** Maybe you didn't like working in an office and having to deal with others' problems, but not having anyone to bounce ideas off of or talk to can be worse. Participating on discussion boards can take up a lot of the slack in this area, but only to a certain extent.

3. **House distractions:** If you're like many self-employed people, your office will be in your home. Until you start spending significant time there, there's no way to know how many

distractions a house can contain. There's television to watch, laundry to do, pets to play with, furniture to dust . . . the list is endless. What's more, you can always find something about your house, something that absolutely needs to be done now, when you're procrastinating. The problem is obvious: The more time and energy you give to your distractions, the more you let them pull you away from your work, the less you'll get done. As your productivity goes down, so will your feelings of success.

4. **Not being able to leave work at a reasonable time, or not being able to leave it behind at all:** Your work becomes all-encompassing, and, since it's right there and some aspect of it always needs some level of attention, you can't leave it alone.

This last point—not being able to leave work behind—is a key one when it comes to avoiding burnout. You simply *must* learn how to put your work aside, and for most people, it *is* a learning process. It's also a discipline process. But it's absolutely necessary. No amount of work and no amount of success can make up for what you stand to lose if you don't put your business in its proper perspective. At a minimum, you'll get stale and tired, and you'll start to ask yourself if it's all worth it. But it can get worse—far worse—from here. You can lose your family, your friends, and your health, both physical and mental.

Don't tell yourself that it can't or won't happen to you. It definitely can, and whether it can—or will—is largely up to you.

Avoiding the Burnout Cycle

Many self-employed people wait until they get to the burnout stage before they take steps to get out of it. When they've absolutely worked themselves into the ground, they take some time to repair and recuperate, but they don't address the underlying causes that created the problem in the first place. Then they go back to work, and the entire cycle repeats itself. This approach isn't necessarily the worst thing in the world, as it does include a repair and recuperation phase, albeit a forced one, but it can wear you down physically and emotionally if you go through the work/burnout/repair cycle too many times.

Inside Track	A Plea for a Balanced Life

Why is it that we tend to be our own worst enemies? We know what we should do to keep ourselves healthy and happy, but do we do it?

Questions like these prompted the following post on one of eBay's discussion boards: "Did you once have a life that included things such as going out with friends, on dates, exploring, exercising, dancing, going on carousel rides, hiking, horseback riding, having great conversations with friends and/or your significant other until the wee hours?

"Have you developed an eBay butt?

"In other words, are we neglecting ourselves? For me, the answer is a big ol' YES, and I'm tired of it. I don't feel that great, emotionally and physically, and heck even spiritually, and somehow I don't think I'm the only one.

"I love selling, don't get me wrong. It's wonderful to love what you do, but dang, I want balance in my life. I'm neglecting myself. I need a manicure, pedicure, hair cut, and to get dressed nicely and get the heck out of here.

"So whaddya say? Anyone else feel like their life has been hijacked by eBay and want to take it back and have some fun ourselves?"

There are lots of clues to what can be done to avoid the burnout cycle depicted in this seller's impassioned words, but the basic answer to the problem is also the simplest one: Take control of your eBay life instead of letting it control you.

A better approach is to put systems and routines in place to avoid burning out and to do so before problems set in. Most small business owners, however, have a hard time doing this until something forces their hand and makes it imperative that they take control over their work instead of letting it control them.

Balancing Work, Family, and Friends

Taking control of your work means putting your work into its proper perspective. Doing so will allow you to incorporate the other things you need to have to keep you happy and healthy—the friends and family part. Also, it will free up time to do things for and with them, as well as for yourself.

According to bestselling author and time-management consultant Julie Morgenstern, organizing your time is a big key to striking a balanced life. Letting time control you instead of you taking control of it is a waste of one of your most precious resources—time itself!

Organizing Time and Space

Morgenstern takes a somewhat interesting approach to time management. She equates it to space management. From her perspective, if you think of time as space—let's say, like a drawer or a closet—you can organize it. To take this concept a step further, think of time as a container. All the tasks that you put into it during the course of a day will take up a certain amount of space. The idea is to keep the container from overflowing.

To get an idea of how this works, let's take a look at two daily schedules of two eBay sellers. One seller lets time control her. As such, her day is hectic, whirlwind, crammed full of more things than she really can handle easily, and looks decidedly out of control to those around her. The other thinks of time as space and organizes it along these lines. Her day is ordered, orderly, and definitely not out of control.

Here's a typical daily schedule for eBay seller number one:

7–8 A.M.: Up, threw on clothes, got kids to school. Ate.

8 A.M.–2:30 P.M.: eBay stuff. Answered emails, worked on some listings, watched some TV. Went shopping for inventory, etc., etc. Went to bank, post office. Went back home to pick up checks for deposit that I left on the kitchen counter. Packed a few things before I left again.

2:30: Picked up kids from school.

3–5: Kid stuff, packed some eBay stuff, made dinner. Oh yeah, had to go back to post office to mail some things I forgot this morning, and had to send DH to the grocery store to pick up some ingredients for dinner.

7–10: Worked on listings, answered e-mails.

10: Bed.

11: Couldn't sleep, went back to office and posted to the boards for a couple of hours. Fixed the register cover that's been rattling and driving me crazy.

Here's a typical daily schedule for eBay seller number two:

7–7:30 A.M.: Get up, shower, dress.

7:30–8: Breakfast, get kids ready for school.

8–8:30: Answer e-mails.

8:30–9: eBay research.

9–10: Pack and label auction wins.

10 A.M.–12 P.M.: Set up and take photos.

12–12:30: Light snack.

12:30–2: Yoga class.

2–2:30: Light lunch.

2:30–3: Check and answer e-mails.

3–5: Soccer game with kids.

5–6: Prepare dinner, supervise homework.

6–7: Dinner, dishes.

7–9: Family time.

9–9:30: Check and answer e-mails, post to the boards.

9:30–10: Lay out kids' clothes for next day, fold some laundry.

10: Bed.

On this particular day, this seller is done with eBay-related activities by noon, with the exception of checking and answering e-mails.

Seller Two's day might seem overly regimented and a bit unrealistic when compared to Seller One's, but it illustrates Morgenstern's concept of putting time into containers, as you would space. The following are specific examples of how this seller implements this time-management approach:

- **Answering e-mail three times a day for one-half hour each session:** At the end of the half hour, she moves on to the next thing on her schedule. If she has more to answer, she'll do them during her next session.
- **Scheduling the majority of the work that needs to be done when she's most productive:** From experience, this seller knows she's more on task in the mornings, so she typically schedules most of the eBay activities that take more attention, like bookkeeping, in the mornings.
- **Putting out what the kids will wear the night before:** This helps minimize the early-morning craziness that can set in far too easily no matter what you do.
- **Saving routine chores for low-productivity times:** Things like folding the laundry or general tidying up can be done anytime; doing them at the end of the day can even be relaxing.
- **Regimenting responsibilities:** This seller didn't hit every aspect of her eBay business on this particular day, nor did she have to, as she has them planned for other days of the week.

This schedule also illustrates a certain amount of delegation. Note how there's nothing in it about picking up the kids or putting them to bed. Her husband did both. This might not be the case every day—some days they might switch off, and he'll do a post-office run while she picks up the kids.

Cleaning Out Your Time Closet

If you have a haphazard schedule, your schedule will control you, not the other way around. But if you can learn to think of time like space, you can control and organize it to meet your needs. Doing so, however, means doing the same thing you'd do when organizing a closet—you have to pull out everything first.

When it comes to time management, this means coming up with an activity log, or, as Morgenstern calls it, a "time map," which is exactly what it looks like—a map of how you spend your time. Doing so will give you a greater awareness of how you spend your time and help you determine how you can spend it better.

This doesn't have to be an elaborate project, but you do have to keep it going for a certain period of time, and you need to be honest about it. Just like keeping a food journal when you're watching what you eat, it doesn't do you any good to cheat on it.

All you have to do is list your activities for two weeks. Start with the basics—when you get up, when you eat, and when you go to bed. Then jot down everything else that you do and how long you did it for. At this point, don't stop and analyze anything. Just write it all down. As you do, key your activities like this:

- ➲ Put a "B" beside everything you do on a regular basis that's business related.
- ➲ Put an "S" beside one-time events—not things you do as part of your regular routine—that are business related.
- ➲ Put an "M" beside everything you do for yourself.
- ➲ Put an "F" beside every family-related activity.

At the end of the two-week period, go through your log and add up your letters. This should show you where you're spending your time. Next, look at the specific activities in each category, and see if you're spending your time wisely on them. The answer is probably no if you haven't been paying much attention to how you spend your days and, again, if you've allowed your work to control you instead of the other way around.

Group similar items so you can work toward batching your efforts—making all of your calls at one time instead of interspersed during the day, running all of your errands on one circuit instead of going on some, coming home, and going out again. Doing so maximizes your use of time and space.

Other batches to look for and consider include the following:

- ➲ **Organizing your office:** It's a good idea to straighten things up a bit at the end of every work day, as coming in to a clean, organized desk simply starts the day off the right way. Save everything beyond basic tidying up for a day of your choice, once a week, and schedule the time for doing it. Or delegate this responsibility and hire someone to do it.
- ➲ **Working on your business's books:** Again, this is something you might have to devote some time to each day. If so, schedule it and group all bookkeeping and accounting tasks into this time-frame instead of spread out over the day. Or, again, delegate the responsibility, and hire a bookkeeper.
- ➲ **Preparing for auctions:** Finding time for various stages of readying things for auction—research, photography, writing descriptions—is a common complaint among eBay sellers. If you're like them, figure out which preparation step you dislike the most, and schedule time for it first. Don't move on to the other stages until you complete this one.

Focus on One Thing, Not Twenty

According to new research, multitasking doesn't work. In fact, scientists have found that it takes the brain four times longer to process everything it receives when it's forced to switch back and forth from one task to another. If you're working ten- to twelve-hour days, eliminating multitasking can cut your workday by at least two hours, which equates to at least ten hours a week you'll have to devote to something other than work.

Once you have a better idea of how you spend your time, you can develop a schedule that makes better use of your productive periods and cuts down on time wasters that rob you of your time.

Here are some basic pointers for putting together your schedule:

1. Start with a basic to-do list that includes everything you have to accomplish in a day. Put your priorities—the things you absolutely have to get done—at the top of the list.

2. Determine how much time you think it will take you to accomplish the top items on your to-do list, and block out the necessary time on your schedule for them. Schedule things that require the highest levels of mental acuity during your most productive times, be they morning, afternoon, or evening.

3. When you have the highest priorities in place, move down to the next items on your list. Determine which of them you have to get done on this particular day and which can wait. Slot them in accordingly.

Again, look for ways to group your activities as well as things you might be able to delegate.

Making the 80/20 Rule Work for You

▶▶**The 80/20 rule goes like this: 80 percent of your results are driven by 20 percent of your efforts.** Recognizing and focusing on how this equation plays out in your life can help you make the most effective use of your time.

The 80/20 rule is derived from the Pareto principle, which was developed by an Italian economist named Vilfredo Pareto in the late 1800s, after he observed that 80 percent of the land in England was owned by 20 percent of the people.

The underlying theory, called predictable imbalance, states that the relationship between input and output rarely if ever balances. The Pareto principle holds true today and has been applied to almost every aspect of modern life, including time management.

Applying the 80/20 rule to time management simply calls for developing a better awareness of how you spend your time and how the results match your needs. When you do this, you'll probably find that of all the things you do during the day, only about 20 percent of them really make a difference. These are the areas where you want to devote 80 percent of your time.

Here are some examples of how the 80/20 rule might play out in your life:

1. You spend more time dealing with a few difficult customers than working on ways to retain your good ones. This is a classic 80/20 example. Yes, good customer service is important, but spending hours trying to make a small percentage of your buyers happy is simply a waste of time. They're not the ones who are going to drive your business success. Your satisfied customers are. So flip the equation around. Find or develop ways to minimize the time and energy you have to devote to the bad eggs.

2. You do your own bookkeeping, even though you hate it and it takes you forever. This is another classic 80/20 example. Way too many small-business owners spend far too much time on things they either aren't very good at or that they simply don't like doing. This approach not only forces you to focus on the parts of your business that don't bring you much satisfaction, it also compromises your ability to focus your energies on things that can have a greater impact on your bottom line, like looking for new products or honing your photography skills. The solution here should be obvious: Delegate your bookkeeping. Or determine what of it, if any, you are good at and you don't mind doing, and find someone else to do the rest.

3. You like to post to discussion boards, and you post to almost every topic when you're on them. Yes, getting to know others online is fun, and you can learn a lot from them, too, but it's also very easy to allow the 80/20 rule to swing the other way here and to spend a lot of your time weighing in on subjects that aren't that important to you. To make the most of your time online, devote the majority of it to posts that benefit your business. Try to limit the time you spend posting to threads just for the heck of it.

The bottom line here is this. You'll derive greater value and enjoy your life a lot more if you devote 80 percent of your time to the things that really matter and to the people who support and satisfy you the most.

Dividing and Conquering

When it comes to time management, dividing and conquering has two meanings: splitting up work into manageable segments so you can more easily accomplish what you need to get done and delegating certain tasks that really don't need your attention.

Every job you can delegate typically frees up an hour of time that you can spend on more productive activities. But delegation can be extremely difficult, especially for small-business owners imbued with the entrepreneurial spirit that makes it difficult not to be involved in the minutiae of running every aspect of their business.

Julie Morgenstern says that of all time-management approaches, delegation is psychologically the most difficult due to our need to, well, control things. That said, if you can find someone who can do it better, easier, faster—let them.

Putting Systems and Programs to Work for You

Technology can work in your favor when it comes to keeping life sane, but you have to learn how to work it. Also, you have to find the systems and programs that work for you. Here are a few approaches to consider:

- Do the majority of your shipping online, and schedule pickups from shippers as much as possible.
- Bank online as much as possible. If the bank you currently use doesn't offer online bill payment, consider switching to one that does.
- Consider grocery-shopping on line, if this is a task that you don't like and you can't delegate it to anyone else.

➲ Use selling tools like bulk listers, automated e-mail for auto response, and after-auction management programs.

➲ Make sure your business equipment meets your needs. If it doesn't, consider replacing or upgrading the things that are lagging behind. As an example, if you're still using your inkjet or laser printer for labels, maybe it's time to add a label printer to your setup. Are you tired of having to switch out USB devices? Buy a hub.

▶▶ Test Drive

Right now, list four things that you can do to nurture yourself. Things to consider include these:

1. Schedule private time every day, even if it's just a few minutes. It's important, and yes, you need to do this.

2. Take a lunch break every day. Not a working lunch, either. Step away from the desk!

3. Don't sweat the small stuff. That includes nasty e-mails and other little things that can so easily get under your skin. In the broad scheme of things, they don't matter much. Give yourself the time to deal with them; realize you don't have to do everything right away.

4. Walk away from things that aren't working and come back to them later. This is kind of a Zen approach to problems, but it works with anything from stuck jar lids to misfiring computers. Try it and see.

Transaction Troubles

As hard as you'll work to keep it from happening, it will. You'll have a sale go bad. Or you'll have a string of them go less smoothly than they should, each for different reasons, each with its own little problems. They might not be huge issues, but taken together they add up and become big enough to make you wonder what you're doing wrong.

It's important to remember that this happens to everyone. You're far from alone, so don't beat yourself up over it. Instead, do your best to troubleshoot the immediate issues, and learn from the experience so you can prevent the same or similar from occurring in the future.

Asking for Help

When you're in the midst of a crisis—and bad transactions can definitely feel like crises—it can seem like your usual support systems have left you to fend for yourself and you have nowhere to go for help. Fortunately, this is far from the truth. In fact, you might find your best support system for times like these right on eBay.

Even if you don't regularly post to any of eBay's Discussion Boards, they can be a great source of advice and support. Look for a board that fits your problem, or, if you're a "boardie"—a regular on one or more boards—throw your problem on the board you know the best and where you feel the most comfortable, and see what others think.

To save others from the tedium of seeing the same questions posted over and over again, do a subject search before you post. There's a good chance that you're not the only one who has experienced this particular problem, and there might already be a thread on it. If there isn't, post away.

Analyzing the Problem

Transaction problems can happen randomly, but they can also follow a pattern. If yours do, it's probably time to see what, if anything, is causing the disconnect between you and your customers. If you're successful in identifying the cause, the next step is determining a solution. If it's eluding you, once again, eBay's Discussion Boards can be a good source of advice and inspiration.

The Case of the Mis-sent Sweater

Inside Track

The more transactions you have, the more likely the odds of something going wrong, and of it being your fault. I knew it would happen to me eventually, and it did, right before Christmas 2004. I was selling a bunch of vintage ski sweaters. Two of them were almost identical, so I listed them at the same time and used the same description on each with some minor changes.

They sold on BINs within hours (yes, it told me I wasn't asking enough for them, but I had priced them low to move them out before the holidays). One buyer paid right away, and I was headed to the post office anyway, so I grabbed her sweater, packed it up, printed out the postage and label, and hustled off.

The problem was, I grabbed the wrong sweater. I didn't realize it until the second buyer paid the next day and mentioned a feature on the sweater she bought in an e-mail to me.

I immediately contacted buyer number one via e-mail, apologized profusely, and told her I'd pay for her to either send the sweater back to me or to send it directly to the other buyer, and that I'd cover all shipping charges (this meant free shipping on *her* sweater) to make it worth her while. She said she'd be glad to send it directly to the other buyer. We agreed that I'd pay her when she sent me the delivery confirmation number on the package.

Problem solved? Not quite yet. The transaction was out of my hands at this point, and I had to rely on her to do what she said she'd do. Fortunately, she did, and pretty quickly, too. Then the problem was, indeed, solved.

This isn't necessarily a great approach. It worked here because everyone involved had the same goal—untangling a mix-up quickly and easily. If you should find yourself in a similar situation, don't just offer the simplest solution right off the bat. Take some time to check out the other parties involved. If they're newcomers or have questionable feedback, or you simply don't get a good feeling about the situation, do your best to take as much control over the situation as you can.

Depending on what your sleuthing turns up, you might have to make some changes in one or more of the following areas:

 Auction listing format
 Auction listing copy
 Terms of service

⮫ Your "About Me" page
⮫ Payment options and/or procedures
⮫ Buyer notification system
⮫ Shipping procedures

Deadbeat Buyers

On eBay, deadbeat buyers basically fall into two categories—nonpaying bidders, also known as NPBs, or general troublemakers. NPBs flame out fairly quickly, as eBay kicks them out once they amass enough negative feedback and/or accumulate enough strikes against them to warrant expulsion.

Troublemakers also tend to burn out in time, but they can hang around long enough to cause lots of damage before they do. Among their various pranks are things like bidding on auctions for the sole purpose of leaving negative feedback, turning BIN auctions into regular auctions just for sport, and bid shielding—a particularly nasty practice where two bidders manipulate auctions to discourage other bidders from joining in.

And that's just on the front end. They can also cause a whole host of problems for sellers on the auctions they win. They can drag payment out for weeks on end, make unreasonable shipping requests, want to return items for no reason, ask for partial refunds, and so on.

Both categories are definitely in the minority, but you can count on having to deal with them, quite possibly more often than you'd like, depending on the categories you sell in. ▶▶**Some categories—electronics and video games among them—are notorious for attracting flakes and troublemakers.** If you sell in these categories, you'll have to accept the fact that these individuals are part of the territory and learn how to deal with them accordingly. However, no category is immune.

Handling NPBs

As mentioned, NPBs tend to disappear almost as fast as they come. Bids are binding, and buyers are expected to follow through. If they don't, they're not destined to be part of eBay for long. While life can happen to anyone and turn even the best-intentioned buyers into NPBs, some people seemingly do it for sport—it's the only plausible reason that comes to mind when you see someone rack up multiple auction wins and multiple negative feedbacks at the same time. And they keep on coming back for more. When they kill off one User ID, they simply sign up a new one. Yes, it's against the rules, but it does happen, and more often than it should.

Some sellers get pretty nasty with NPBs, but it's really a waste of time. If people aren't going to pay, they aren't going to pay. Threatening them doesn't accomplish anything beyond maybe some much-needed venting for you. These "buyers" already know the consequences, and they don't care.

In the long run, it's easier to treat all buyers the same, even the problem children. As one seller put it:

> **❝I also try to treat** everyone with respect, dignity, and warmth, and this includes nonpaying bidders. You never know what the problem is. Maybe the person really had good intentions, but could not follow through. Maybe they landed in the hospital. Even if they were simply irresponsible, I still am kind, and tell them I am sorry we could not do business, perhaps another time. Often, they will come through and pay after this, or apologize. I never treat them with firmness, as if they are a disobedient child. The response would not be good. Dignity for all.❞

Some sellers don't file negative feedback against NPBs, fearing retaliation from them. But doing so will help boot them out faster and can save other sellers from having to deal with these particular deadbeats.

If you get caught in a transaction with an NPB, you do have some recourse beyond leaving the individual the appropriate feedback and filing an NPB report. You can file a request for a final-value fees credit, relist the item or, if you had multiple bids, offer it as a second chance to the next highest bidder on the list.

Taking the Air Out of Troublemakers

Troublemakers are a bigger problem, as they can cause trouble in so many ways and can be extremely sneaky about it. The best way to avoid them is to nip their activities in the bud whenever possible when they come your way. How can you identify these problem children? There's no sure-fire approach that will work all the time, but one of the best ways to spot them is to check their feedback. This includes not just what they have received but what they've left for others. If you see a string of negatives going one or both ways, you should think twice about doing business with these individuals. While you're checking their feedback, take a look at their bid retractions. Lots of them spell trouble, too, as it can indicate bid shielding.

Dealing with Newbies

Newcomers to eBay often face a certain amount of discrimination from sellers who have had NPB problems with newbies. While they're not that much more likely to be bad buyers, a fair number of them are. Before you decide to categorically block newbies from your auctions, remember that everyone has to start somewhere. If there's no other reason to say no beyond the fact that they're new, think twice about it. Give them the opportunity to bid on your items, and you might win some very loyal customers.

If you don't catch a potential problem child in time, and he or she bids on one of your auctions, cancel the bid if you can (depending on the time left, you might not be able to), and put the bidder on your blocked bidder list immediately. This is a seller tool to know about, and you can find it through Seller-Related Links on your "My eBay" page.

If one slips past you and wins one of your auctions, do everything you can to avoid trouble. Keep everything on a highly professional level even if you're seething inside. Be courteous in your communications, respond promptly to theirs, and ship as soon as you can after you receive payment. Print out and keep a copy of your auction description and images, and be sure to document every step of the transaction to cover yourself. Doing so will definitely be to your advantage should trouble erupt. No matter what you do, problems can still arise. Many sellers can tell horror stories of buyers threatening to turn them in to "the authorities" or wanting partial or full refunds for a whole host of bogus reasons.

Not all troublemaker buyers do what they do intentionally. Some are just harder to please than others. Being a little finicky shouldn't turn into major heartache, but it can. It happens more often than it should, unfortunately, for one simple reason—buyers aren't always right, but they're always in control.

Sometimes sellers who have encountered troublemaker bidders will post a heads-up on eBay's discussion boards. This is another good reason for visiting the boards on a regular basis.

Payment Problems

Auction payments are an area in which the Peter Principle—"If something can go wrong, it will"—seems to proliferate in spades. People and money seem to be a fatal combination, or at least one destined for trouble more often than not.

Payment problems tend to fall into the following areas:

➡ **Using a payment method you don't accept:** You have a couple of options here—keeping the money or returning it to the sender and asking him or her to remit the funds using a method you do accept. This isn't the greatest customer relations move, however. After all, you have the money—the buyer just didn't play by your rules. If you have the money, regardless of how you got it, you're better off honoring your side of the transaction and shipping the merchandise.

➡ **Insufficient funds:** You take checks, and one of your buyers bounced one on you. Give the buyer a chance to make things right, including any fees you might have incurred at your bank as a result of the problem. Chances are good that you'll get your money as it's a bigger problem for your buyer than it is for you—he or she risks a big fat negative from you for not completing the sale. You, on the other hand, can relist the item and file for a final-value fees refund on the previous sale.

➡ **Not paying enough:** Shorting a payment amount can be an honest mistake, but it's also a fairly interesting scam that makes its rounds on eBay from time to time. Again, you have some options here. If you're dealing with a negligible amount—say a dollar or two—it might be best to just let it go. If it's more than this, you can send the payment back and request the correct amount.

Shipping Woes

Shipping problems are another area in which the Peter Principle manifests itself in spades. Packages get lost, merchandise arrives damaged or broken, the wrong item is sent, you name it.

Here's how to avoid the majority of problems in this arena:

1. Confirm the buyer's address via e-mail if it doesn't look right for any reason. As an example, let's say a buyer has provided an address that looks like a college dormitory, but it's the holiday season and you're concerned that the shipment won't get there before the place shuts down for the year. This definitely warrants an e-mail. If you're really concerned, call.

2. For buyers paying through PayPal, ship to confirmed addresses if at all possible. This is the only way that PayPal's seller protection program will cover you. However, be a little flexible about this. PayPal won't confirm foreign addresses. Some buyers have more than one residence or are temporarily residing somewhere other than at their confirmed address. If they ask you to ship to an unconfirmed address and everything about them seems okay, honoring their request might win you some very loyal customers.

3. Check your e-mail for communications from the buyer before sending the merchandise.

4. Use delivery confirmation on everything you possibly can. However, keep in mind that delivery confirmation isn't a tracking system. It simply records when packages arrive at post offices and when they're delivered to their final destination. Not all packages are scanned in, either, though most are.

5. On big-ticket items—that is, anything whose replacement costs you wouldn't want to cover out of your own pocket—insist that buyers pay for insurance, or set your shipping fees high enough to cover it and include it automatically. You can also consider shipping these items via UPS or FedEx. Both services include a certain amount of coverage in their fees, and you can buy more if necessary.

6. Pack appropriately, and overpack fragile items. If you're not sure if items are cushioned well enough, check the shipper's pack and ship guidelines. They're available online at each shipper's Web site.

▶▶**If you're the cause of the shipping problem, try to make things right as quickly and completely as you can.** If you sent the wrong item, pay the buyer to ship it back, or come up with another solution that's agreeable to both of you. If you didn't pack the item properly and it arrived broken, offer a refund or replacement. As long as you take the attitude that problems can be solved, they typically can.

"It Just Isn't Me"

Buyer's remorse happens. Sometimes it's legitimate, sometimes it's not. Spend enough time on certain boards—clothing-related ones in particular—and you'll see sellers complain about buyers wanting to return their purchases under the guise of "it didn't fit right" or "the item isn't as represented."

The best way to deal with buyer's remorse is to have a solid return policy in your terms and conditions that is well worded and easy for buyers to find. Include an abbreviated version of it in all of your auctions as well. eBay requires it, but many sellers neglect to do it. This way, buyers know what to expect before they bid.

The simplest, easiest policy is "Items sold as is, all sales final, no returns," and you'll come across a lot of eBay sellers who use it. But one-size-fits-all policies like these aren't necessarily the way to go. Some would argue against them entirely as they don't score very high on customer-service points.

That said, it's up to you to decide how you want to handle returns. Whatever approach you take, make sure it's one that fits your overall business strategy and your pocketbook. While it might be nice to offer a blanket "If you don't like it, send it back" policy, it won't work if you can't afford it. However, if you're doing things right on the front end, chances are good that you won't have to deal with many returns anyway.

Here are some options:

- Allow returns, and reimburse shipping both ways if there's a significant fault in the item that wasn't covered in the listing description. The key word here is "significant." If your pictures are good and your descriptions are accurate, returns for this reason should be rare.
- If the fault is listed but the buyer decides he or she doesn't want the item after seeing it, accept the return under buyer's remorse. The customer is out shipping both ways.
- Allow returns, but charge a restocking fee. Many electronics and camera retailers have taken this approach for years. Restocking fees typically run anywhere from 15 to 25 percent.

Regardless of the approach you choose, always notify the buyer right away if you come across something about the item that constitutes a condition change prior to shipping. You can offer a few options, such as canceling the sale, issuing a partial refund, or paying for shipping.

▶▶**Buyer's remorse can set in before the buyer even gets the merchandise.** If it does, there are ways to handle it then, too. Buyers can retract their bids, or you can mutually agree not to complete the transaction. Neither approach will affect your feedback or the buyer's in any way, but bid retractions will show up on the buyer's feedback page, which, as previously noted, can work against them.

Using eBay's Buyer Management Tools

As previously discussed, one way you can avoid buyers you'd rather not deal with for some reason is by using eBay's Buyer Management Tools. These tools, which give you greater control over buyers and protect you from ones that might push you beyond where you want to go as a seller, let you block buyers who meet the following criteria:

- Live in countries you don't want to ship to
- Have negative feedback scores
- Have Unpaid Item strikes (meaning they're NPBs)
- Don't have PayPal accounts
- Are on buying sprees

Again, you'll find the console for Buyer Management Tools through Seller-Related Links on your "My eBay" page. You can move buyers on or off your list whenever you want.

Contacting eBay

eBay's position as a transaction facilitator puts it squarely in a neutral corner. In other words, it's not the place to go for most of your problems, as the company prefers not to get involved. They'd rather you work things out on your own or directly with your trading partners. That said, there are still times when it is appropriate to contact eBay. However, unless the issue concerns something like problems with your billing statement, consider it a last resort.

There's no denying that eBay has its good and bad points, but this is an area where eBay itself could take a few lessons from its users, or, at the very least, practice what it preaches. Like many large companies, eBay has established an almost impenetrable wall between itself and its customers. Because of this, communications with eBay will often leave you less than satisfied. You'll find yourself wishing you could just pick up the phone and call them instead of working through their e-mail system. If you're a silver level or higher PowerSeller, by the way, you can do exactly that—it's one of the perks of getting to this level. What's more, eBay even gives you a toll-free number to call. If you're not, well . . . there's e-mail. Answers are typically canned and often entirely miss the point, and the response time isn't what anyone would call speedy. Again, however, if you're a PowerSeller, you also get priority e-mail support.

It is possible to get a fairly rapid response from someone on the other end who knows what he or she is doing and does care, even if you aren't a PowerSeller. At the same time, the chances of your dealing with the same person twice are virtually nil. If follow-up is required, you might have to start all over again.

There's also eBay Live Help, which puts you in touch with a real live person. However, this service is only available between 5 A.M. and 6 P.M. Pacific time. If you decide to try it, just click on Live Help link on the upper righthand corner of eBay's home page.

Dispute Resolution Approaches

While no one likes conflict, a certain amount of it is unavoidable when people have to deal with each other. No two people see things exactly the same way, and a meeting of the minds doesn't always come easily. **▶▶If your business model is based on the belief that problems can be solved, you can usually find a way to solve them.** And if you can't, you can at least feel confident that you put your best efforts toward finding a solution.

Always tackle issues head on. Yes, it can be painful, but you won't make things any better by letting problems fester. Doing so is almost guaranteed to turn little problems into big ones.

Poor communication between buyers and sellers is the leading cause of disputes. Sometimes a fast response can be worse than none at all, however, especially if you're angry and you fire off something that you shouldn't say. Never answer disgruntled buyers if you're angry and upset. Step away from things, and take some time to think about what's really going on. Draft your response when you're feeling calmer, and send it only when you're ready. Remember, you can't erase e-mail. Once it's sent, it's sent.

Other conflict-resolution tips to keep in mind include these:

1. Don't counter a threat with another threat. Let the buyer huff and puff all he wants. But if the tone of the communications toward you concerns or frightens you in any way, don't hesitate to take appropriate steps, which might include contacting local authorities and does include contacting eBay. The company doesn't take this kind of stuff lightly. Actions it might take range from limits on account privileges to permanent suspension from the site. Also contact your ISP, if the threat was made via e-mail, or your phone company if it was made by phone.

2. If a buyer continues to harass you once you've reached a resolution, report it to eBay and block his or her e-mail from your server.

3. Again, if you're ever in a situation where you fear for your safety, do not hesitate to do what you think is appropriate to protect yourself and others around you. It's always better to be safe than sorry.

Understanding Square Trade

Nipping little problems in the bud before they become big ones is always a good approach. However, sometimes problems escalate into disputes no matter what you do. Settling conflicts directly without having to involve third parties is always the best approach, but sometimes things simply don't go in this direction.

If after you've tried everything in your arsenal and you're still left with a customer who's vastly displeased, you might have to call in an expert. On eBay, Square Trade can be that expert. Square Trade settles disputes between trading partners for a fee—$20—which can be paid by either party or jointly. When a complaint is filed, the company assigns a professional arbitrator who listens to both sides of the story and comes up with a best remedy/solution for the dispute. It can be disconcerting to have a

SquareTrade case opened against you, but it's sometimes the only way to communicate and come to a resolution with a difficult buyer.

▶▶ Test Drive

Go back through this chapter, and identify any areas in which you could see trouble brewing for you. Think about actions you can take now to avert disaster. Do you need a stronger return policy? Do you need to fine-tune your buyer controls? Change your shipping procedures? Remember, it's always a good idea to put the best possible solutions in place before trouble happens.

APPENDIXES

Appendix One
Glossary

Appendix Two
Further Reading

Appendix Three
Resources

Appendix One
Glossary

About Me
A personal home page that's available for every eBay user.

Affiliate programs
Programs that allow individuals to endorse products and/or services via Web site links and that pay commissions when purchases are made.

Bid cancellation
Canceling a buyer's bid.

Bid history
The list of people who bid on an item, and the amounts they bid.

Bid increment
The amount by which bids go up.

Bid retraction
Withdrawing a bid.

Bid shielding
Using secondary user IDs or other eBay members to artificially raise bid levels, done to protect another eBayer's low bid.

Blocked bidder list (BBL)
A list of eBayers who are blocked from bidding on certain auctions. Each seller can have his or her own blocked bidder list.

Brick and mortar
The real world, as opposed to cyberspace.

Buy It Now (BIN)
An eBay auction format offering the option of bidding on items or buying them at a fixed price.

Category listings
How items on eBay are sorted and organized.

Completed search
Search results that reflect expired listings.

Consignment selling
Selling merchandise for others.

Co-op advertising
Funds paid to sellers to cover the cost of advertising another entity's goods.

Cost of goods
How much merchandise costs, plus shipping costs.

Drop shipping
Shipping items directly to customers from a location other than your own.

Dutch auction
Selling two or more identical items in the same auction. Also known as a Multiple Item Auction.

Escrow
A payment service that acts as an intermediary between buyers and sellers.

eBay Store
A specialized eBay area where sellers can offer fixed-price inventory.

eBayer
An eBay user.

eBaying
Using the eBay site.

Featured Listings

Special sections on eBay that prominently display certain listings.

Feedback

Comments that eBayers make about trading with other eBayers.

Final value

The final bid on an auction; what an item sells for.

Final-value fee

The percentage of the final value of what items sell for paid to eBay as part of seller's fees.

Fixed-price sale

Selling an item or items on eBay at a set price with no auction option.

FTP

File transfer protocol. Online protocol used to transfer files from one computer to another.

Gallery

Listing option that includes thumbnail pictures of sellers' items displayed next to their titles in the category list.

HTML

Hyper-text markup language; a programming language used to create Web pages.

ID Verify

Independent verification service that confirms users' personal information if they don't want to provide bank or credit card information.

Insertion fee

The nonrefundable fee eBay charges for listing items.

Merchant account

A bank account that allows businesses to accept credit cards for payment.

Minimum bid

The lowest bid amount. Also known as opening value or starting price.

My eBay

A page that eBayers can use to track their buying and selling activities.

NARU

Acronym for "Not A Registered User."

Navigation bar

A graphic with clickable links at the top of every eBay page.

Opt in

Requesting to be put on a mailing list.

PowerSeller

eBay program that recognizes the site's most successful sellers.

Private Auction

Auctions where the bidders' identities are not visible to anyone other than the seller.

Proxy bidding

Bidding system used on all eBay auction listings except Multiple Item.

Reserve price

The minimum amount the seller is willing to accept for an item listed at auction.

Second-chance offer

Offering a non-winning bidder a chance to purchase an item.

Shill bidding

Deliberately placing bids to artificially raise the price of an item.

Sniping

Bidding at the last possible second of an auction.

Terms of service

Seller's guidelines on how sales will be handled.

Trading Assistant

eBay seller who sells for other people.

User ID

Unique nicknames chosen by eBayers when they register.

Appendix Two
Further Reading

Bursch, David D. *The eBay Myth-Buster: Turn 199 Misconceptions into Money!* Wiley, 2004.

Some of the myths that Bursch busts are somewhat contrived, such as #131: You can't create your own items to sell on eBay. That said, some eBay myths have reached mythical proportions, and Bursch does a good job of busting them down to reality.

Cagan, Michele, C.P.A. *Streetwise Structuring Your Business.* Adams Media, 2004.

This entry in the Streetwise series walks you through everything you need to know about the different business structures—sole proprietorships, partnerships, LLCs, and others—you have to choose from, along with their tax and liability implications.

Collier, Marsha. *eBay Timesaving Techniques for Dummies: Expert Insights That Help You Work Like a Pro!*

Collier, a long-time eBay seller, has written a number of books on various aspects of eBay. This one offers some good pointers on streamlining the online selling process, but you have to wade through the artificially jokey tone that dominates this series to get to them.

Gianforte, Greg, and Gibson, Marcus. *Bootstrapping Your Business: Start and Grow a Successful Company with Almost No Money.* Adams Media, 2005.

A book on the advantages and possible pitfalls of starting a business with little or no outside financing.

Griffith, Jim "Griff." *The Official eBay Bible: The Most Up-to-Date, Comprehensive, How-to Manual for Everyone from First-Time Users to People Who Want to Run Their Own Business.* Gotham, 2003.

A good basic primer on how eBay works. More for newcomers than experienced sellers.

Joyner, Amy. *The eBay Millionaire: Titanium PowerSeller Secrets for Building a Big Online Business.* John Wiley & Sons, 2005.

If you're looking for some inspiration, there's lots of it in this inside peek into the lives of eighteen Titanium PowerSellers—people who have reached eBay's most elite selling status.

Koch, Richard. *The 80/20 Principle: The Secret to Success by Achieving More with Less.* Currency, 1999.

Advice on how to put the 80/20 rule to use from a top time-management expert.

Morgenstern, Julie. *Organizing from the Inside Out.* Henry Holt and Company, 2004.

Work through Morgenstern's organizational tips, and you'll be able to maximize the time you spend on your business. Also worth picking up is Morgenstern's *Time Management from the Inside Out.*

Peters, Paula. *The Ultimate Marketing Toolkit.* Adams Media, 2006.

Practical advice for the small business owner on low-cost ways to create a business identity and how to get the word out to potential customers.

Peters, Tom. *The Brand You 50 (Reinventing Work): Fifty Ways to Transform Yourself from an "Employee" into a Brand That Shouts Distinction, Commitment, and Passion.* Knopf, 1999.

Not sure how to establish "you" as a brand? Peters will show you how.

Steiner, Ina. *The eBay Seller's Guide to Sales Research and Analysis.* McGraw-Hill Osborne Media, 2005.

The skinny on capturing and analyzing eBay sales data and using it to improve your online business, written by the editor of Auctionbytes .com.

Appendix Three
Resources

Web Sites

Search Engine Watch. Free site with tips and information on the search engine industry.
🖱*www.searchenginewatch.com*

Search Engine Guide. Info on the smaller search engines, plus where you should submit to get better ranking with the big guys.
🖱*www.searchengineguide.com*

Software

Auction Software

The following listings include some, but by no means all, of the software available to help you manage various aspects of your auctions. All have different fee structures and features. Many offer a short free trial or other incentives for trying them out.

Auction Genie
🖱*www.luxcentral.com/auctiongenie*

AuctionHawk
🖱*www.auctionhawk.com*

AuctionHelper
🖱*www.auctionhelper.com*

Auction Wizard 2000
www.auctionwizard.com

Auctiva
www.auctiva.com

ChannelAdvisor
Pro.channeladvisor.com/pro

Inkfrog
www.inkfrog.com

PriceMiner
www.priceminer.com

Sellathon (Viewtracker)
www.sellathon.com

The Seller Sourcebook
www.sellersourcebook.com

Shooting Star
www.foodogsoftware.com

SpareDollar
www.sparedollar.com

Vendio
www.vendio.com

Search-Engine Optimization Software

Wordtracker
www.wordtracker.com

Optilink
www.optilinksoftware.com

WebPosition Gold
www.webposition.com

Other Resources

www.auctionbytes.com
There are plenty of sites that discuss the online auction world, but this is the one that's definitely worth knowing about. Sign up for free e-mail newsletters to keep on top of industry news and announcements, new products, and basically anything and everything having to do with online sales.

www.auctionsoftwarereview.com
Reviews on eBay-related software products.

eBayers to Know About

There are many talented and helpful people on eBay. One of the best when it comes to photography is camerajim, aka Jim Salvas. The best place to access his knowledge is through his "About Me" page, which you can reach by going to Home>eBay Stores>CameraJim. You can also do a seller search on eBay for camerajim, or check the Photos & HTML board, where he hangs out regularly.

Lesley Feeney (lesley_feeney) offers template design services in her eBay store—Lesley's Auction Template Designs—and a bunch of good information on making your listings stand out visually through her "About

Me" page. You can find her by doing a seller search for lesley_feeney or by searching for her store.

Sniping Services
🖰 *www.powersnipe.com*
🖰 *www.AgentProxy.com*

Information on Business Plans

🖰 *www.sba.gov/starting_business/planning/basic.html*

Index

V

Verified Rights Owner (VeRo), 20, 136

W

warranty programs, 236–37
Web hosting services, 291–92
Web-site design companies, 286–87
Web sites
    Affiliate program, 292–93
    domain names, 290–91
    linking to eBay listings from, 292
    search engine optimization, 288–89
    setting up own, 284–90
wholesaler lists, 66
workshop calendars, 39

Y

Yahoo! Auctions, 5

Z

zoning laws, 108–10

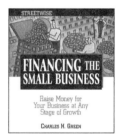

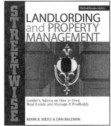

Streetwise® Managing a Nonprofit
John Riddle
$19.95; ISBN 10: 1-58062-698-X

Streetwise® Managing People
Bob Adams, et al.
$19.95; ISBN 10: 1-55850-726-4

Streetwise® Marketing Plan
Don Debelak
$19.95; ISBN 10: 1-58062-268-2

Streetwise® Maximize Web Site Traffic
Nobles and O'Neil
$19.95; ISBN 10: 1-58062-369-7

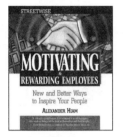

Streetwise® Motivating & Rewarding Employees
Alexander Hiam
$19.95; ISBN 10: 1-58062-130-9

Streetwise® Project Management
Michael Dobson
$19.95; ISBN 10: 1-58062-770-6

Streetwise® Restaurant Management
John James & Dan Baldwin
$19.95; ISBN 10: 1-58062-781-1

Streetwise® Sales Letters with CD
Reynard and Weiss
$29.95; ISBN 10: 1-58062-440-5

Streetwise® Selling on eBay®
Sonia Weiss
$19.95; ISBN 10: 1-59337-610-3

Streetwise® Small Business Book of Lists
Edited by Gene Marks
$19.95; ISBN 10: 1-59337-684-7

Streetwise® Small Business Start-Up
Bob Adams
$19.95; ISBN 10: 1-55850-581-4

Streetwise® Start Your Own Business Workbook
Gina Marie Mangiamele
$9.95; ISBN 10: 1-58062-506-1

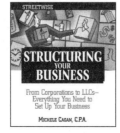

Streetwise® Structuring Your Business
Michele Cagan
$19.95; ISBN 10: 1-59337-177-2

Streetwise® Time Management
Marshall Cook
$19.95; ISBN 10: 1-58062-131-7

About the Author

SONIA WEISS turned her love for bargain hunting at garage sales and thrift stores into a thriving eBay® business. A recognized industry expert who has advised eBay® sellers on establishing their businesses and maximizing their profits, Weiss also works as a writer. Her works include *The Pocket Idiot's Guide to Garage and Yard Sales* and *The Unofficial Guide to Collecting Antiques.*